Spoken English on Computer

SPOKEN ENGLISH ON COMPUTER

Transcription, mark-up and application

EDITED BY **GEOFFREY LEECH, GREG MYERS, JENNY THOMAS**

Longman Group Limited,
Longman House, Burnt Mill,
Harlow, Essex CM20 2JE, England
and Associated Companies throughout the world.

Published in the United States of America
by Longman Publishing, New York

© Longman Group Limited 1995

All rights reserved; no part of this publication may be
reproduced, stored in a retrieval system, or transmitted
in any form or by any means, electronic, mechanical,
photocopying, recording, or otherwise without either the
prior written permission of the Publishers or a licence
permitting restricted copying in the United Kingdom
issued by the Copyright Licensing Agency Ltd.,
90 Tottenham Court Road, London W1P 9HE.

First published 1995

ISBN 0 582 250218 PPR

British Library Cataloguing-in-Publication Data

A catalogue record for this book is
available from the British Library

Library of Congress Cataloging-in-Publication Data
Spoken English on computer: transcription, mark-up, and application/
edited by Geoffrey N. Leech, Greg Myers, and Jenny Thomas.
    p. cm.
Includes bibliographical references and index.
ISBN 0-582-25021-8 (pbk.)
  1. Natural language processing (Computer science)
2. Computational linguistics. I. Leech, Geoffrey N. II. Myers,
Greg, 1954- . III. Thomas, Jenny, 1948- .
QA76.9.N38S76   1995
420'.285'572–dc20   94-41504
                                                                     CIP

Set in 10/12pt Times by 8
Produced through Longman Malaysia, PP

Contents

List of contributors	viii
List of abbreviations and acronyms	x
Editors' general introduction	1

Part A: Issues and practices

Introduction   15

1. Principles and alternative systems in the transcription, coding and mark-up of spoken discourse
   JANE A. EDWARDS   19

2. Theoretical issues: transcribing the untranscribable
   GUY COOK   35

3. Adequacy, user-friendliness, and practicality in transcribing
   WALLACE CHAFE   54

4. Whole-text analysis in computerized spoken discourse
   JAMES MONAGHAN   62

5. The Text Encoding Initiative: an overview
   LOU BURNARD   69

6. The approach of the Text Encoding Initiative to the encoding of spoken discourse
   STIG JOHANSSON   82

7. From theory to practice
   JOHN SINCLAIR   99

Part B: Applications and more specialized uses

Introduction — 113

8. Transcription, segmentation and analysis: corpora from the language-impaired
   PAUL FLETCHER and MICHAEL GARMAN — 116

9. Corpora of disordered spoken language
   MICK PERKINS — 128

10. Discourse considerations in transcription and analysis
    CHRISTINE CHEEPEN — 135

11. Code switching: a problem for transcription and text encoding
    MARK SEBBA — 144

12. Linking prosodic transcription to the time dimension
    PETER ROACH and SIMON ARNFIELD — 149

13. Grammatical tagging of the spoken part of the British National Corpus: a progress report
    ROGER GARSIDE — 161

14. Publishing a spoken and written corpus on CD-ROM: the HCRC Map Task experience
    HENRY S. THOMPSON, ANNE H. ANDERSON and MILES BADER — 168

Part C: Samples and systems of transcription

Introduction — 183

15. The Survey of English Usage and the London–Lund Corpus: computerizing manual prosodic transcription
    SUE PEPPÉ — 187

16. The COBUILD spoken corpus: transcription conventions
    JONATHAN PAYNE — 203

17. Converting a corpus into a relational database: SEC becomes MARSEC
    GERRY KNOWLES — 208

18. The International Corpus of English: mark-up for spoken language
    GERALD NELSON — 220

19. The BNC spoken corpus
    STEVE CROWDY — 224

20. The Bergen Corpus of London Teenager Language (COLT)
    VIBECKE HASLERUD and ANNA-BRITA STENSTRÖM — 235

Bibliographical references	243
Author index	255
Subject index	258

List of contributors

ANNE H. ANDERSON, Human Communication Research Centre, Department of Psychology, University of Glasgow, UK.

SIMON ARNFIELD, Department of Linguistic Science, University of Reading, UK.

MILES BADER, Human Communication Research Centre, University of Edinburgh, UK.

LOU BURNARD, Oxford University Computing Services, Oxford, UK.

WALLACE CHAFE, Department of Linguistics, University of California, Santa Barbara.

CHRISTINE CHEEPEN, School of Humanities, University of Hertfordshire, UK.

GUY COOK, Department of English for Speakers of Other Languages, Institute of Education, University of London.

STEVE CROWDY, Longman Group Limited, Harlow, UK.

JANE A. EDWARDS, Institute of Cognitive Studies, University of California, Berkeley.

PAUL FLETCHER, Department of Linguistic Science, University of Reading, UK.

MICHAEL GARMAN, Department of Linguistic Science, University of Reading, UK.

ROGER GARSIDE, Department of Computing, Lancaster University, UK.

VIBECKE HASLERUD, Department of English, University of Bergen, Norway.

STIG JOHANSSON, Department of British and American Studies, University of Oslo, Norway.

GERRY KNOWLES, Department of Linguistics and Modern English Language, Lancaster University, UK.

GEOFFREY LEECH, Department of Linguistics and Modern English Language, Lancaster University, UK.

JAMES MONAGHAN, School of Humanities, University of Hertfordshire, UK.

GREG MYERS, Department of Linguistics and Modern English Language, Lancaster University, UK.

GERALD NELSON, Survey of English Usage, University College London.

JONATHAN PAYNE, School of English, University of Birmingham, UK.

SUE PEPPÉ, National Hospital's College of Speech Sciences, London.

MICK PERKINS, Department of Speech Science, Department of Psychology, University of Sheffield, UK.

PETER ROACH, Department of Linguistic Science, University of Reading, UK.

MARK SEBBA, Department of Linguistics and Modern English Language, Lancaster University, UK.

JOHN SINCLAIR, School of English, Corpus Linguistics, University of Birmingham, UK.

ANNA-BRITA STENSTRÖM, Department of English, University of Bergen, Norway.

JENNY THOMAS, Department of Linguistics and Modern English Language, Lancaster University, UK.

HENRY S. THOMPSON, Human Communication Research Centre, Centre for Cognitive Science and Department of Artificial Intelligence, University of Edinburgh, UK.

List of abbreviations and acronyms

AACR	Anglo American Cataloguing Rules
ACL/DCI	Association of Computational Linguistics/Data Collection Initiative
ALEP	Advanced Language Engineering Platform
ASCII	American Standard Code for Information Interchange
BNC	British National Corpus
CD-ROM	Compact disk – read only memory
CHAT	Codes for Human Analysis of Transcripts (the mark-up adopted by CHILDES)
CHILDES	Child Language Data Exchange System
COBUILD	Collins/Birmingham University International Language Database
COLT	Corpus of London Teenager Language
CSAE	Corpus of Spoken American English
DAT	Digital Audio Tape
dtd	document type description (in TEI)
EAGLES	Expert Advisory Groups on Language Engineering Standards (European Union)
FIFO	First In First Out
ftp	file transfer protocol
HCRC	Human Communication Research Centre, Edinburgh and Glasgow
HMM	Hidden Markov Model
HTK	HMM Tool Kit
ICE	International Corpus of English
itu	incomplete tone unit
LARSP	Language Assessment Remediation and Screening Procedure
LLC	London–Lund Corpus

LOB	Lancaster-Oslo/Bergen Corpus
MARC	Machine Readable Catalogue
MARSEC	Machine Readable Spoken English Corpus (see SEC)
MIT	Massachusetts Institute of Technology
MLU	Mean Length of Utterance
NERC	Network of European Reference Corpora
NFS	Network File Server
SALT	Systematic Analysis of Language Transcripts
SALT Club	Speech and Language Technology Club
SAM	Speech Assessment Methodology (an EC programme for assessment of speech technology)
SEC	IBM/Lancaster Spoken English Corpus
SEU	Survey of English Usage, University College London
SGML	Standard Generalized Mark-up Language
SPE	The Sound Pattern of English (Chomsky and Hallé, 1968)
SUMLARSP	a program for providing data from LARSP
TEI	Text Encoding Initiative
TIMIT	a US corpus of spoken data
ToBI	Tones and Break Indices
tsm	tonetic stress marks
UCREL	Unit for Computer Research on the English Language

Editors' general introduction

1 Defining the field

This book is concerned with the development and exploitation of *computer corpora of spoken discourse* ('corpora' being the plural of 'corpus', refers to a body of language samples). Condensed into a single phrase like this, the field appears to be technical and mystifying. But let us begin by reconstructing its development from a number of simpler and more familiar processes:

1. Someone, somewhere (let us call this Person A) decides to undertake the *recording* of natural spoken discourse, which may be everyday conversation, or some other variety of spoken language. The purposes of doing this are many: for example, they could be to study the language itself (particularly the spoken variety), to study the nature of conversation as a social activity, to help build better dictionaries, or to help build improved machines which will talk or understand speech.

2. Person B (who is perhaps the same as Person A) sets about *transcribing* the above recording. This person should ideally be highly trained in phonetics and linguistics, but often is not. Person B has to decide on a set of conventions for transcribing speech, which means deciding which sorts of information from the speech signal should be retained as important, and which should be disregarded. For instance, if the speaker makes a noise like 'um', should that be transcribed or ignored? And if it should be transcribed, how?

3. Person C (perhaps the same person as A and B) decides to *computerize* Person B's transcriptions; that is, to convert them to an electronic form that can be read, stored, or processed by computer. At this stage, decisions have to be made about how to make use of the computer's symbolization potential (the letters, numbers, and other symbols such as > and %) to represent some, or all of the information in the transcription. (This is known as *mark-up* – see Edwards, Chapter 1.)

2 *Editors' general introduction*

4. Person D decides to make this resource more useful by adding information which was not in the original transcription itself, but could be derived from it, plus a knowledge of the language and the contexts of its use. This amounts to an *enrichment* of the corpus as a resource, by adding extra layers of information, for example, on the grammatical classes of words, or on the classes of speech acts which have taken place in the course of the transcribed speech. This process of adding enriching information may be termed *coding* or *annotation*. Once the corpus has been coded with useful information, the results of the coding can, again, be 'ploughed back' into the corpus for other users to benefit from.
5. Person E decides to make use of the corpus (perhaps with various types of codings added) by *applying* it to a specialized area of research, with practical benefits in mind. The areas of application can be varied. For example, they may include social areas of application, such as investigating the nature of language disabilities, or technological ones, such as building better speaking and listening machines (i.e. speech synthesizers and speech recognizers).

Whatever the application, it is quite likely that Person E will not be content to use the corpus resources which are already available: he or she will often need to adapt or supplement those resources, for example by providing a different kind of information through transcription, a different kind of representation through mark-up, or a different kind of enrichment through coding. In other words, Person E will probably need to be a corpus compiler and developer, as well as a corpus user. In this way, corpus resources will become further extended.

Why, it may be asked, does Person C bother to computerize the transcriptions? The main reasons are:

1. The computer enables a corpus of language data to be precisely copied and transferred to other users' computers: in effect, it provides a vehicle for publication by electronic means.
2. The computer enables the corpus to be easily processed: for example, to be automatically converted into different formats for different users' needs. Through various kinds of automatic processing, many purposes may be served. For example, the computer can retrieve from the corpus all occurrences of a particular phenomenon (such as the string *sort of* followed immediately by a verb) in context and, if required, display them to the user (concordancing). It can derive the frequency of particular features of spoken language in different types of data. It can discover significant patterns of cooccurrence – e.g. between the gender of the speaker, and turn-taking phenomena such as interruption.
3. The linking of (1) and (2) illustrates a combinatorial power which comes with the advantages of computerization. By means of automatic copying and distribution (1), the results of processing (2) can be passed on to multitudes of other users, who can then make use of these results. We

can then see the outcome of Person C's work as a corpus to be used as a flexible resource by a whole crowd of people for a wide range of research purposes throughout the world.

4. The use of a corpus as a common resource, as described in (3), serves the purposes of scientific endeavour in a further way. While the data on which research is based remains private, there is no way in which the analysis of that data, and the conclusion drawn from that analysis, can be challenged by another person. But if the source of data is generally available, in the form of an electronic corpus, then the analysis can be replicated by another person, who may or may not agree with the original researcher's findings. Thus the corpus of spoken discourse can become a testing ground, against which people's research claims can be evaluated.

But for the moment, let us look at the five people, Persons A–E, not as individuals, but as representing five kinds of activity which we can see as forming a logical sequence:

1. recording
2. transcription
3. representation (mark-up)
4. coding (or annotation)
5. application

If we see these processes in their historical context, there is also a progression through time:

1. Speech recording began to be widespread, through tape recording, in the 1950s.
2. Transcription of speech from recordings began on a substantial scale in the 1960s (see Peppé, Chapter 15).
3. The electronic mark-up of spoken language transcriptions began in the 1970s (see Peppé, Chapter 15).
4, 5. In the 1980s and 1990s, work has begun to gather momentum on the coding of spoken corpora, and the application of spoken corpora in various practical areas of research (see especially Part B).

On the other hand, instead of looking back on these processes historically, we may now see them as coming together synchronically in a collaborative research effort: there is an emerging research community working on spoken language corpora. The object of the research community can be seen as the creation of a many-channelled information exchange system, where each component process directly or indirectly determines the nature of others. This system is illustrated in Fig. 0.1. For example, it is obvious that the quality of a recording will determine how much information is passed on to the transcription stage, and how reliable that information is. In Fig. 0.1, this dependence is represented by the solid arrow

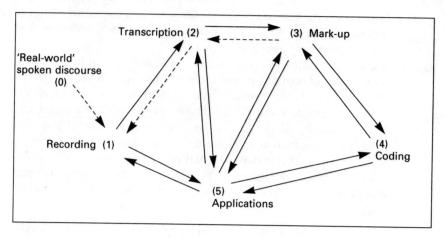

Figure 0.1

between (1) and (2). In return, the broken arrow pointing back from (2) to (1) represents the feedback from transcription to recording, in the sense that what information we need at the transcription stage will determine the quality of reproduction we aim to provide at the recording stage. Similarly, there is a feedback arrow from (3) to (2), to show not only that the mark-up needs to be able to represent any of the information provided in a transcription, but that the requirements of a given mark-up scheme may in turn require us to adapt transcription practice – say, to restrict the transcription symbols to those available on the normal computer keyboard. In contrast, the backward arrow from (4) to (3) is a solid one, showing a more substantial relation of mutual dependence between mark-up and annotation. The coding of linguistic features such as parts of speech has to be directly representable in the mark-up scheme: enrichment of the corpus implies enrichment of mark-up.

On the left of Fig. 0.1 is a further element of the picture: (0) – the real-world speech events which have been recorded, and which form the starting point of the whole information system. As far as our present research field is concerned, there is no feedback arrow between (1) and (0), because the aim is to record, as far as possible, naturally occurring spoken discourse, ideally uncontaminated by the influence of artificial requirements of recording, transcription, or any other research activities to the right of it in the diagram. (In practice, of course, the fact of recording *can* influence the events, and much thought has to be put into the issue of how to obtain a record of *natural* speech.)

However, we should note an important point here. There are computer databases of recorded speech known as *speech corpora*, which are used as resources in speech science and speech technology, and which frequently, if not typically, contain artificially contrived language material, for example decontextualized sentences designed to represent certain phonetic combinations of sound, rather than naturally occurring spoken language. These speech corpora (such as the TIMIT database – see p.150) also typically contain material recorded in highly artificial circumstances, to prevent unwanted noise from interfering with the acoustic signal. Such 'laboratory recording' techniques are necessary if the acoustic properties of the speech signal are to be studied with sufficient precision to serve the purpose of the new speech technologies. Our concerns in this book exclude such speech corpora, but if they were included, then there would be a reason to add the omitted feedback arrow between (1) and (0), to show that considerations of recording quality, of transcription quality, and so on, may affect the nature of the speech event to be recorded. To avoid confusion with such speech corpora, we will avoid using the term 'speech corpora' for the bodies of naturally occurring spoken data we are concerned with, and will use 'corpora of spoken discourse' or 'spoken language corpora' instead.

This book is mainly concerned with the central area of Fig. 0.1: with transcription (2), mark-up (3) and their relation to applications (5). Virtually no attention will be given to recording (1), and coding (4) will also be less central (see, however, the contributions of Jane Edwards (Chapter 1) and Fletcher and Garman (Chapter 8) and Roger Garside (Chapter 13)).

In the areas of transcription and mark-up in particular, consideration has to be given to important issues both of principle and of practice, which it will be the business of this book to explore. In earlier times, when transcribers typically made transcriptions for their own research purposes only, there was little reason to worry unduly about the selection of features of transcription and their representation by symbols on paper. But the advent of the computer corpus means that transcriptions can easily become part of a public resource – a corpus or database. Also, because transcription is a skilled, costly and time-consuming activity, it increasingly makes sense to make use of other researchers' spoken language material, now becoming available on a scale undreamed of a few years ago, rather than to embark on one's own corpus-building activity. The huge advantage the computer offers in terms of *reusability of resources* (a common buzz-phrase in speech and language technology these days) also brings to the corpus compiler the responsibility of devising systems of transcription and mark-up which will be optimally useful to others. This, in turn, creates the need to work towards a *common interchange format* (another present-day buzz-phrase) for transcriptions of spoken discourse, and more generally for language corpora, to aid exchange of data between research groups. Researchers typically have strong reservations about notions of standardization, seeing them as constraining research. But the need to converge towards a standard, or (to weaken the concept) towards agreed guidelines, is becoming a matter of practical urgency. The issue of practicality, however, cannot be divorced from a range of general issues of theory and principle, which will inevitably receive prominent attention from the contributors to this book.

The word 'corpus' and its plural 'corpora' will also provide a recurrent theme in this book: a corpus is generally understood to be a body of language materials containing a range of different samples: for example, not just a single transcription, but a whole collection of transcriptions, perhaps sampled systematically in order to be representative of a language, of its spoken variety, or of some other varieties of it. Within a corpus, the same transcription and mark-up conventions will typically be used for all sample texts (note the use of the term 'text' here includes spoken as well as written language). As already noted, we have largely left behind us the days when individual researchers collected and worked on their own data with little thought of distributing it to others. The computer has provided the means to collect, store, and re-use large quantities of data laboriously and expensively collected and transcribed by others. Hence, for the first time a considerable number of corpora containing or consisting of spoken discourse have been compiled or are in the process of compilation on computer. One of the purposes of this book is to give an overview of a number of important corpora – to illustrate and describe their contents and their transcription schemes: see particularly Part C.

2   Why this book at this time?

Spoken language corpora at present are at the point of intersection of many avenues of research, and we may look forward to a future in which they are likely to be the regular and accepted resource for studies of spoken language broadly across the spectrum of disciplines, from the humanities through social sciences to science and information engineering.

At present, the field is 'taking off' for a number of reasons:

1. *Technological progress* It is now commonplace that a transcription can easily be stored and circulated in electronic form, simply by virtue of being typed on a word-processor. There is also the increasing availability of appropriately powerful hardware and software, as well as of effective and relatively inexpensive data transfer devices such as CD-ROMs ('Compact disk – read only memory').

2. *Development and influence of corpus-based methodologies in speech and language technology* Up to 10 years ago, the use of computer corpora, whether of spoken or of written language, was a field of endeavour largely ignored by theoretical and computational linguists. Since that time, a revolution has taken place: corpus-based studies have moved to the centre of the stage, particularly in speech and language technology (see Church and Mercer 1993, Leech and Fligelstone 1992). The earliest available computer corpora (e.g. the Brown Corpus, see Francis and Kučera 1979) were corpora of written language, and written language materials have continued to be by far to be the most abundant and readily available, especially because they are easy to collect and computerize through the use of scanners and of electronic text preparation. As far as current technologies allow, however, there is increasing

recognition of the need for spoken language to catch up, in this respect, with written language.

3. *Need to collect together data of past research projects before they vanish* In areas such as sociolinguistics, dialectology and discourse analysis, many research projects over the past 20 or so years have involved the collection of spoken language data in the form of recordings and transcriptions. Much data of this kind could be lying around untended – perhaps languishing in bottom drawers of filing cabinets – and there is an obvious benefit in recovering this material for the use of the wider research community. It was concern for the continuing availability of individual collections of data which led, in part, to the initiative of MacWhinney and others (MacWhinney and Snow 1990; see also Fletcher and Garman, Chapter 8) in putting together, for data interchange, a computer archive of data of child language, known as the Child Language Data Exchange System (CHILDES) database.[1]

4. *Current initiatives, such as the TEI, BNC, EAGLES, etc.* At present, there are a number of large-scale research initiatives which will leave their mark on the field of spoken language corpora. The Text Encoding Initiative (TEI) (see Burnard, Chapter 5), begun in in the late 1980s, is in the course of producing detailed guidelines for electronic text encoding and interchange. Among its recently published provisional recommendations have been guidelines for spoken language mark-up (see Johansson, Chapter 6), which are extremely relevant to the task of selecting a markup scheme for spoken corpora. Other initiatives to take account of are large-scale corpus compilation projects, which include a spoken language component; for example the British National Corpus (BNC) (see Crowdy, Chapter 19, and Garside, Chapter 13), which contains 10 million words of spoken English discourse – this compares poorly, though, with the BNC's 90 million words of the written language. Another English language project, the International Corpus of English (ICE) (see Nelson, Chapter 18) extends the coverage of the English language to many different national varieties, each to be represented by a million-word corpus, half of which will consist of spoken discourse. Whereas the BNC and ICE consist exclusively of English language material, a more recent standard-setting initiative within the European Union, known as EAGLES, covers the range of EU languages in its recommendations. EAGLES (Expert Advisory Group on Language Engineering Standards) contains a working group of specialists on text corpora, and one adjoined group is concerned with the treatment of spoken language (see Sinclair, Chapter 7). EAGLES aims at achieving guidelines, commonly agreed across language frontiers, for the development of language resources, and its work will impinge on one of the major themes of this book: that of seeking agreement on a common interchange format. These are only four major examples of the initiatives taking place at present.

8   Editors' general introduction

We have seen from the above discussion why the past and the present concerns have led to a convergence of interests and initiatives, focusing on spoken language corpora. From now on, we may look forward to a diversification of studies, based increasingly on commonly agreed guidelines, in the future. This diversification will no doubt take place mainly through the proliferation of applications and of specialized corpora. For example, among contributions to the present volume we have chapters on such specialized areas as teenage discourse (Haslerud and Stenström, Chapter 20), bilingual discourse (Sebba, Chapter 11), discourse associated child language impairment (Fletcher and Garman, Chapter 8) and with aphasic discourse (Perkins, Chapter 9). These applications have a social science orientation, whereas others have more of a bias towards speech and information technology applications (see the contributions of Thompson et al., Chapter 14 and of Roach and Arnfield, Chapter 12). Each application tends to bring its own priorities regarding transcription and mark-up, and often also the need for a specialized corpus dedicated to that application.

In conclusion, spoken language corpora are now at a point of junction between many strands of research – strands converging from the past, and strands diverging into the future. The time is right for a book of this kind.[2]

3   The Workshop on which the book is based

The book originated in the proceedings of a Workshop on Computerized Spoken Discourse, held at the Lancaster House Hotel (adjoining the campus of Lancaster University) on 25–27 September 1993. The Workshop was supported by a grant from the Economic and Social Research Council (ESRC), the British research council responsible for supporting research in the social sciences.[3]

Participants in the Workshop included many leading specialists in the field, and particularly representatives of current research projects and initiatives. Since the support came from the ESRC, it was natural that most participants were from the United Kingdom, although our funding also allowed us to invite several participants from overseas (Wallace Chafe, Stig Johansson and Anna-Brita Stenström). Unfortunately, it was not possible to collect together all the important scholars, or representatives of all important research projects. To make the book a more comprehensive record of the state of the art in spoken corpus collection and research, we invited additional contributors, to whom we are grateful for their prompt response to our appeal. We are particularly grateful to Jane Edwards for contributing, at short notice, the initial scene-setting chapter to this volume.

One limitation of the Workshop was that its focus, as it turned out, was almost exclusively on just one of the world's languages – English. Although we advertised the wish to extend the field to other languages, there were virtually no takers. This is, of course, from many points of view an unfortunate restriction. By way of excuse, we can point out that most research in this area has so far been on English, and most computerized spoken corpora have so far been of this language. Furthermore, whatever the loss of concentrating on one language, a mitigating factor is that the concentration has enabled us to widen the scope of discussion to a very broad range of issues. It is arguable that by using one language as our proving-ground, we were able to throw the spotlight on differences of philosophy, methodology, and descriptive practice in a particularly concentrated way which would have been impossible otherwise.[4]

4   The plan of this book

The book, after this introduction, is divided into three parts, each of which is prefaced by an editorial introduction.

Part A addresses fundamental issues which are recurrent through the book, and so prepares the ground for the more specific topics which follow in Parts B and C. They are issues of theory, issues of practice, and above all, issues of how theory and practice are to be reconciled. Two contributions to Part A (those of Burnard and Johansson, Chapters 5 and 6) are concerned specifically with the provisional recommendations of the Text Encoding Initiative (TEI), and their implications for the representation of spoken discourse.

Part B illustrates the wide range of applications of computerized spoken corpora, some of them being explored here in print (to our knowledge) for the first time. On the one hand, there are the many possibilities of developing specialized corpora for different areas of research (e.g. corpora of children's language, of language disability, of bilingual data – including code-switching), and these bring with them particular priorities and particular difficulties regarding transcription and representation. On the other hand, there are applications to speech and language technology, using corpora for the computer modelling of the speech behaviour of the human subject, notably in the areas of speech synthesis, speech recognition, and human-machine dialogue. For these purposes, again, it is necessary to develop corpora containing special kinds of information: for example, grammatical and prosodic information.

Part C takes us one stage further down the road from theory to practice. In this part are assembled a range of descriptions of corpora which are either complete or in the making. They begin with the London–Lund Corpus (LLC), the oldest and best-known of spoken corpora, itself based on the yet older pre-electronic corpus of the Survey of English Usage at London. They end with the recently collected Corpus of London Teenager Language (COLT). One thing that will strike and perhaps puzzle a newcomer to the field is the variable degree of interest in detail reflected in the various corpora. There is a world of difference between a fine-textured transcription giving prosodic detail of features such as stress and intonation on the one hand, and a 'broad' transcription which gives little information beyond the verbatim record of what was said. This variability of detail naturally correlates with the amount of data transcribed and the cost of transcriptions. For the compilers of a spoken corpus such as that of (COBUILD) The Collins/Birmingham University International Learners' Dictionary or the BNC, the aim is to transcribe millions of words within a relatively short time, notably for lexicographic purposes, so transcription has to be pared down to a bare minimum of information. On the other hand, for a corpus like LLC, the Lancaster/IBM Spoken English Corpus (SEC), or the Corpus of Spoken American English (CSAE), the amount of data transcribed takes second place to the need for a relatively precise and painstaking record of *how* what was said was said.

5 Conclusion: looking ahead

The field is developing fast. We are reaching a time when very large quantities of spoken data will be widely available. But there is a trade-off between quantity and quality: there will remain a place, for many years to come, for the painstakingly transcribed corpus – the hand-crafted product. There is also going to be a new tendency for the development of tools which will automate, or at least speed up, the transcription process – a move in the opposite direction of mass-production. We note the great scope for advances along this 'automation' route, but there are also manifest dangers in editing out many layers of meaningful information from the original speech signal, and then treating the transcribed, computerized record as the 'real thing' to be studied.

Thus, another avenue of future development is to give the corpus user the ability to cross-refer back and forth when desired, between the transcribed record and the original audio-recording. Digitization technology allows the sound to be computerized, as well as the transcription. The techniques of 'timestamping' (see Thompson et al., Chapter 14) and alignment allow instant cross-reference between the recording and the transcription/mark-up. Conversion of a corpus into a relational database allows cross-reference between other levels of the corpus record, where they exist, as well. These emerging technologies are demonstrated, for example, in the Edinburgh Map Task Corpus (see Thompson et al., Chapter 14), and the MARSEC database of the Lancaster/IBM Spoken English Corpus (see Knowles, Chapter 17). In this way, the information lost between recording, transcription and annotation can be recovered whenever wanted. Following this line of thinking, one can foresee a situation in which the computerized transcription is accepted as a first level of information, to which the individual researcher can add more detailed transcription features – by reference to the original recording – as needs arise.

6 Acknowledgements

First, we thank the Economic and Social Research Council for its generous support of the Workshop on Computerized Spoken Discourse (see section 3 above). We are also grateful to those members of Lancaster University staff who helped us to run the workshop: Freda Gidlow, Graeme Hughes and Steve Fligelstone. Our thanks to Freda are particularly heartfelt: she played an important role not only at the workshop itself, but in its preparation, and in the preparation of this book.

Finally, we wish to thank all the participants in the Workshop on Computerized Spoken Discourse, and particularly those, whether participants or not, who have contributed to this book. The workshop would not have been true to its purpose if it had not represented important differences of viewpoint. But these differences, even though they were sometimes expressed forcefully, were good-humoured, and did not detract from the sense that we were engaged in a common endeavour, with shared goals and shared enthusiasms. We have not been able to include here any of the discussions which took place, but, in spite of that omission, we believe that the good qualities of the workshop have been faithfully captured in this volume.

Notes

1. Here it may be useful to distinguish between a computer *corpus* – which is normally a collection of texts or text samples selected systematically by one research team according to a particular plan or design – and a computer *archive* of language data, which is an open-ended collection of texts, samples, or corpora assembled from different sources, and extended as opportunities arise. The CHILDES database may be defined, in this sense, as an archive, although without emphasis on the historical record-keeping function traditionally associated with archives. The CHILDES database (a database only in the loosest sense) has as its function a pooling of data by different researchers who want to be able to share in such common resources through an interchange system. As such, CHILDES fulfils many of the functions of a spoken language corpus, as discussed in this introduction. In the present context, it is best to avoid terminological pedantry, and we will use the term 'corpus' in a loose and general sense, for any collection of texts or text samples (including transcriptions of spoken material).
2. This is not the only book recently published on the theme of computerized spoken discourse. We recommend, as collateral reading, Edwards and Lampert 1993.
3. It is significant that, in addition to its support by the ESRC, the Workshop included among its participants representatives of two other British research grant-giving bodies, the Science and Engineering Research Council, and the British Academy (responsible for research grants in the Humanities). The keen interest in the subject of the Workshop shown by these three research bodies was symbolic of the very broad interdisciplinary relevance of the study of spoken discourse corpora.
4. We may hope for a successor to this volume, which will explore these issues with reference to different languages around the world.

Part A

Issues and practices

Introduction

The first four chapters in this section deal with theoretical and practical issues relating to the transcription and coding of spoken language in machine-readable form. *Transcription* is the process of representing spoken language in written form: how broad/narrow should that representation be? How can transcription be made useful to/usable by a wide range of users? How can we overcome the limitations of the written medium? *Coding* (also known as 'tagging' or 'annotation') relates to more abstract attributes of the text: for example, you might want to label grammatical, semantic, pragmatic or discoursal categories (to indicate, for example, that a word is a proper noun, that its use is restricted in some way, that a particular utterance was said in a sarcastic manner, or that it was used to bring an interaction to a close). Chapters 5 and 6 focus on issues of *mark-up* – the process of making texts machine-readable in ways which facilitate the interchange of data between users. The final chapter is rather different in nature – it is an edited transcript of an unscripted talk delivered interactively at the Lancaster Workshop on Computerized Spoken Discourse, held in September 1993. In this chapter, John Sinclair responds to the issues raised in the previous chapters. If we were constructing corpora in an ideal world, the issues raised in the first six chapters regarding delicacy of transcription and coding and detailed mark-up might all be taken on board. However, Sinclair speaking from his experience of many years working with large corpora of spoken language, discusses how in practice issues of cost and usability affect the transcription, coding and mark-up of very large corpora.

Three of the contributors to this section draw attention to Ochs's (1979) paper, in which she observes that transcription (and to transcription we can now add coding) becomes data. The use of the computer, in spite of the many advantages and new possibilities which it opens up, does not resolve the problems of the relationship between the original speech event and the transcription, nor does it obviate the problem of representing spoken language in written form (indeed, in some ways it exacerbates these problems). Decisions made at the time of transcription and coding will affect the entire process of data analysis. Carefully thought out transcription can greatly aid analysis; poor decision-making early on can make the subsequent analysis difficult or worthless. Chapters 1 to 4 raise many issues which need to be taken into account when transcribing and coding a corpus.

In the first chapter, Jane Edwards focuses in particular on issues of coding. In a discussion which will prove invaluable to corpus researchers for years to come, she examines the principles underlying the design and implementation of transcription and coding, the principles of designing coding categories, the implementation of coding (applying the design to the data), ways of optimizing readability for human users while at the same time creating a system which is computationally tractable.

In Chapter 2, Guy Cook argues that while the use of the computer offers new possibilities for the researcher (particularly in terms of data retrieval and statistical analysis) it does not solve the initial problem of representing spoken language in written form. Underlying everything must be a sound theory and practice of transcription. He warns against treating speech as if it were writing. In particular he notes the tremendous importance of including contextual and other information when dealing with spoken data and the danger of focusing on purely linguistic features, at the expense of discourse phenomena, simply because the former are easier to handle. In discourse analysis and pragmatics we are dealing not with words alone, but with utterance-context pairings – *how* something is said, and the *context* in which it is said, may be as important as the words themselves. In relation to this Cook discusses the problems of how to represent paralinguistic and other non-linguistic features as well as background knowledge, while at the same time being aware of the problems of producing transcriptions which are so elaborate that the user becomes lost in a welter of detail. He argues (cf. Burnard and Johansson in Chapters 6 and 7) that it would be a mistake to assume that elaborate coding systems mean that we now have everything under control – many issues still remain to be resolved.

In Chapter 3, Wallace Chafe picks up many of the issues raised in the first two contributions. He is concerned with the representation of spoken language in a written format which optimizes its usefulness to the human reader. Transcription of spoken language is done for the specific purposes of the original transcriber, but ideally should be usable by a broad range of other users. Like Edwards, Chafe stresses the importance of building on the interpretive skills readers already have, and to this end discusses ways in which transcriptions can exploit such features of written language as different fonts and iconic symbols. He discusses in detail features of intonation and how to represent them and the importance of distinguishing between what *can* be measured (e.g. the precise length of a pause) and what is actually significant to participants in the original interaction and to the analysts of that interaction. Finally, in a discussion which looks forward to issues raised in Parts B and C, Chafe suggests that many of the problems raised so far can be mitigated by issuing corpora on CD-ROM which can also include the original recording in addition to the transcription and other information (such as digitized waveforms).

In Chapter 4, James Monaghan focuses on the importance of considering the end-user of the corpus and the importance of designing corpora in such a way that it is possible to access whole text structures, as well as lower level phenomena.

Chapters 5 and 6 deal with issues of transcription, coding and mark-up as they relate specifically to *electronic storage* and data interchange. Lou Burnard discusses in detail the requirements for encoding *all* types of text in order to conform to the requirements of the Text Encoding Initiative (TEI), regardless of the domain of application, or of the hardware and software the individual may be using. Johansson, in Chapter 6, deals specifically with the distinctions necessary for representing spoken discourse so that it conforms with TEI requirements. He argues that there is no necessary conflict between what are often seen as the very demanding requirements of TEI-conformant mark-up and the limited resources of the individual corpus-builder, nor between TEI and a reader-friendly/transcriber-friendly system. Provided the necessary software is developed, the underlying TEI representation can be transferred into any form convenient for an individual project.

In Chapter 7, the final chapter of this section, John Sinclair voices the worries of people involved in constructing large corpora who are alarmed by the demands of making their transcriptions TEI-conformant. These worries can be grouped under three main headings:

1. Picking up the final point made in Johansson's chapter, Sinclair raises the question of transcriptions for humans, versus those suitable for machines. Like Cook, Sinclair is concerned that end-users will become lost in a welter of detail. Several contributors to the conference raised the possibility of associating transcription with either waveforms or sound recordings by means of hypertext or CD-ROM (see Johansson, Roach, Chafe and Cook, this volume) thereby offering access to greater detail as *an option*, although the relevant software and hardware are not yet widely available.
2. If TEI-conformant transcriptions are difficult to read to most users, their production also makes totally unrealistic demands on most transcribers. For those involved in the production of very large corpora (and it must be remembered that the size of the corpus is not a trivial matter, but crucially affects the types of linguistic generalizations and claims which can be made) the cost-effectiveness of TEI must be challenged. Although it is clearly of great importance that the basic data be available for other researchers to use, is it really the case that others will want to use your corpus annotations?
3. Sinclair challenges the way in which the requirements of TEI will operate in practice. His worry is that instead of individuals being able to operate within the inherent (indeed, almost unlimited) flexibility of TEI,

as outlined in Chapters 5 and 6, we shall in practice be forced to operate within a very limited subset. We shall end up distorting our data in order to fit it into a straitjacket designed by computer buffs. Sinclair argues strongly in favour of the much weaker notion of *compatibility* (rather than *conformity*) with TEI.

Like many contributors to this book and to the conference, John Sinclair underlines the need for software interpreters to be produced – not just an interpreter which will render your TEI marked-up text readable to ordinary users, but one which will translate 'ordinary' transcripts into TEI format. Mark-up must remain user-friendly, without costing too much, and this is undoubtedly the direction in which things will develop in the future. These issues are not only of interest to designers of corpora. But as the chapters in this section show, issues of mark-up relate to long-debated issues on the transcription and interpretation of speech.

1 Principles and alternative systems in the transcription, coding and mark-up of spoken discourse

JANE A. EDWARDS

Far from being an objective and exhaustive mirroring of events of an interaction, a transcript is fundamentally selective and interpretive. The transcriber is constantly making choices concerning what information to include, what descriptive categories to use (e.g. what length pause constitutes a 'short' pause), which aspects of the interaction are interrelated and which are the most important, and how to express all of this within the limits of the graphemic/spatial medium of the transcript. If well chosen for the researcher's goals and theoretical orientation, a transcript can greatly help in finding regularities of interest free from the distraction of irrelevant detail. If not, it can hinder detection of patterns of interest, and give rise to directly misleading impressions.

For example, Ochs (1979) notes that displaying speaker turns one above the other (i.e. what I call 'vertical' format) gives rise to the perception that the speakers are equal contributors to the conversation. While useful for adult–adult conversation, this would be problematic for conversations with very young children, since these tend to be more child-controlled and child-centred. In that case, Ochs recommended putting turns by different speakers in different columns (i.e. columnar format), to suggest they are unequal contributors, and placing the child's utterances in the leftmost column, to counteract the bias towards perceiving the adult as the more dominant of the two.

Format-based biases, such as the above, can be adjusted by reformatting, if one notices them. In contrast, content-based biases involve information loss, and cannot be helped by reformatting but only by returning to the audio recordings and re-encoding the relevant aspects of the data. These include the total absence of some type of information not thought to be important initially (e.g. no prosodic marking),[1] or faulty choice of descriptive categories for the question at hand (e.g. measuring pause length as raw duration instead of adjusting for speaker's articulation rate, or the reverse).

The same types of biases are involved in the other two processes of data encoding: coding and mark-up (defined below).

20 Issues and practices

The present chapter seeks to provide a brief survey of types of encoding alternatives and what they imply, along with general principles underlying the design and use of transcription, coding and mark-up systems.

Definitions

The three encoding processes of transcription, coding, and mark-up are defined as follows.

'Transcription' involves capturing who said what, in what manner (e.g. prosody, pause, voice quality), to whom, under what circumstances (e.g. setting, activity, participant characteristics and relationships to one another). It includes preservation of various temporal aspects (e.g. pause duration, sequence of events, and simultaneity or overlap of speaker turns or speech and gestures), and some metacomments, or interpretive 'annotations'. A 'broad transcription' provides a level of detail similar to that found in scripts of plays and in courtroom proceedings. A 'narrow transcription' provides a high degree of detail regarding aspects such as stress and intonation, gesture, voice quality and phonetic/phonemic details of pronunciation, that is, regarding acoustic or non-verbal aspects of the discourse, typically in the form of punctuation marks or other non-alphanumeric characters. An example of an extremely narrow transcription is that of Pittenger et al. (1960), in which the transcript and field notes for five minutes of interaction require 183 pages.

'Coding' (also called 'tagging' or 'annotation') differs from transcription in its content and degree of structuring. Rather than capturing the overtly observable acoustic and non-verbal aspects of the interaction, coding focuses on events which bear a more abstract relationship to each other, that is, on syntactic, semantic and pragmatic categories. Whereas events tied together by transcription categories tend to share some physical similarities (e.g. all instances of 'short pause' involve the absence of vocalization of less than some specified raw or adjusted duration), the events grouped together by coding categories may have little or no physical similarity, as for example, the word strings 'ice cream' and 'Senate Appropriations Committee' which are both instances of category 'Noun Phrase'. In an electronic text, all instances sharing a code can be retrieved to-gether, so in a sense, coding serves to create physical similarity (i.e. the code or tag), which can be used in considering them jointly and in distributional analyses. Finally, except for the exploratory phase of research (during which a coding system is expanded and developed), coding involves a tightly specified set of categories, usually encoded as abbreviations (e.g. 'N' for 'noun'; 'V' for 'verb').

'Mark-up' originated in the marks used by typesetters to signal the structural units and fonts of a document. As defined here,[2] it concerns *format-relevant* specifications intended to be interpreted by a *typesetter or computer software*, for proper segmentation of the text and cataloguing of its parts, in the service of formatting, retrieval, tabulation or related processes. The best-known mark-up system is the Standard Generalized Mark-up Language (SGML), developed by

the publishing industry so that texts submitted by diverse sources could be conformant with the same software without the need for expensive hand-editing. The Text Encoding Initiative (TEI) (see Burnard, Chapter 5) has extended SGML to apply to a wide range of texts, from historical, to poetic, to spoken language and a number of others. SGML is a *metalanguage*. That is, it concerns how to symbolize general types of information; not the specific substantive distinctions which are made. Thus, as Johansson notes in Chapter 6, the TEI proposal for spoken language indicates <s> and </s> as one type of marker for the boundaries of text units, but leaves it up to the researcher to decide what substantive type of units those will be (i.e. syntactically defined, prosodically defined). Because mark-up systems are intended to be read most immediately by a computer rather than a person, readability is less of a concern than computational tractability. Consequently they often involve lengthy control strings which would be difficult for people to process efficiently, and tend to be proposed in conjunction with a software environment, or 'user interface', which hides the cumbersome mark-up strings from the user and renders them instead into a more person-friendly format, as selected by the user. Rather than its readability or specific content choices, what determines the adequacy of a mark-up system is its exhaustiveness in allowing for the full range of types of format-relevant distinctions users may wish to make. For this reason, the TEI proposal for spoken language (Johansson, Chapter 6) began with a compilation of transcription and coding systems from a wide range of disciplines (summarized in Johansson et al. 1992), and was devised to allow for all major *types of encoding* encountered, without advocating a particular set of substantive categories they are to encode.

The discussion which follows is divided into four sections:

1. principles underlying design of transcription, coding, and mark-up systems;
2. contrasting systems of transcription and coding;
3. principles of implementation, that is, applying a designed system to actual data;
4. principles underlying the use of computerized archives.

What is intended here is a general overview. References to fuller discussions of related points are provided in each section.

1 Principles underlying the design of encoding systems

Three types of general design principles pertain to the design of adequate encoding systems, regardless of content domain or research focus. These are: principles of category design, readability, and computational tractability.

1.1 Principles of category design

All systematic description (either format-relevant or content-relevant) depends on three principles of categorization. In designing a category set for describing a dimension of interest, three properties are particularly important. First, the categories must be *systematically discriminable*. That is, it must be clear for each event in the data and each category whether or not the category applies. In the classification of pause length, for example, there must be some basis for deciding between 'short' or 'long' pauses. Second, the categories need to be *exhaustive*. That is, for each particular case in the data, there must be a category which fits (even if only 'miscellaneous'). Third, and most important, the categories must be *systematically contrastive*. This requires further discussion.

When categories are treated as mutually exclusive alternatives – that is, if only one can apply to any particular case in the data – the categories partially determine each other's boundaries. For example, the upper boundary of 'short' pause depends on the lower boundary of 'long' pause in the system, and this may differ greatly across projects. This is a property of language more generally (e.g. Lyons 1977) – for example, the meaning of a spatial preposition is partly determined by the other prepositions it contrasts with within the language. It means that two transcription systems which both have a category of 'final intonation' may mean something different by it, if there are five other intonational categories in one system and nine others in the other system.

When categories are not mutually exclusive, as with speech act categories (i.e. the utterance 'It's cold in here' can be interpreted as either an assertion about temperature or a polite request to close the door, or both), there is an implicit contrast between the presence and the absence of each individual conceptual property (e.g. presence vs. absence of 'assertion'; presence vs. absence of 'indirect request').

The researcher's task in choosing a set of descriptive categories for *transcription* and *coding*, or format-relevant categories for *mark-up* and data display is to exploit the contrastiveness of categories, that is, to choose categories which contrast in ways which are most likely to reveal the properties of interest in the research.

For example, in their research on speech acts, Lampert and Ervin-Tripp (1993) began by consideration of Searle's (1976) taxonomy:

1. *Representatives* Speech that commits a speaker to the truth of the expressed proposition (e.g. assertions, suggestions, conclusions).
2. *Directives* Speech where a speaker attempts to get an addressee to act (e.g. requests, prohibitions, questions).
3. *Commissives* Speech that commits a speaker to some future action (e.g. promises, offers, threats).
4. *Expressives* Speech that reveals a speaker's current psychological state (e.g. apologies, greetings, thanks).
5. *Declarations* Speech that immediately changes a current state of affairs (e.g. christenings, firings).

However, since their focus was on *children's acquisition* of methods of affecting other people through interaction, or '*control acts*', the following taxonomy was more useful for their purposes:

1. *Directives or positive requests* Utterances that require that an addressee act to provide either goods or services.
2. *Prohibitions or negative requests* Utterances that require that an addressee stop or avoid a line of action.
3. *Permissions or allowances* Utterances that either request from or grant to an addressee permission to obtain goods or services.
4. *Intentions* Utterances that commit the speaker to a line of action that an addressee is expected either to facilitate or at least not block.
5. *Claims* Utterances that require an addressee to recognize a speaker's right to certain goods, activities, or services.
6. *Offers* Utterances that invite an addressee to accept goods or services.

1.2   Readability

If a transcript is to be analysed mainly by reading through it line by line (for coding, or interpretive analysis), it is important that information be preserved in a form which enables the researcher to extract the main information as quickly as possible without overburdening short-term memory.

In approaching a transcript, readers necessarily bring with them strategies developed in the course of extensive experience with other types of written materials (e.g. books, newspapers, train schedules, advertisements, personal letters). It makes sense for transcript designers to draw upon reader expectations in their choice of conventions, in part because readers are good at extracting information in these ways from other written materials, but also because strategies based on reading habits are not necessarily subject to conscious awareness and may be difficult to suspend when reading a transcript, even if it is desirable to do so.

Two cues used widely in print to channel reader attention and shape perceptions of the relative importance of different types of information and their degree of interrelationship are: *visual prominence* (e.g. bold face, underlining, font size) and *spatial arrangement* (e.g. nearness to other parts of the text, spatial precedence left to right or top to bottom). For example, chapter titles are expected to be printed in a large font, possibly centred or ruled off, and placed above the body of the text at some vertical distance, rather than, say, being embedded in the body of a text and in the same font size and type. Despite great differences in orientation and research purpose, in looking across transcripts of various types, one notices some recurring uses of these cues in transcripts, to highlight information and relationships of interest. In what follows, I briefly summarize six of them (treated in greater detail in Edwards 1992b, 1993b). Some of these overlap with properties discussed by Du Bois (1991) and Johansson (1991).

The principles of readability described below can be met in a computerized text either by direct encoding (i.e. having the input format be considered to be also the format the reader is to read), or through the mediation of a mark-up language, and associated reformatting software (as discussed above regarding compensating for format-based biases).

Issues and practices

Proximity of related events

Events or types of information which are more closely related to each other tend to be placed spatially closer to each other than those that are less closely related. For example, prosodic information may be placed immediately beside the relevant segment of an utterance, as in the following, from the London–Lund Corpus, in which the direction of nuclear pitch change is indicated by nonletter characters inserted before the relevant vowel (i.e. rise '/', fall '\', and fall-rise '\/'):

(1) Svartvik and Quirk (1980), text S.1.3
1 3 7212280 1 1 A   11 and at ^\/home# .
1 3 7212290 1 1 A   11 she`s not a ^b\it the way she is at c/ollege#

Visual separability of unlike events

Readability is improved if events or types of information that are qualitatively different (e.g. spoken words and researcher comments, codes, and categories) are encoded in distinctly different ways, for example, upper vs. lower case letters, enclosed in parentheses vs. not, letters vs. non-letter characters (as in Example (1)), full words vs. abbreviations. These can enable the reader to know what kind of information is involved before actually reading it, and in this way can greatly speed interpretation of a text and minimize false attributions (such as perceiving a word as having been spoken when it is actually part of the contextual specifications or research comments).

Time–space iconicity

Typically in transcripts, temporally prior events are encountered earlier on the page (top to bottom, or left to right) than temporally later events. This can include utterances, pauses, gestures, door slams, laughs, coughs, and so forth. In this way, temporal sequence is represented relatively directly in the form of spatial sequence:

(2) From Heath (1984):
1   (door opening)
2   (0.5)
3   D: Hello
4   (2.3)
5   D: Mohammed Oola?
6   P: Yes
7   D: Yes could you sit down (.) please
8   (7.3)

(3) From Jefferson (1984): Tom: I used to ((cough)) smoke a lot.

Logical priority

Logically prerequisite information for interpreting utterances tends to be encountered earlier on the page than the utterance or utterances to which it is relevant.

Information concerning the circumstances of data gathering and the relationships among the speakers tends to be given at the top of the transcript, whereas changes in circumstances or activities during the course of the interaction tend to precede the utterances they contextualize or potentially influence.

Mnemonic marking

Categories are encoded either in directly interpretable abbreviations or in symbolically iconic ways in order to expedite recovery of their meaning during rapid reading. An example of this is the use of a slash (/) for rising tone and backslash (\) for falling tone, rather than vice versa or instead of arbitrary numerical codes (e.g. '106' for 'rising'). Another source of direct interpretability is a high level of familiarity from other written materials. Du Bois (1991) notes that a number of transcription conventions derive from literary conventions found in novels and plays – conventions with which readers have extensive experience independently of transcript data. Some examples are the use of three dots (. . .) for pauses, or a dash (–) for interrupted thoughts or interrupted utterances. In a sense, time–space iconicity and logical priority could also be considered as borrowings from familiar literary conventions.

Efficiency and compactness

Reading speed can also be increased by marking coded distinctions with as few symbols as possible, so long as meaning is easily recoverable (i.e. encoded mnemonically), to minimize non-essential and distracting clutter in the transcript. For example, the use of slash (/) for rising tone is more compact and efficiently read than would be the use of the full word *rising*. The encoding of spoken words and prosodic information on the same line instead of on separate lines is also a type of compactness.

1.3   Computational tractability

Computers interpret things literally. Unlike people, they will not detect the similarity between, for example, 'you know' and 'y'know' unless provided with explicit instructions or functional heuristics to do so. For this reason, two properties needed in computerized data are: *systematic encoding*, that is, avoidance of non-meaningful variability (e.g. in spelling, spacing, capitalization), and *predictable encoding*, that is, use of systematicities that the researchers can successfully extend in guessing how a form of interest is probably encoded, prior to specifying a search command to find it. If the researcher knows of only one variant form when there are several, the computer search will retrieve only a subset of relevant instances, and the results may be seriously compromised from sampling error. This problem and strategies for avoiding it are discussed in detail in the final section.

2 Contrasting systems of transcription and coding

With these general design principles in mind, we turn now to substantive differences among transcription and coding systems, focusing first on type and level of description, and then on spatial arrangement of information.[3]

2.1 Level and type of description

Table 1.1 summarizes several major alternatives in transcriptional categories. For reasons of space, I will only discuss two: pauses and units of analysis. Discussion and examples of the others are found in Edwards (1993b).

Table 1.1 Some content-related alternatives (reproduced from Edwards 1993b)

Notation of words: orthography, eye-dialect, phonetic/phonemic
Unit of analysis: defined by intonation, pauses, syntax
Prosodics: Intonation: contours vs. levels
Pauses: physically measured vs. adjusted for speech rate
Prominence: pitch vs. loudness vs. lengthening
Turn taking: latching encoded explicitly vs. by default
Kinesics: gesture globally described vs. analysed into components

Pauses

Different research perspectives classify the same domain in different ways. In research on information flow, all perceived pauses are preserved (e.g. Chafe 1993), whereas, in focusing on miscommunication or coordination of turns, the only pauses of interest may be those which are longer or shorter than expected, relative to interlocutors' shared cultural norms (e.g. Gumperz and Berenz 1993). In the former, the minimum pause may be 0.2 seconds, in the latter, 0.5 seconds. Researchers also differ in whether they measure pauses in physical time or in number of beats relative to speaker's articulation rate. Each of these choices is justified with respect to some theoretical framework.

Units of analysis

Researchers use different criteria in dividing the text into segments useful for coding and analysis. Discourse researchers may employ units which are based on intonation (e.g. 'tone units' or 'intonation units') or bounded by pauses (e.g. the 'production units' in Gee and Grosjean 1983). If they are defined syntactically, the definition may differ depending upon whether the project involves only English or also other languages, only adults or also children, and the type of discourse involved (e.g. dialogue or narrative). Berman and Slobin (1986) used discourse-functional criteria in defining 'clause' for purposes of cross-linguistic research on children's narratives: 'We define a clause as any unit containing a *unified* predicate. By *unified*, we mean a predicate that expresses a *single* situation (activity, event, state)' (Slobin 1993: 211).

Comparisons of units of different types and their interrelationships are found in Chafe (1987), Cruttenden (1986), Du Bois and Schuetze-Coburn (1993), Edwards (1989, 1991, 1993b), Schuetze-Coburn et al. (1991), and Svartvik (1990).

2.2 Spatial arrangement

Another set of decisions with content implications are decisions of spatial arrangement, especially with respect to: (a) arrangement of turns by different speakers, and (b) placement of contextual comments, gestures, prosody, and coding, relative to utterances.

Spatial arrangement of speakers' turns

The arrangement of turns one above the other ('vertical' format) implies equal influence of the speakers, whereas arranging turns in separate columns ('columnar' format) implies unequal influence, with the speaker in the leftmost column being the more dominant. 'Partiture' format is similar to the format used in choral music, in which the voices are given always in the same order within the staff (soprano, alto, tenor, bass), and continue all the way to the right margin, rather than only up to the first utterance or turn boundary. This is the best of the three for display of densely overlapping events, including verbal and non-verbal, if used with specialized software (as in Ehlich 1993).

Placement of comments, non-verbal events, prosody and coding, relative to the spoken utterances

This involves actually two independent choices: (a) the placement of non-utterance events (i.e. non-verbal actions or contextual events) relative to utterances, and (b) the placement of specifications relative to the utterance, non-verbal action, or contextual event being specified.

The arrangement of non-utterance events relative to utterances

There are two alternatives. *Running text* (*RT*) format is the most versatile and widely used. Based on methods used for preserving conversations in literary works (e.g. novels and plays), RT format maintains time-space iconicity for non-utterances as well as for utterances. That is, all events are arranged on the page in the same order as they occur in time (left to right; bottom to top), as in Examples (2) and (3) and the following:

(4) Bloom (1973, Alison, third data session):
     (M and A sitting on chair; A wearing half-zippered jacket;
     fingers in her mouth)

M: What did you see? What did you see over there?
(M points to monitor)
(A looking at monitor with fingers in her mouth)
A: Mommy/

Its systematic ordering amounts to anchoring all events to an external reference frame, namely the time line. The specification of the time line ranges from simple ordering of events to systematic time tags throughout the discourse (e.g. Bloom, 1993; Johansson, Chapter 6), which are useful in linking the transcript with videotape or digitized speech records. The uniform temporal treatment of utterance and non-utterance events eases perception of temporal structuring of utterances relative to non-utterance events (overlap, sequencing, rhythmic and other properties), and presents utterances and non-utterances as being potentially of equal communicative significance in the interaction.

In *Utterance-plus-clarification* (or UPC) format, non-verbal and contextual events are treated as clarificational information, and are placed on dependent tiers beneath the utterances, labelled as to type (e.g. 'sit' for 'situational', 'gpx' for 'gestural-proxemic' in the following example):

(5) UPC version of Example (4)
  *MOT: what did you see?
  %sit: Mother and Alison sitting on chair; Alison wearing half-zippered jacket; fingers in her mouth
  *MOT: what did you see over there?
  %gpx: <aft> points to monitor
  *ALI: Mommy.
  %gpx: looking at monitor with fingers in her mouth

In contrast to RT, which is event-based, UPC is utterance-based, and maintains time–space iconicity only for utterances. UPC is intended to enable each utterance to be retrieved with any additional information needed for interpreting it, and is a viable option when the analyst is interested only in utterance-level phenomena. But the decision of which non-verbal events are and are not relevant to each particular utterance involves an extra set of interpretive decisions beyond those in RT. It is, of course, difficult to see temporal structuring of verbal relative to non-verbal events in this format, and the absence of information regarding the relative ordering of non-verbal events prevents translation from UPC to RT format where they could be more easily expressed. Finally, the implied subordination of non-verbal to verbal events makes it difficult to preserve discourse types in which non-verbal information supplements the content of utterances to any great degree, such as when a gesture occurs without an utterance, or in the retelling of highly visual events, such as silent films, cartoons, and so on.

Placement of analytic specification

Specificational information includes narrow transcription (e.g. details of prosody or non-verbal actions) and coding (e.g. semantic, syntactic or pragmatic coding).

Unlike the preceding distinction, it concerns co-temporaneous rather than temporally ordered information.

If the information can be compactly and distinctively encoded, it can be interleaved with the basic level description of the utterance, action or event it specifies, i.e. *'Interspersed'* format. An example of this is the use of non-letters for prosodic encoding shown in Example (1).

As the level of complexity increases, or when users plan to focus selectively on some layers to the exclusion of others, it is common to place the specification on separate tiers, labelled as to type, i.e. *'Segment-plus-specification'* (or SPS) format. For example, in the following, the 'S:' tier contains the orthographic rendering of the utterance, the 'm:' tier, its morphological rendering, and the 's:' tier, its syntactic word classes, constituent structure and deep semantic case:

(6)   From Fillmore et al. (1982):
        S: He wen' (=went) out./
        m: he *went out
        s: (n1a PN.3.M) (v *V PT)

SPS format can also be used for purposes of 'narrow' transcription. For example, in the Tones and Break Indices (ToBI) system of prosodic encoding proposed by Victor Zue and associates (Silverman et al. 1992), the orthographic rendering of the utterance is followed by three specification tiers: a tone tier, a break-index tier, and a tier for miscellaneous annotations. The difference between SPS and the other tier-based format, UPC, is that the events in SPS are co-temporaneous, so they can still be uniformly related to a time line.

Either Interspersed or SPS format can be used with either RT or UPC format.

Descriptor scope

A descriptive category can be left to 'float' in a region of general applicability in transcription, or it may be tied more closely to a specific unit of analysis. The most common methods for indicating the scope of relevance of descriptors are:

(a)   placing the descriptor next to the relevant item on the text line;
(b)   repeating the relevant item on a separate tier next to the descriptor;
(c)   using computer-generated numerical tags to all words in the discourse (as in Du Bois and Schuetze-Coburn 1993);
(d)   explicit time tags, as to when the coded event occurred (as in Bloom 1993); or
(e)   bracketing and/or spacing practices.

The following is an example of bracketing and spacing.

(7)   From the Penn Treebank
       (S (NP (NP Composer
                   (NP Marc Marder))

         ,
        (NP (NP a college friend

```
            (PP of
                (NP
                    (NP Mr. Lane)
                    's)))
        (SBARQ
        (WHNP who)
        (S (NP T)
            (VP earns
                (NP his living)
                (S (NP *)
                    (VP playing
                        (NP the double bass)
                        (PP in
                            (NP classical music ensembles))))))))
```

A recurrent challenge is how to specify the scope of codes when they pertain to non-adjacent elements in the discourse. For example, in coding the verb phrase 'picked ... out', in 'They picked the kittens out', an adequate method would involve indicating not only that both 'picked' and 'out' are parts of a verb phrase, but also co-referencing of some sort to show that they are part of the *same* verb phrase. While the brackets and spacing of Example (7) preserve this kind of discontinuous constituency, it is often desirable to attach yet further levels of coding to verb phrases and this requires additional mechanisms. Du Bois and Schuetze-Coburn (1993) accomplish this by means of co-indexing within the context of a relational database. The constituents of a phrase are co-indexed (in whatever way is appropriate for a given language), and further levels of specifications can then be attached as needed to either the elements or the phrase as a whole.

3   Principles of implementation

Various factors can contribute to a mismatch between the distinctions intended in the manuals for an encoding system and their actual realization when applied to actual data. These include such things as underspecified documentation, inadequate coder training, lack of systematic checks on intercoder agreement.

Lampert and Ervin-Tripp (1993) note that learning to use a coding system is similar to learning a second language in that in both cases, the learner must learn how to extend what is already known in useful ways. Problems can arise when the distinctions of importance rest on cultural or age-based assumptions other than those the coder shares (e.g. politeness norms), or when the distinctions to be made are highly subjective in other ways.

In documenting a coding system, the alternatives which contrast with each other within a particular content area need to be given conceptual definitions, contrasted with each other, and illustrated by core and boundary examples (to bracket the concept), as in the following example.

(8)   Types of speech acts (Lampert and Ervin-Tripp 1993).
    Code (abbreviation): D
    Category: Directive or Positive Request
    Category definition: An action is required or requested of the hearer, involving goods or services. These may have similar surface forms to codes of Topic 10, but unlike that Topic, the focus here is who is going to act. If it is the addressee, it is a directive, etc.
    Example: Can I have some of that?

For prosodic distinctions, audio tapes also help to clarify the intended distinction, such as those prepared by Cruttenden (1986) and Du Bois et al. (1993).

Lampert and Ervin-Tripp discuss at length various other factors which affect the match between the distinctions intended by the researcher and those actually made in the data. Among other things, they advise the following: use of multiple coders, from differing backgrounds, trained in groups, with concrete materials, and periodically checked for intercoder agreement, using such statistics as Cohen's Kappa (see Lampert and Ervin-Tripp 1993 for details).

4   Principles for the use of computerized language archives

Difficulties with validity and reliability may arise within a computerized archive, especially if the data come from different sources.

Validity: comparability of encoded distinctions across projects

For computational ease, archives sometimes convert data from different sources to a single encoding standard. In the absence of audio tapes, this is done by assigning to each category in each data set the seeming 'nearest translational equivalent' in the encoding standard. But as in foreign languages, the nearest one still need not be very close in meaning. The categories from different projects may then be the same in symbol only. For example, although '. .' may stand for 'short pause' for all the data sets in the archive, for some projects that may mean 0.2 of a second and in others, 0.5 of a second. This can be determined by referring to the manuals from the different projects. Determining the number and nature of categories of a particular type can also help determine the likely comparability of nearest equivalents. In all but lexical studies, it is generally safest to assume that 'related categories' from different sources are *not* the same (see Edwards 1992a, 1993a for discussion and examples).

Reliability: consistency of encoded distinctions within and across projects

Two main hazards in the use of computerized archives are: *overselection*, that is, the retrieval of more instances than are desired due to using an overly general search pattern (e.g. retrieving *only* and *one* when searching for instances of the preposition *on*), and *underselection*, that is, the retrieval of only a subset of the relevant instances, due to neglect of some relevant variants in the data. Whereas the former can be costly in time and effort; the latter can actually jeopardize the validity of research findings, and is the focus of the remaining discussion.

Unlike random sampling error in psychological experiments, the inconsistencies in data archives arise from human hands, and need not be either rare or random. Fortunately, they can be counteracted with use of an exhaustive listing of forms in the data, as described below.

Figure 1.1 on page 33 presents actual data from an archive, relevant to the question of when a child acquires uncontracted-*not* (e.g. *cannot*) and contracted-*not* (e.g. *can't*). The two forms: *n't* and -*'nt* mean the same thing, namely contracted-*not*, and arose from coder error. If the researcher knew of only one of them, research results would differ greatly, since they are distributed differently with respect to the other variable of interest, namely, time. The -*'nt* variant is abundant from the first data file, but the *n't* variant does not become abundant until the 27th data file, when the child is *seven months older*.

This kind of coding inconsistency happens to some degree in any archive, but need not affect results if the researcher can detect all the variants prior to computer search, and include them in the search. An exhaustive listing of wordforms in the data is highly useful for this purpose. This was the method used in the present case, and led to detecting not only the above two variants but also 12 further variants: *can'*, *can(t)*, *&can*, *di'n(t>*, *di(d)n*, *didn*, *don'*, *don*, *&don*, *won*, *won'*, and *&won*, which account for an additional 58 cases or 12 per cent of the total number of contracted negatives in the data, and would be important to include, for example, for determining which particular verbs are first to appear in contracted form.

Exhaustive listings of forms can be obtained by using computer programs, such as the *freq* program available in the HUM package via anonymous ftp from the ICAME archive (nora.hd.uib.no). Where homographs arise, a concordance program such as *kwal* is useful, providing the utterances containing each form.

Conclusion

This chapter has examined principles underlying the design and implementation of transcription, coding and mark-up systems, and surveyed format- and content-relevant differences between transcription and coding systems. It described some hazards encountered in the use of computerized data archives, and strategies for minimizing their impact on research results. The use of computers in discourse research offers many new possibilities, but depends on data accountability and effective user strategies. The present chapter is intended as a contribution to the continuing development of methodology in this area.

Figure 1.1 Occurrences of full-not, and two encodings of contracted-not (n't, and -'nt) in child utterances in the data from an electronic archive.

File	Age	not	n't	-'nt
01	2;02		l	lxxx
02	2;02	ooo	l	lx
03	2;03	oo	lxx	lxx
04	2;03	o	l	lxxx
05	2;03		lxx	lxxx
06	2;03	o	lx	lxx
07	2;04	oooooooo	l	lxxxxxxxx
08	2;04		l	lxx
10	2;05	oo	l	l
11	2;05	oo	l	lxxxxx
12	2;05	oooooooooooo	lx	lxxxxxxxxxx
13	2;05	oooooooooooooo	l	lxxxx
14	2;05		lx	lxx
15	2;06	oooooooooo	lxx	lxxxx
16	2;06	oooooooooooooooo	lx	lxxxxxxxxxx
17	2;07	oooooooooooo	l	lxxxxxxxxx
18	2;07	oooooooo	lxxx	lxxxxxxx
19	2;07	ooooooo	lx	lxxxx
20	2;08	ooooooo	lx	lxxxxxxxxxxxxx
21a	2;08	o	l	lxx
21b	2;08	oooo	l	l
22a	2;08	ooo	lxx	lxxxxxxxxx
22b	2;08	o	l	lxxxxxx
23	2;08	oo	lx	lxxxxxxx
24	2;09	oooooo	lx	lxxx
25	2;09	oooo	l	lx
26	2;09	oooooo	lxxxx	l
27a	2;09	oooooooooo	lxxxxxxxx	lx
27b	2;09	ooo	lxxxxxxxxxxxxx	lx
28b	2;10	oooo	lxxxxxxxx	l
29	2;10		lxxxxxxxx	l
30a	2;10	o	lxxxx	l
30b	2;10	oo	lxxxxxxxxx	lx
31a	2;11	oo	lx	lx
31b	2;11	oo	lxx	l
32a	2;11		lxxx	lxxxxx
32b	2;11		lxx	lx
33	2;11	oooooooooooooooooooo	lxxxxxxxxxxxxx	lxx
34	3;00	ooooo	lxxxxxxxxxxx	lxxxxx
35	3;00	oooooooooooo	lxxxxxxxxxxxxxxxxxxxxxxxxx	lxxx
36	3;00	ooooo	lxxxxxxxxxxxxxx	lxxxxxxx
37	3;01	ooo	lxxxxxxxxxxxxxxxxxx	lxx
38	3;01	oooo	l	lxxxxxxxxxxx
39	3;01	oooooooo	lxx	lxxxxxxxxxxxxxxxxxxx
40	3;02	oooooooooo	lx	lxxxxxxxxxxxxxxxxxxxxxxxxxx
Totals:		235	180	219

Notes

1. This may even include the exclusion of repeated utterances, as noted by Perkins (this volume), and as was the practice of child language researchers in the 1960s (e.g. the Roger Brown corpus).
2. Two other definitions of mark-up warrant brief mention. First, some authors use 'mark-up' as a superordinate to both transcription and coding, but I prefer to use 'encoding' as the superordinate because it focuses attention on the mediating function of a string of characters rather than on the string itself. Thus, referring to '..' as 'one way of *encoding* a pause', has a different sense than referring to '..' as 'one way of *marking up* a pause'.

    Second, some authors define 'mark-up' as any conventions that are not part of standard orthographic practice. In a publishing context, this would mean any marks an editor adds in ink for the benefit of a typesetter, and would be functionally motivated. But the distinction between what is or is not part of mark-up breaks down when applied to spoken language texts for several reasons:

    (a) In a spoken language transcript, the class of conventions that depart from standard orthographic practice includes not just format specifications, but also types of information which pertain to the unique properties of spoken discourse as distinguished from written language: prosody, turn-taking, and non-verbal events. To treat these as part of 'mark-up', on analogy with typesetter's marks, implies a view of spoken language as being basically the same as written language, but with (optional) embellishment. This is a theoretical position which few would intentionally embrace.

    (b) It obscures the fact that interpretive choice is involved even when standard orthographic conventions are used in transcript. Encoding a spoken word via standard spelling rather than via the International Phonetic Alphabet (IPA) presupposes that details of the speaker's pronunciation are not important for the research at hand. This is an interpretive judgement which may be false in some cases and lead to neglect of what may turn out later to be important clues to structure.

    (c) Finally, it overlooks the possibility that characters within standard orthography can themselves serve a mark-up function in conjunction with a computer program that recognizes them as such. For example, some computer programs interpret the sequence: period, two spaces, capital letter, as boundary markers in the same way as other programs interpret the explicit boundary markers, <s> and </s>.

    Thus, a different separation of mark-up and non-mark-up would be involved for each encoding system, and the distinction between mark-up and non-mark-up is arbitrary rather than corresponding to natural classes of events in discourse.
3. Mark-up is not mentioned in this section because the content is secondary to the processes of transcription and coding. But mark-up can play a vital role with software in enabling alternative visual displays of the same data and should be thought of below wherever format-relevant choices are involved, especially concerning spatial arrangement.

2 Theoretical issues: transcribing the untranscribable

GUY COOK

1 Introduction

Although the possibilities offered by computerized corpora of spoken discourse for advancing understanding are beyond question both exciting and promising, it would be self-defeating to suppose that the problems of the relationship between transcriptions and original speech events are solved by the storage of transcriptions on computer. To take full advantage of the opportunity offered by computerized corpora, we need to intensify, rather than sidestep, our scepticism about this relationship.

The advantages of establishing a standardized notation for computerized transcription may be stated simply. It would enable analysis of more data, making possible an improvement in the understanding of spoken discourse. The tremendous effects of increased quantity should not be belittled. In the analysis of linguistic features, the fashionable ethnographic division between qualitative and quantitative research is overstated. Increase in quantity *can* provide the basis for an increase in quality. Yet this gain arises because quantity enables analysts to distinguish regularities from idiosyncrasies more successfully; it is not because corpora change the nature of transcription, nor because computer storage magically converts subjective and impressionistic judgements into objective facts.

In the analysis of a corpus of spoken discourse, the computer can be used in two ways:

1. to retrieve and present transcriptions for analysis;
2. to abstract statistics from the corpus or a designated part of it.

It is important to distinguish these two quite separate uses, for they often present quite different problems. Each use also demands its own distinct criterion of readability: on the one hand for humans, and on the other for computer programs.

For the first use the computer serves only to store and relay the transcription. The result is still presented in writing and read by a human being, albeit on screen rather than paper. Although the quantity of transcription may be greater and more quickly retrieved and manipulated, the problems inherent in representing speech in writing remain; analyses of the theoretical issues in transcription on to paper (Ochs 1979, Cook 1990, Edwards 1992b) are thus not superseded, but remain as relevant as ever.

The second use does indeed introduce new possibilities, new problems and new solutions not dealt with in earlier discussions; but the statistical analysis, however skilfully programmed, will be invalidated if the text and notation it searches are flawed. Both uses of the computer and both types of readability remain dependent upon a sound theory and practice of transcription whose principles are unaffected by the technology of storage, retrieval and analysis. It is issues concerning these underlying principles which this chapter seeks to address.

It is in the nature of human communication to be in part vague and indeterminate. The conflictual and socially dangerous nature of much interaction (Lecercle 1990, Shippey 1993) makes it advantageous for speakers to court such indeterminacy, in order that they may retreat behind pleas of misunderstanding if challenged. This endemic vagueness creates considerable problems for both transcription and analysis.

In transcription, there is an inevitable conflict between those elements which can be transcribed most exactly and those which must remain impressionistic, elusive and subjective. Analysis finds itself in a dilemma. A first option (characteristic of periods when the study of language is seeking to identify itself as a science) is to limit enquiry to exact and measurable elements where hypotheses can be made and falsified. A second option is to extend analysis to those areas whose description must remain intuitive and speculative, but which are nevertheless often essential to an understanding of certain aspects of communication.

It is not the intention of this chapter to attack either option. Spoken interaction is of its nature both precise (in order to promote communication and cooperation) and imprecise (as a strategy for defending territory), and to do justice to both tendencies, analysis must accept two separate routes for description and assessment: the one precise, statistical, factual; the other conjectural and philosophical.

A problem, however, arises when the two areas and two types of description are confused. An example is provided by Tannen (1992: 189–92) in her discussion of a controversial subject: whether men interrupt women more than women interrupt men. She observes that if 'interruption' is defined only as a linguistic phenomenon, in which one participant begins to speak during another's utterance, then interruptions can be quantified. Yet if 'interruption' is defined psychologically, as intrusive speech perceived as offensive, then it cannot be quantified from transcriptions alone. There are linguistic interruptions which are perceived as affectionate or supportive, and therefore do not count as psychological interruptions at all.

Corpora of transcribed spoken discourse present a temptation to such confusion, especially when one considers the kinds of questions to which people with access to corpora will be asked to provide answers. The expense of time and effort will put analysis under pressure to overreach itself by trying to extend objective judgements from areas which are quantifiable into areas which are not. Undoubtedly, for example, a corpus of spoken discourse will be used to quantify the correlation between conversational behaviour and social groups. It is essential for analysts not to fall into the trap exemplified by Tannen. Limitations must be accepted if important advances are not to be discredited. Automatic searching of a computerized corpus cannot provide statistics about psychologically defined discourse phenomena, though it can provide a starting point for further investigation.

1.1   Elements of spoken interaction

The problems of transcription, and the distinction between measurable and immeasurable phenomena, may be clarified by a classification of elements in the original speech event. The classification adopted here is as follows:

A   Linguistic features:
   1. the *words* under consideration at any given time;
   2. *preceding words*: speech occurring earlier in the same event and its transcription.
B   Contextual features:
   3. *paralanguage*: any meaningful behaviour preceding or interpolating the words, such as voice quality, gestures, facial expressions and touch;
   4. *situation*: features of the immediate physical surroundings including features of the participants;
   5. *participant knowledge* of the cultural context including knowledge of other participants, and of other speech events and written texts affecting interpretation;
   6. *participant attitudes* towards all of these.

The general organization of this chapter is based upon consideration of each of these in turn and of the interaction between them.

The apparently naive terms 'words' and 'preceding words' are used in preference to 'text' and 'co-text' on the grounds that the latter associate too readily with writing. As one of the main arguments I wish to advance is against the treatment of speech as though it were writing, 'text' and 'co-text' are reserved for reference to transcription. In this terminology, it is perception as *words* which links (via the intermediate levels of phonology and graphology) the *speech* of the original event to the *text* of the transcription which contains the same words. Though words must be realized physically in either speech or writing, yet they may reasonably be said to have a psychological existence independent of either; if this were not the case, it would be impossible to read aloud or to write down speech. In lay transcriptions, such as those of court cases and parliamentary proceedings, the stenographer's aim is to make the identity and order of written words correspond exactly to the order and identity of those spoken. For linguistics, however, this is only a beginning.

38 *Issues and practices*

The first central problem of transcription, often overlooked by a linguistics designed for the analysis of invented or written data, is to relate linguistic to contextual features. For whereas in writing, contextual features are either irrelevant to the meaning, or – when they are relevant – textually encoded, in speech they are often manifest to participants and therefore unmentioned. Perhaps the best known illustration is deixis. Whereas in speech I might say 'Give me that', the same message in writing, to make any sense at all, would have to specify referents for 'me', 'that' and the ellipted 'you'.

The second central problem derives from the first. The fact that relevant elements of context are less likely to be given linguistic realization in speech because they are evident to participants, intensifies the likelihood of divergent interpretation. To a greater or lesser degree in all my categories of context, there is the possibility of a difference between transcriber's and participants' perceptions. To confuse the two is itself inherited from the tendency to analyse speech as though it were writing, for whereas anyone who reads a written text becomes a participant, the transcribers of spoken discourse, or the readers of their transcriptions, remain outsiders: voyeurs rather than participants. Yet where there is a difference between participant and observer perceptions, it is essential, though difficult, for the transcription to reflect only the former. There is very little point in transcribing any contextual information unless it is noticed and considered significant by the participants. Unfortunately many elaborate transcription systems pay little attention to this principle (Birdwhistell 1973, Jefferson 1984).[1] The ethnographic notion (that the use of participants as transcribers or commentators eliminates this problem) overlooks the difference between recalled judgements and immediate ones, and also limits the conversations considered to those which include ethnographers!

2   The words

This problem of discrepancy between transcriber and participant is, however, far less problematic in the first category[2] (words) than in the remainder. Here the view that 'all transcription is interpretation' or 'the text is already mark-up' (Editors' comment: this refers to a point made by James Monaghan in discussion, see also Chapter 4) is a simplification, confounding two very different meanings of 'interpretation'. When a group of literate native (or similarly expert) users[3] of a language write down the utterance of another expert user, the words on their separate pages are in most circumstances exactly the same. This is because there are fairly universal procedures for the idealisation of speech into writing which are inculcated into literate people through education, and the degree of difference between transcriptions of the words is generally exaggerated.[4] Literate expert speakers of a language cannot help understanding what is said and, in almost all cases, segmenting it into the same words as other speakers.[5] This is inevitable unless there is some interference in the channel or the speech is too fast to transcribe. Yet neither of these circumstances is irremediable. In face-to-face

Theoretical issues: transcribing the untranscribable 39

interaction channel interference can be rectified by participants' requests for clarification (though they may well remain unclear for the transcriber). The problem of speed is largely solved by the tape recorder: a piece of technology whose impact on linguistics (Halliday 1985: xxiii) probably remains greater than that of the computer.

In claiming that the words of transcription and original speech event can be the same, I believe it right to reassert the relevance of the Saussurean insights which are the foundation of modern linguistics (de Saussure [1916] 1974), and to do this against those critics of them (Vološinov [1929] 1973; Bakhtin [1936] 1986; Derrida [1967] 1976) whose emphasis on the receiver- and context-relativity of interpretation has recently become fashionable. The phonetic sound of the speech and the graphetic form of a transcription may be unique and individual, but all participants who know the language will perceive an element of sameness in what is said or what is written, identifying in the physical substance the same *emic* units as other users, and combining them into the same linguistic units at higher levels. That is what 'knowing a language' (albeit with some circularity of definition) means. This ability to perceive and reproduce sameness in difference is a prerequisite of human language use, and this commonality of perception by users of a given language means that on one level the transcription of the words in a speech event is *not* an interpretation or systematic translation from one mode to another, but a repetition.

This view does not imply, however, that words reside in the physical form of the message independent of interpretation. Words are not the sound waves of speech, nor the marks of writing, but the interaction of those physical phenomena with the competence of a receiver. Among literate expert users this is uniform enough to create a core of agreement comprising both the linguistic forms and their denotations. There *is* interpretation involved, but of so particular and uniform a kind, that it may in practice be discounted, and the word 'interpretation' reserved for those further aspects of meaning (such as connotations, illocutions, perlocutions and schematic associations) on which expert users disagree.

There is, then, sufficient constancy and reliability in the perception of words for them to be treated as independent of interpretation, and it is partly this relative stability of the words which has made them the central and sometimes only concern in the analysis of oral communication, and encouraged the relegation of other aspects of the speech event, such as paralanguage, situation, and participants' interpretations, to the status of mere extras. The Text Encoding Initiative (TEI) (see Burnard, Chapter 5 and Johansson, Chapter 6) has enshrined this notion of the centrality of the text (i.e. a written record of the words) in the metaphor of transcription as 'a Chicago Pizza' (Burnard 1993). The text is analogous to the pizza base to which various toppings (mushrooms, olives, ham, etc.) may be optionally added. In transcription the toppings to the text might include a selection of phonemic transcription, intonation patterns, notes on the situation, participant relationships, etc. Alternative culinary metaphors are 'the set-menu transcription' in which the same elements of the speech event are always represented in the same combination, and 'the Chinese-meal transcription' in which different elements can be combined in different ways, with no single element obligatory. Both are rejected by the TEI in favour of the pizza metaphor whose central notion is that, whatever else there may be in a transcription, there must always be the words. This implies that on occasion there may be *only* words. A pizza is still a pizza even with nothing on it.

A similar strategy of giving priority to the words is advocated and practised by COBUILD. Both practice and rationale however are different from the TEI, and more consistent with the aims of the project. Rather than allowing for the addition of extra toppings in the future, the COBUILD conventions for transcribing speech impose a leaner regime from the outset. In keeping with what Sinclair describes as 'clean text' (Sinclair 1991: 21), transcriptions keep non-linguistic information to a minimum.[6] The reasons for this leanness are twofold: first, to allow the rapid building of large corpora; second, because non-linguistic elements are too elusive and problematic to be transcribed and assessed accurately.

Text is safe and objective, but it is not sufficient for certain types of analysis. Although a pizza base of plain text will suffice for the analysis of purely *linguistic* phenomena such as lexical frequency, density and collocation, there are other *discourse* phenomena to which non-linguistic elements are essential, elusive as they may be. In the case of COBUILD, whose aim is textual rather than discourse analysis, it is these linguistic phenomena which are the object of research, and so the approach is justified: there is no claim to comment on those areas which are left out of transcription. In the TEI, where there is no specified object of research, though contextual data can be presented, they are relegated to secondary status by being presented only optionally. Yet for discourse analysis, the problem with making the words the central or only object of analysis is that this overlooks the obvious point that in a good deal of spoken discourse words do not carry meaning as autonomously as in writing but only in conjunction with context.

If there is a degree of justice in ignoring the context in the discourse analysis of some written texts because it is marginalized and deemed unimportant, there can be no justification for this in the transcription of speech. In many spoken discourses how something is said outweighs what is said; the interpersonal dominates the ideational. The effect of the paralinguistic message which accompanies every linguistic message provides an example. For when the paralinguistic contradicts the linguistic message, it is usually the former which is believed, presumably because we know it is harder to control. (To see the truth of this, one has only to imagine someone saying 'I'm terribly sorry' in a loud and sarcastic voice, or sobbing while saying 'I don't mind if I'm not invited'.)

This is not only intuitively true: it is borne out by experimental evidence as well. Argyle et al. (1970, 1971) describe how undergraduate subjects, under the false impression that they were taking part in a quite different experiment, were told one of two things afterwards: to leave quickly so as not to waste the researchers' time, or to stay and chat, as the researchers were always pleased to meet students. These two linguistic messages were combined with two paralinguistic messages, with a similar polarity of meaning. Either the experimenters shook the subjects' hands, smiled, and looked them in the eye while speaking; or they avoided eye contact and touch, and wore unfriendly facial expressions. Each subject thus experienced one of four possible combinations of behaviour (see Fig. 2.1).

verbal behaviour	paralinguistic behaviour	overall effect
+	+	+
+	−	−
−	+	+
−	−	−
(+ = friendly, − = unfriendly)		

Figure 2.1

When subjects were asked, some time later, to recall whether they had been treated in a friendly or unfriendly manner, their replies correlated only with the paralinguistic behaviour. It did not matter what had been said to them, but only what had been done.

This attested communicative weight of non-linguistic information has severe implications for the use of a Chicago pizza transcription in which toppings are optional. To make the base the words implies the primacy of language over paralanguage in spoken discourse on all occasions. Spoken discourse, unfortunately for transcribers, is arguably inherently more like a Chinese menu (the analogy rejected in TEI) in which any dish can be removed from the table. Sometimes one element is important sometimes another. The same meal may be perceived as rice with chicken or chicken with rice. There are interactions in which the words are the least important feature or even do not matter at all: interchanges involving foreign speakers or small children who do not understand what is being said, but who do understand the social function (that this is a greeting or a threat or a joke for example). There are many discourses where some of the language is specialized so as to be incomprehensible to some participants. And even when participants do understand the words, they are not always the most important elements. In such situations, we should not impose a method of transcription which elevates the text simply because it is easier to handle.

I am aware that it may seem odd to question the centrality of words to transcription in a book whose proclaimed concern is the analysis of language (rather than the kinesics, proxemics, etc.). It might be argued that, whatever else is included or omitted, the words must always appear. Yet against this it may be said that the assumption that the language of oral interaction can be analysed as words abstracted and isolated from other features of the original event may fundamentally distort the object of analysis, imposing upon it a feature of written communication which is alien to the nature of oral interaction. The pizza analogy and the concept of plain text are misleading, for in speech the non-verbal aspects of interaction are not mere toppings, but essential, even constitutive of what is happening. For transcribers and analysts, this is inconvenient but unavoidable. There is also a danger that making the centrality of the words an international standard imposes a particular theoretical stance upon all transcribers who wish to contribute to and benefit from the opportunities offered by shared computerized corpora.

2.1   Speech and writing

Transcription's conversion of speech into writing may be necessary for analysis, but need not entail an easy slippage into regarding spoken language as though it were identical with the writing derived from it. This distortion, however, has a long history in linguistics, which, since Saussure, has professed two incompatible beliefs. The first is the doctrine that language is primarily speech and that writing is merely secondary, a representation of speech, appearing later, if at all, in both ontogenetic and phylogenetic development (Lyons 1968: 38). The second is that language is separable, not only from other mental activities, but also from its physical instantiation, the circumstances of its realization, and the other communicative behaviour which inevitably accompanies it. (To use the current jargon, language is modular.) Most famously, this second belief appears in Saussure's notion of *langue* ([1916] 1974: 9), Chomsky's notion of competence (Chomsky 1965: 3–10), and in the tradition of idealizing recorded speech for linguistic analysis (Lyons 1977: 585–9). Yet there is an ironic contradiction between these two doctrines: the primacy of speech and the modularity of language. For the second view is far more tenable with regard to writing than it is to speech, and when applied to the analysis of spoken discourse, it has the effect of treating speech as though it were writing (Vološinov [1929] 1973: 71). Indeed it has been argued that, as awareness of the nature of speech came into existence through writing, in a sense it is writing which precedes speech (Derrida [1967] 1976).

As stressed in many recent works on orality and literacy (e.g. Ong 1982, Olson and Torrance 1991), in writing the circumstances of production are often of little interest. In discussing the merits of a novel we are unlikely to be affected by whether the particular copy we read was hardback or paperback, was typeset in a particular typeface, or was printed in London or Hong Kong. Though each written text *is* produced in a particular situation by a particular person, and has a physical form, these features are frequently unimportant to the reader. We regard one written text as the same as another, even when they are physically very different. So whereas writing encourages the notion that language may be divorced from the circumstances of its production, and can often be understood without reference to them, speech is as often inseparable from these circumstances, and can only be apprehended in the context of the knowledge of the participants, their paralanguage and the situation. By modularizing language, linguistics has been guilty of an Orwellian doublespeak: professing the primacy of speech, practising the primacy of writing.

3 Preceding words

It is a truism of discourse analysis that the meaning of the words in any part of a discourse will be affected by the words in other parts: an insight which reflects the popular wisdom that remarks should not be interpreted 'out of context'. In discourse analysis words in other parts of the same discourse are referred to as co-text (following Halliday et al. 1964: 125). Although co-text is often treated as an element of context (and indeed the term 'context' is sometimes used to mean co-text) I shall reserve the term context only to refer to those elements relevant to analysis, such as paralanguage and situation, which are perceived in parallel with the words.

I have also chosen, when referring to speech and transcriptions, to use the term 'preceding words' rather than 'co-text' in order to underline an obvious but often neglected distinction between writing and speech. Writing removes the receiver of language from the obligation to process temporally and enables the reader to move backwards and forwards in the text. This means that the interpretation of any given section may be affected by what comes afterwards as well as what comes before. In speech this is not the case, unless the event is one of those surprisingly common speech genres, such as prayers and songs, which are repeated verbatim (Cook 1992: 227, 1994a). Although there is following co-text in a transcription it must remain irrelevant to analysis. Faced with a transcription of speech it is easy to overlook this very basic difference, illustrated in Fig. 2.2, and vigilance is needed on the part of the analyst.

SPEECH:	preceding speech	speech	NO EQUIVALENT
PERCEPTION:	preceding words	words	NO EQUIVALENT
TRANSCRIPTION:	co–text	text	irrelevant co–text
WRITING:	co–text	text	co–text

Figure 2.2

The need to present preceding words in order to aid the interpretation of the words under consideration is in conflict with the need to present information about the context which is present in parallel with them. As the interpretation is aided by the inclusion of both, and the whole has to be readable, an inherent problem arises. Given a finite time for transcribing or reading, then the quantity of context and the quantity of preceding words must be in inverse proportion: the more of one the less of the other. This can be represented diagrammatically as in

Fig. 2.3, in which the preceding words are represented horizontally and context vertically, and a given reading or transcribing time is represented by a constant area.

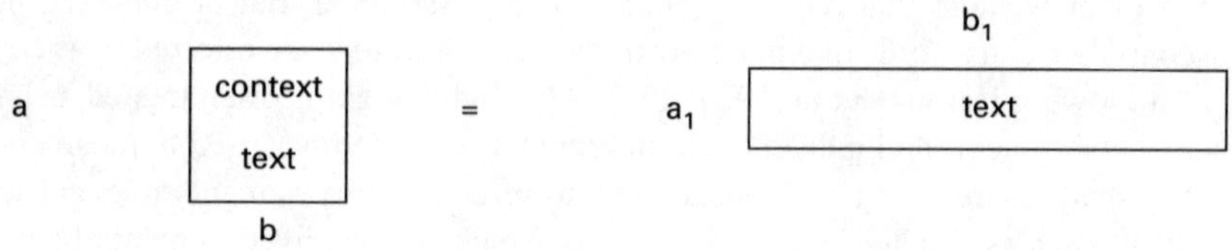

$$a \begin{array}{|c|} \hline \text{context} \\ \text{text} \\ \hline \end{array} b \quad = \quad a_1 \begin{array}{|c|} \hline \text{text} \\ \hline \end{array} b_1$$

reading time, transcribing time: $a \times b = a1 \times b1$

Figure 2.3

Here, however, we encounter a genuine and indisputable advantage of computer storage, for the problems of quantity posed by these two inversely proportionate needs, though they remain problematic for the human reader and transcriber, are far less so for the computer abstracting statistics from computerized corpora. (This relates to the second use of the computer described above.) On the other hand, as transcription is still done by humans and the human resources available are finite, the inclusion of context diminishes the amount of transcription that can be done.

The inclusion of preceding words in transcriptions presupposes the establishment of where each discourse begins. As has often been remarked, this identification of boundaries in discourse analysis is far from simple (Reichman 1985). Although some discourses have apparently clear beginnings and endings marked by, say, the picking up or putting down of a telephone receiver, the ringing of a school bell, or the scrolling credits on a cinema screen, such apparently clear markers may easily be overridden. The 'same lesson' may continue in another school period (Sinclair and Coulthard 1975: 24); a telephone call may be terminated but the 'same conversation' be continued in a subsequent one (as indicated by formulaic openings such as 'Now where were we...'); a film may have a sequel, and so on.

4   Paralanguage

The frequent inseparability of speech and the circumstances of its production means that for certain types of analysis these circumstances will often need to be represented in some way in transcription. This in turn creates problems quite different from those concerned with the representation of the words. For whereas the words, as argued above, are in some senses repeated, the representation of other elements cannot be so.

The problems of transcribing paralanguage (the next element on the list) will illustrate a problem which is inherent in all the other categories of context: the relation of graded to discrete signs. Many paralinguistic signs, unlike linguistic ones, are graded rather than discrete, creating meaning by being more or less, rather than either/or.[7] It follows that they cannot be represented in a semiotic system using discrete signs without simplification and approximation.[8] Whereas in the transcription of the words, there is only one set and order which correspond to those of the original, in the transcription of paralanguage there are many valid representations of the same phenomena.

In these respects the transcription of graded paralanguage is analogous to the mapping of the earth's surface. This must also reduce graded variation along a continuum to a series of finite points, yielding different if equally valid results according to the scale, the symbols used, and the projection. Mapping is thus quite different from the transcription of words in which there is often only one possible version. In making maps, as in making transcriptions, especially with the help of powerful technology such as computers, there is always a temptation to believe that the greater the degree of detail, the better the map, and the closer the approximation to the original. To yield to this temptation, however, is to misunderstand the inevitable nature of map making: a point presented dramatically in Lewis Carroll's neglected novel *Sylvie and Bruno Concluded* when two characters competitively discuss the scale of maps used in their respective countries.

'That's another thing we've learned from your nation,' said Mein Herr, 'map making. But we've carried it much further than you. What do you consider the *largest* map that would really be useful?'
'About six inches to the mile.'
'Only *six inches*!' exclaimed Mein Herr. 'We very soon got to six yards to the mile. Then we tried a *hundred* yards to the mile. And then came the grandest idea of all. We actually made a map of the country on the scale of a *mile to a mile*.'
'Have you ever used it much?' I enquired.
'It has never been spread out yet,' said Mein Herr. 'The farmers objected: they said it would cover the whole country, and shut out the sunlight! So we now use the country itself, as its own map, and I assure you it does nearly as well.'

(Carroll [1893] 1982: 556)

The map described here is not only a bad map in the sense that it is impractical, it is arguably not a map at all. Good map making, in linguistics as in geography, is the result of determining what to miss out rather than what to include; being 'good' is not an absolute quality in a map but always relative to the needs of its users (Batstone 1994: 24).

This problem of the relationship between graded and discrete phenomena remains, whatever the symbols which are used or the areas and level of detail which are fixed upon. A good deal of the discussion in this book is given over to the practical issues of which discrete symbols to use. Though necessary, this discussion does not solve the problem of the discrete/graded relationship, for it concerns only the signifier rather than the signified. The signifiers being arbitrary, all that is at stake is establishing the convention that they are used by everyone in the same way.

Languages themselves are mapping devices which simplify complex phenomena and they too have words signifying types of paralanguage. The relation of such words to the paralinguistic phenomena they describe, is the same as that of transcription symbols. Take for example the representation of laughter, a task which exemplifies many of the problems associated with the transcription of paralanguage in general (Jefferson 1985). Laughter has many different forms and languages have many different words for types of laugh. Thus in English we have among others: titter, giggle, snigger, cackle, chuckle, guffaw. To some degree, the different types of laughter denoted by these terms may be defined by reference to gradable physical parameters such as loudness, pitch, frequency of exhalation. Thus it might seem reasonable to use these words accordingly in transcription, or substitute for each word a symbol which stands for it. We might even seek to improve on the distinctions offered by English or some other natural language by offering some more delicate distinctions of our own. But it is important to remain aware that these substitutions or additions do not alter the nature of the representation which is to translate the virtually infinite points on a graded line into discrete units. We are always and inevitably simplifying. Moreover, words or other symbols referring to types of laugh, denote far more than a section of gradient acoustic phenomena. They say something about the intention and attitude of the person laughing, and the perceiver's perception of it. Exactly the same physical sound may be described by one person as a 'giggle' and by another as a 'snigger'. We cannot avoid this by retreating into some pseudo-scientific neo-behaviourist pretence that the transcriber should represent only an objectively verifiable physical phenomenon. It is not a question of one perception being right and the other wrong. Perception in discourse is self-fulfilling: if someone perceives a laugh as a snigger, then it *is* a snigger for them. Clearly what matters in laughter – as in other aspects of communication – is not only the physical form it takes, but the intention behind it and the effect which it has. To indicate only the sound is to say almost nothing.

This argument is supported by practice in translation and lexicography, two other areas of applied linguistics which, like transcription, need to define types of laughter verbally. Dictionaries tend to define laughter words by combining reference to physical form with reference to intention and effect. This applies both to traditional dictionaries and to modern ones based upon computer corpora. Thus COBUILD's definitions for snigger and giggle are as follows:

Snigger: If you snigger, you laugh quietly and disrespectfully, for example at something rude or at someone's misfortune.
Giggle: If you giggle, you make quiet and repeated laughing noises, because you are happy or occasionally because you are nervous or embarrassed ... If someone has the giggles they cannot stop giggling.

More sonorously and less effectively the 1944 edition of the Shorter Oxford English dictionary defines the same words as:

snigger: To laugh continuously in a manner suggestive of foolish levity or of uncontrollable amusement.

Theoretical issues: transcribing the untranscribable 47

giggle: To laugh in a half-suppressed, light or covert manner.

In all four definitions, it is the reference to intention and effect which most successfully conveys the meaning. Similarly, in translation, where a laugh with the same physical form may have quite different communicative effect in the speech communities of the source and the target text, it would be quite misleading to give the translation equivalent of the physical form.

4.1   Possible solutions in representing paralanguage

The problems of the transcription of paralanguage then derive from the problems inherent in the conversion of graded signals into discrete signs, the inescapably subjective nature of the interpretation, and the temptation to answer these problems by using ever more delicate categories with the result that the transcription may be swamped, becoming something like the unusable monster map described by Lewis Carroll.

In this volume two solutions are suggested to this problem of proliferation. Wallace Chafe imaginatively suggests that a graded phenomenon in the original speech event may be represented iconically by a graded phenomenon in the transcription. The louder the volume of a word for example the darker the letters in the transcription. (Though Chafe is thinking more of the pencil than the computer there is no reason in principle why computers could not be programmed to produce the same effect.) But though attractive in its whimsicality, this suggestion only delays facing up to the problem. To be written or read with any consistency, points of contact between the two gradients would have to be established: a procedure which would involve in effect the division of that gradient into discrete units, as well as imposing on transcriber and reader a formidable learning task. The abstraction of any statistics from computer corpora must likewise involve this division and must also work with discrete rather than graded phenomena. Moreover, the whole operation begs the question which often arises when transcription becomes too delicate: why not just play a recording?

One other solution to the burgeoning of contextual detail is to leave certain areas hidden on screen to be summoned up only by those who have an interest in examining that area. In its most radical form, this approach would present only the words and change of speakers; specified keyboard commands would summon up notation of other features such as phonetic or phonemic transcription, intonation, other paralanguage, description of the situation and so on. Undoubtedly, this *is* the great advantage of the computer over paper in presenting written information and it would go some way to remedying the tendency of current transcriptions to be simply unreadable. This feature of computer presentation is praised in many of the chapters of this book. Nevertheless, despite obvious advantages, there are some reservations. If we are to examine the transcriptions not as text only but as records of communication – as discourse – then this hiding of information would allow analysts to ignore features which may in fact be crucial to an understanding. To those with a narrow approach this narrowness would simply be reinforced.

5   Situation

If the central problem in transcribing paralanguage derives from the potential infinity of detail entailed by extending the delicacy of description, the remaining categories of relevant context (situation, participant knowledge and participant attitude) both present the same problem and add to it another one: that of a capability for infinite expansion. The category of situation is a case in point. Even if a definition of situation as 'immediate physical surroundings' is considered unproblematic and the boundaries of that physical setting are regarded as fixed in the same place for all participants and transcribers, then within that finite space there are virtually infinite possibilities for inclusion of detail and delicacy of description. This, however, is only the beginning of the problem.

Establishing boundaries is as troublesome for situation as for preceding words. If one imagines a conversation taking place inside a room with drawn curtains, the problem may not seem so insurmountable. But what if the curtains are open and one of the participants is looking out of the window, or if the conversation takes place in the open air in front of a panoramic view, or if the interaction is being filmed for broadcasting? Where then does the situation end? The same problematic principle is as unavoidable here as in other categories: what matters is participant and not observer perception. Situation is not only physical but psychological, with consequent differences among participants, and between participants and transcriber. We are all familiar with situations in which one participant has noticed something affecting interaction which others have not. For example, I was recently invited to a restaurant meal to honour the head of a language school. This guest of honour and his wife were late. Seated opposite the window, I could see the latecomers pacing up and down the pavement outside arguing and delaying their entry. Clearly the boundaries of the relevant physical situation were different for me than for the other people at the table (and who knows what they may have seen that I did not). In such cases whose situation should be transcribed? Are there as many subjective situations as there are participants? In discourse analysis this issue has been ignored, as though the visual perspective of the transcriber and of all participants were the same. Once again, this reflects a bias towards writing where situation, if relevant, is encoded from the perspective of the writer, who is often the only sender. Consideration of the multiple senders, and consequent multiple perspectives, in spoken interaction reveals the fallacy of believing that a video recording can capture a situation as an objective reality: it does not film all perspectives, and even if the lens were fixed in the same place as the eyes of one participant, it would not indicate what had caught his or her attention.

The problems raised by such considerations are insoluble. We cannot know how each participant perceives the situation, and even if we could, we should not be able to transcribe it accurately. Even if we *could* know it and transcribe it accurately, we should produce a transcript so detailed that nobody would have time to read it. So I am not advocating that transcribers should in practice do anything differently than they have in the past: make an *ad hoc* selection of elements intuitively felt to be important in a loosely defined situation. But I am arguing that this selection of elements of situation should be recognized for what it is: a matter of expediency. There is no theoretically rigorous basis for it.

6   Participant knowledge

As we move through the elements of the speech event (listed in Section 1.1), problems of subjectivity, infinite delicacy, infinite expansion, and subjective variation become more and more striking. When faced with the problem of transcribing participant knowledge and attitude, these problems take a quantum leap. It might seem wiser perhaps not to include these categories at all in an inquiry with pretensions to objectivity. Yet participant knowledge cannot be left out of account, and recognition of its essential contribution to discourse understanding has been a salient feature of approaches to discourse in the last three decades. Pragmatics and especially speech act theory (Austin 1962; Searle 1969), schema theory (Schank and Abelson 1977; Sanford and Garrod 1981), relevance theory (Sperber and Wilson 1986), genre analysis (Swales 1990) as well as literary theories such as reader-response (Freund 1987) and reception theory (Holub 1984) not only recognize the essential contribution of pre-existing knowledge to any understanding, but also that the same words will have different 'meanings' in interaction with different pre-existing knowledge. Understanding is not only the result of systemic knowledge of a linguistic code, but also of schematic knowledge of the world (Widdowson 1990: 102–14).

Attempts to describe or even reproduce the interaction of knowledge and language, however, while they may capture aspects and advance partial understanding of communication, are strikingly impoverished in comparison with the vastness, indeterminacy and unpredictability of the knowledge which, as introspection tells us, is employed in any actual human understanding (Cook 1994b). The listing of felicity conditions, relevant propositions or schematic defaults cannot do justice to the profusion of personal memories and erratic associations which are activated by participation in discourse. Here again, description is capable of infinite expansion, if only because minds wander and each thought evoked by the discourse may give rise to another leading down paths of anarchic association which may finish literally anywhere, potentially evoking any part of each participant's knowledge. This proliferation is often dismissed in the rather glib observation that discourse is interpreted in the light of cultural knowledge, an observation which both ignores the individual quirkiness of interpretation and also hides behind the vagueness of the meaning of 'culture'. For when culture comes to mean, as if often does, something as all-inclusive as the totality of beliefs and behaviour in a community, then to say that it is employed in understanding is no more than to state the obvious, while avoiding the more interesting if unanswerable question of precisely which bits of cultural knowledge are evoked in which individuals, in which circumstances, and why.

Another problem with the description of activated knowledge is that associations may be of different strengths. There is a vague notion in circulation that connectionist models of thought (with weightings rather than on/off connections) may do more justice to the weakness and simultaneity of associations than the notion of processing as a mechanical serial neatly bounded operation (Martindale 1991). But appeal to connectionism, though fruitful in other ways, does nothing to explain either how associations may be detected, graded or represented in transcriptions. Transcriptions, moreover, still have to be produced and processed serially.

The potential for a virtually infinite explosion of relevant detail once participant knowledge is considered necessary to interpretation is well illustrated by the observation that the understanding of any discourse is effected by knowledge of other similar or related discourses. This may take either the form of association with particular discourses, or of association with more general classes of discourse, now widely known as genres (Swales 1990).

Alertness to inter-discoursal echoes and genre identification are undoubtedly crucial to understanding; both therefore should presumably be included in transcription. Parody for example cannot be understood without an awareness of other specific discourses, and in transcription it might be essential for an utterance or set of utterances to be identified as parodic, if serious misjudgements about a given speaker's style are to be avoided. The words of a teenager who imitates the teacher may not tell us anything directly about the sentiments or discourse of teenagers. Similarly, an indication of genre identification by participants may completely alter assessment of a transcript. A series of bald personal questions about sexual behaviour will have quite different force in a medical consultation and a casual conversation. To acknowledge the importance of particular and generic associations with other discourses, however, says little about how they might be presented in transcription. How are we to identify which aspects of which other discourse are activated for which individuals when and by what? The evocation of other relevant discourses is open-ended too, for they themselves will give rise to echoes of others, until the entire discoursal knowledge of an individual is potentially involved. Genres and discourses, like the signs of language, relate to each other in a system in which meaning is defined by difference and therefore eternally deferred (Derrida [1967] 1976).

7   Participant attitudes

Despite the problems of identifying relevant knowledge, there is at least the possibility of representing some part of it as a series of propositions. For the transcription of participant attitudes and emotions, however, not even the rudiments of a terminology exist which could reflect the nuances and variations. Yet attitude and emotion may account for far more of discourse interpretation than such mechanical procedures as those postulated by schema theory, speech act theory or relevance theory. Is it not more likely that the leap from locution to illocution, the separation of what is relevant from what is irrelevant, or the pinpointing of unmentioned schematic defaults, derives often from an emotional predisposition to interpret certain utterances or certain people in certain ways, rather than from any logical or schematic procedure?

8   Relating the elements

I have so far examined the elements of relevant context as discrete components and said nothing about the interaction of these elements and the presentation of this in transcription. The problems of context transcription do not merely concern principles for selection and representation, but also ways of relating context to words which reflect their relationship for the participants in the original speech event. Here the central problem is that whereas in face-to-face interaction various communicative channels are processed simultaneously, writing is processed linearly. Ochs (1979) has commented on how this leads particular transcription conventions to attribute more importance to one element than another. In a left-to-right writing system, what is presented on the left will be perceived as more important than what is on the right. If words are transcribed in a column on the left and contextual information on the right, this can make language seem more important than context. Similarly, in adult–child discourse transcription, putting the adult's words on the left presents the interaction from an adult point of view. Yet it would be mistaken to suppose that such biases *can* ever be corrected; they are rather an inevitable consequence of transferring speech into writing. It is true that the computer could remedy emphases which are frozen and immutable on paper, perhaps through a facility for on-screen presentation capable of switching the order. Yet it is in the nature of reading that something has to be read first, and whatever the arrangement on the page or screen, one of the elements which were in face-to-face interaction simultaneous will be given priority.

In the relationship of paralanguage to words, a further complication arises. It is not simply a question of adjusting the balance between two parallel channels. Although there is paralanguage which is not also language, the reverse is not true: there is no language which is not simultaneously paralanguage. Despite the capacity of the literate scientific mind to marginalise the paralinguistic content of an utterance (making it seem that all that matters is *what* is said, rather than *how*, or *by whom*) every utterance must carry both a paralinguistic and a linguistic message.

9   Conclusion

What I have been arguing throughout this chapter is the necessity of recognizing the paradox that certain elements of spoken communication both must be transcribed and cannot be transcribed. They must be transcribed because they alter the meaning of what is happening for the participants and to exclude them can lead to misunderstanding. They cannot be transcribed because they are graded, because their boundaries are not clear, because they are infinitely extendible, or because they are made up of an unknowable and indescribable subjective reality.

Some readers may find this unacceptable and pessimistic, but it need not be taken as such. The study of language must of its nature straddle the border between scientific and non-scientific enquiry. A part of its object of inquiry is knowable, verifiable and quantifiable; another part is none of these things, yet no less important for being so.

Since the nineteenth century at least, the study of language has always been tempted to associate itself with what it sees as the more secure, prestigious and objective sciences (though ironically those sciences themselves have long since accepted the relativist and unstable basis of their own enterprises). Thus the study of language has at times been seen as analogous to biology, or chemistry, or even law (Winograd 1983: 13). Chomsky has linked linguistics to both genetics and mathematics. Now the association with computer science and with neurology (the two are themselves connected through the computer metaphor of mind and the brain metaphor in connectionist computing) tempts us to yet another such alliance. Every successive metaphor of language has revealed something of its nature, yet left other aspects untamed. There is no reason to suppose that the current generation of linguists will fare better, or worse. Some aspects of spoken communication will yield to computer analysis, but others must remain vague: essential but indescribable elements in interaction. Computer analysis of transcription will lead to many advances in understanding, but the pretence that all is now under control should not be one of them.

Notes

1. Birdwhistell's (1973: 283–5) 'sample conversation' takes three pages to transcribe a conversation of 26 words between a mother and child on a bus. He includes elaborate notation for body postures and eye movements, but does not distinguish between those perceived by observer and those perceived by the participants.
2. Participant recollection of preceding words may be inaccurate, thus creating a great possibility of discrepancy in this category as in the contextual categories 3–6.
3. 'Expert user' is a more accurate term than 'native speaker'. 'Native' confuses acquisition of a language in childhood with proficiency (Rampton 1990). 'Speaker' does not encompass proficiency in both speech and writing.
4. This belief is presumably shared by the collectors of the spoken discourse section of the British National Corpus (Crowdy, Chapter 19) who use transcribers with no specialist training in linguistics or conversation analysis.
5. Scholes and Willis (1991) present evidence that non-literate speakers do not segment speech in the same way as literate ones.
6. Although they do trespass occasionally into territory normally considered

Theoretical issues: transcribing the untranscribable 53

paralinguistic by, for example, including filled pauses on the grounds that they are functionally equivalent as equivalent to lexical items such as 'well' or 'right'.
7. Those that are not graded, but relate clearly to a linguistic sign (such as the thumbs-up signal for 'ok' or the repeatedly bent index finger for 'come here') are more properly described as linguistic.
8. During the workshop on which this book is based it was argued that all graded signs are ultimately reducible to discrete elements. The sensory receptors of graded phenomena (the retina etc.) work with discrete units. This, however, is subconscious; what matters is that the mind perceives the information as graded.

3 Adequacy, user-friendliness, and practicality in transcribing

WALLACE CHAFE

In the process of developing new spoken language corpora that will be of the greatest use to the greatest number and variety of users, we are continually faced with the difficult question of how best to represent spoken language in a visual format. It is interesting at the outset to think about why we should want to do this. Spoken language, after all, comes in the form of sound, and why would not it be enough just to make sound recordings available to our customers? The question is not a frivolous one, and there is a part of me that would be happiest if we confined our efforts to collecting useful recordings and passing them on to whoever might want and be able to use them.

But of course we know that the first thing almost anyone would do upon receiving such recordings would be to transcribe them, in one way or another. In fact, I suspect that all too many spoken language corpus users are quite content to ignore the sound of language completely, doing whatever they do on the basis of transcriptions alone, as if they were dealing with written language. I find that too bad, and am more than a little pleased that future corpora will make it easy to access transcriptions and audio information simultaneously. One might hope that the increased availability of the sound will encourage more users to pay more attention to it.

Why is the Western scientific tradition so much more attuned to visual information than to auditory? Certainly this preference has something to do with the different relations of the two types of information to time. What is heard is, by its very nature, constantly changing, whereas what is seen stays put long enough to be examined, manipulated, and pondered over. To the extent that we can succeed in making spoken language visible, we can subject it at our leisure to kinds of scrutiny and comparison that would be difficult if not impossible with the spoken language itself.

If, then, nearly everyone will want to work largely if not exclusively from transcriptions, it is incumbent on us as corpus developers to keep asking ourselves what the transcriptions should be like. A first question might be whether any transcription system can be ideal. Probably the answer is no. How we transcribe depends on our purposes, which are inevitably going to differ. In spite of that, we have an obligation to provide transcriptions that will be broadly useful to a broad range of users, and I want to pursue here the question of what that might entail. What I will say is much in the spirit of Edwards (1993b); cf. my own contribution in the same volume (Chafe 1993).

Especially interesting to a linguist is the fact that any transcription system is a theory of what is significant about language. Taking transcription seriously can stimulate progress in understanding what language consists of, forcing us to confront questions we might otherwise sweep under the rug. Whatever system we use commits us to a particular understanding of what is important (cf. Ochs 1979). Alphabetic writing is a good example. The way we ordinarily write gives priority to vowels and consonants rather than, say, phonological features or syllables. It also privileges words (with spaces), certain kinds of phrases (with commas), sentences (with capitalizations and full stops), and paragraphs (with indentation and/or spacing). Our attempts to develop more adequate transcription systems are in essence attempts to go beyond what I have just listed, particularly with respect to prosody. If alphabetic writing has contributed a great deal to Western civilization, it has also impeded a more complete understanding of language in all its richness. Like all theories the alphabet has rigidified a commitment to a partial truth, which it should be the goal of more adequate transcription systems to transcend.

In extending the resources provided by ordinary writing, we need of course above all to decide on the kinds of things that should be represented. However, if our transcriptions are going to be maximally usable, we also need to think in terms of transcriptional devices that (a) take advantage of what users already know (see Edwards, Chapter 1) and (b) are easy to manipulate, given the current state of representational technology. On the first point, literate people are already accustomed to interpreting visual representations of language, and transcriptions will be easier to process to the extent that they capitalize on habits already formed. Furthermore, in moving beyond ordinary writing there is an obvious advantage to representations that have an iconic value, resembling to some degree what they represent, so that the burden of learning arbitrary conventions is to that extent mitigated. At the same time we are limited by what our computers and printers are able to do. While there may be increasing flexibility in this regard, particularly with idiosyncratic resources developed by individual projects, widely used corpora must be constrained by options available to large groups of users. We can expect these options to be continually expanding, but their state at any particular time sets practical limits on what we can do.

Keeping in mind these (not always compatible) goals of theoretical cogency, user friendliness, and technical practicality, we can explore a small sample of spoken language from the Corpus of Spoken American English (CSAE) being developed in Santa Barbara. The transcriptional devices I will mention here go beyond what the Santa Barbara project has settled on, for reasons that will be discussed at the end. Some of these devices are idiosyncratic, while others coincide with recommendations of Du Bois et al. (1993). We can begin with a brief segment of speech transcribed with nothing but alphabetic writing and word boundaries:

(1)   the other thing you can do is

and then quickly move on to a slightly more satisfactory representation that includes disfluencies:

(2)   um . . . (0.3) the other thing you can do is

A question raised by (2) is the extent to which linguistic features are categorial as opposed to being gradient (cf. Bolinger 1961). The question is easy to illustrate with the pause following the word *um*, a period of silence that lasted for about a third of a second. Pauses obviously come in a continuum of lengths, and we are now able to measure them accurately. (An accuracy to the nearest tenth of a second is likely to be sufficient.) But is there some basis on which we can validly segment this continuum into, say, significantly brief pauses, normal pauses, and significantly long pauses, or something of the sort? We might then use two dots for minimal pauses, three dots for normal ones, four dots for long ones, or the like. We would have to investigate the different functions of different pause lengths (taking into account the different speaking rates of different speakers), but such a project would undoubtedly be worthwhile. In lieu of further knowledge, I have in my own work been distinguishing between brief breaks in timing of less than a tenth of a second, marked with two dots, and everything longer than that, marked with three dots plus a measurement in parentheses, as in (2).

To turn to another basic issue, it seems unavoidable that transcriptions should appear as lines on a page, however those lines are organized. It is certainly advantageous to use the lines for some purpose, and I believe it is a happy coincidence that language seems to be produced in the format of 'intonation units' (or whatever they may be called) whose length is well suited to a division into separate lines. Speech verbalizes brief foci of consciousness, each expressed in a spurt of language that tends to contain, in English at least, about four or five words. The resulting units have proved rewarding to investigate, not just for their prosodic properties, but also for what they can tell us about the organization of ideas (e.g. Chafe 1994).

Although the matter is not yet settled, it may be the case that intonation units can always be identified from their auditory properties; that is, we can hear them. We do not need to rely on, say, syntax or meaning to tell us where their boundaries are. Most of them are very easy to hear, with boundaries signalled by a combination of prosodic features, among which are terminal pitch contours, resetting of the pitch baseline, pauses, changes in tempo, and changes in voice quality such as creaky voice. The delimitation of intonation units is, of course, easiest when most or all of these features are present, and becomes more difficult when we can find only one or two, but segmenting speech in this way does appear to be a valid and rewarding endeavour.

At the very least, then, there is a value in transcribing speech in the format of intonation units in separate lines, including pauses when they are present. On this basis (2) can be retranscribed as (3), where the *um* is assigned to a separate intonation unit:

(3) a   um
     b   ... (0.3) the other thing you can do is

Intonation units are delimited in part by their termination in one of a number of distinctive pitch contours. Each contour has some semantic, cognitive, evaluative, and/or interactive function. Some contours and their functions are relatively easy to describe, some not. The deeply falling pitch, often accompanied by deceleration and creaky voice, that is characteristic of the ends of declarative sentences is relatively easy to deal with. So is the high rising pitch associated with the ends of yes–no questions. But other contours may be less clearly identifiable, and we still lack an agreed-upon vocabulary with which to characterize their functions.

There are many ways in which pitch contours have been represented visually. Here I want to emphasize the fact that everyone who reads and writes English is accustomed to a rudimentary and imperfect representation of these terminal contours by means of punctuation marks (cf. Chafe 1988). We constantly interpret punctuation in that way, even if inconsistently, and it would surely be an advantage if transcription practice could take advantage of this habit. In the past I have often employed a system that has distinguished between full stop contours, question mark contours, and all others, marked with a comma, an all-purpose symbol for everything I was leaving for another day. In the absence of firm evidence that the task is hopeless, I would suggest the usefulness of extending the range of intonation-unit-final punctuation marks, modifying and supplementing them in the hope that we may one day be able to identify and mark a more complete range of options.

A small illustration is provided by the first four intonation units of our sample, as shown in (4):

(4) a   um:
     b   ... (0.3) the other thing you can do is:
     c   ... (0.5) um;
     d   ... (0.4) as I recall,

The first two intonation units are closed with a colon, the third with a semicolon, and the fourth with a comma. The colon is meant to show a pitch that is perceived as more or less level. This contour in this context seems to convey something similar to the words 'the following', one of the functions of the colon in ordinary orthography. Some intonation units end with a pitch that falls, but not to as deep a level as that which I have been marking with a full stop. Because a semicolon can be regarded as halfway between a full stop and a comma, it seems appropriate at the end of (4)c, where there is an incomplete fall. At the end of (4)d there is a fall-rise pattern on the last syllable, but its initial high pitch can be attributed to the prominence of that syllable, on which more below. The comma at the end of (4)d, then, captures the final rise. There are of course more contours than these, but if the number is not too great we might do well to think about extending the inventory of punctuation marks to accommodate them. It is a project I feel motivated to push as far as I can before giving up, just because using punctuation in this way is so in accord with the habits of literacy.

Besides their final intonation contours, intonation units contain certain words that are more prominent than others. This prominence is above all a matter of pitch, mostly heightened pitch in American English (it may be that British English makes more use of pitch lowering). I have found it useful to distinguish two degrees of pitch prominence, or deviations from a pitch baseline, as illustrated by the acute and grave accent marks in (5):

(5)   ... (0.3) the óther thing you can dò is:

The highest pitch in this intonation unit fell within the word *other*, as shown with the acute accent. A secondary pitch deviation was present in *do*. Humans are better designed to discriminate pitch differences than differences in loudness, but even though loudness may be secondary to pitch it does apparently have some role to play. One iconic way of showing greater loudness is with boldface type, as in (6), where the words *other*, *do*, and *is* are louder than the rest:

(6)   ... (0.3) the **óther** thing you can **dò is:**

There are other features worth representing that fall within the area of duration, which I think has been given less attention than it deserves. Changes in tempo, for example, provide one of the important clues to intonation unit boundaries and may be functional in other ways. One device for showing the lengthening of syllables that is especially common at the ends of intonation units is the equals sign, which can be thought of as a colon stretched out (the colon itself being better reserved for other uses). The last two words in (6) were not only long but were also clearly separated from each other in a 'marcato' style (cf. Du Bois et al. 1993: 69). That kind of pronunciation can be shown iconically with extra spacing between the words. In (7), then, the equals sign shows lengthening and the extra spacing shows the marcato effect:

(7)   ... (0.3) the **óther** thing you can **dò =   i=s:**

We have now arrived at a transcription that captures various meta-alphabetic features of this intonation unit in ways that are both iconic and in accord with habits established by literacy. We can add a few more options by looking at the intonation units that immediately followed (7), considering how other features might be shown in the same spirit:

(8)   a   ... (0.5) **u=m;**
      b   ... (0.4) as I **recá=ll,**
      c   ... (0.3) **one= ca=n lísten [tó=]:**
      d   LINDA: [©]   ©
      e   BOB: ... (0.5) the **túner,**

Adequacy, user-friendliness, and practicality in transcribing   59

The marcato effect can be seen again in the spacing of (8)c. In (8)d Linda cleared her throat twice, as shown with the (hopefully) iconic symbol ©. The spacing of the square brackets shows that the first throat clearing coincided with Bob's word *to*, whereas the second followed that word.

Bob's next intonation unit was spoken with a distinctively lower pitch baseline, as shown by the symbol ↓ at the beginning and end:

(9)   BOB: . . . (0.9) ↓ so= you could pùt on=: ↓

After Linda's backchannel *mhm* in response to what Bob said in (8), Bob continued the idea begun in (9), but then experienced a great deal of disfluency:

(10) a LINDA: mhm:
      b BOB: . . . (0.1) **KDB** ↓ or << I [I] ∧ e >> ↓

Following the confident utterance of the radio call letters *KDB*, he lowered his pitch baseline again. Beginning with the word *I* he lapsed into creaky voice in the stretch bounded by the (again hopefully iconic) symbols << and >>. After repeating the word *I*, he produced two unintelligible vowel sounds shown with the phonetic symbols ∧ and e.

There followed another backchannel response from Linda, and then two intonation units spoken by Bob with both a lowered pitch baseline and creaky voice:

(11) a LINDA: [m;]
      b BOB: ↓ << or there's óne= **Máck likes:** >> ↓
      c   ↓ << *I forget what it's **called**:* >> ↓

In (11)c he moved to a faster tempo, shown with italics, an iconic option if the letters can be thought of as leaning forward when the sounds become more rapid.

The next seven intonation units can be transcribed with conventions already introduced. The reader is invited to recreate with auditory imagery what was said:

(12) a BOB: [But ányhow:]
      b LINDA: [m hm hm]
      c   Ríght.
      d BOB: . . . (0.3) **u=m;**
      e LINDA: ©
      f BOB: . . . Oh he [wánts] to get KFAĆ ↓ << I think it is. >> ↓
      g LINDA: [©]
      h   Yéa=h;

Then came an intonation unit that began with two pulses of laughter, for which smiling faces (generally available with computer systems) might be appropriate:

(13) BOB: . . . (0.2) ☺☺ *Which is kinda* **tóugh:**

60   *Issues and practices*

We can conclude the illustration with five more intonation units that can be accommodated with the conventions already described:

(14) a   **u=m;**
     b   ... (0.2) *So* **yóu** *could* **be lístening** *to the* **rá=dio,**
     c   ... (0.3) **whi=le** táping a CD.
     d LINDA: Mhm=:
     e BOB: ... (0.4) ↓ **You** you *know it allows you to do*
                << *that* >>.↓

To review, I have suggested the following conventions, intended to be both iconic and practical. They are only suggestions, and my higher purpose is to urge transcribers to continue experimenting along these lines.

primary pitch prominence	acute accent
secondary pitch prominence	grave accent
prominence through loudness	boldface
lowered pitch baseline	↓
faster tempo	italics
creaky voice	<< >>
marcato	extra spacing
prosodic lengthening	=
pulse of laughter	☺
throat clearing	©

The entire transcribed sample can now be brought together as follows:

    a BOB: **u=m:**
    b   ... (0.3) The **óther** thing you can **dò=**   i=s:
    c   ... (0.5) **u=m;**
    d   ... (0.4) as I **recá=ll,**
    e   ... (0.3) **one=**   **ca=n**   **lísten**   [**tó=**]:
    f LINDA: [©]   ©
    g BOB: ... (0.5) the **túner,**
    h BOB: ... (0.9) ↓ so= you could pùt on=: ↓
    i LINDA: mhm:
    j BOB: ... (0.1) **KDB** ↓ or << I [I] ʌ e >> ↓
    k LINDA: [m;]
    l BOB: ↓ << or there's óne= **Máck** likes: >> ↓
    m   ↓ << *I forget what it's* **called:** >> ↓
    n BOB: [But **ányhow:**]
    o LINDA: [m hm hm]
    p   Ríght.
    q BOB: ... (0.3) **u=m;**
    r LINDA: ©
    s BOB: .. Oh he [**wánts**] to get KFAĆ ↓ << *I think it is.* >> ↓

t	LINDA:	[☺]
u	Yéa=h;	
v	BOB:	... (0.2)☺☺*Which is kinda **tóugh:***
w		**u=m;**
x		... (0.2) *So **yóu** could **be lístening** to the* **rá=dio,**
y		... (0.3) **whi=le** táping a CD.
z	LINDA:	Mhm=:
aa	BOB:	... (0.4) ↓ **You** you *know it allows you to do* << *that* >>. ↓

Although I believe that something like this representation is worth aiming for, the Santa Barbara corpus has settled on something more modest, with greatest attention being paid to intonation unit boundaries and overlapping speech. One reason for this more limited approach is the difficulty at this stage of achieving a system with which everyone will be satisfied. Another is the fact that this project has been amassing a large amount of material that is being transcribed with great care. The procedure is extremely time-consuming, and it would take an impractical amount of time to transcribe these materials in anything like the manner discussed above, even if the transcribers could all learn to perform such a task to a sufficient standard of reliability.

Offsetting the limitations of our transcription practice is the fact that we are planning to issue the corpus in a CD-ROM format that will allow users immediate access to sound as well as sight. This access creates both a potential for embarrassment and a considerable advantage. Users will be able to check what we have done, and for that reason alone we are hesitant to transcribe features that users might interpret differently. On the other hand, and more importantly, this same availability of the sound will make it easy for users to extend the transcription in any direction they wish. Taking what we provide as a starting point, they will be free to elaborate it in accordance with their own preferences and goals. I hope they will do that.

Such a practice will at least partially alleviate the fundamental problem with transcribed spoken language that I mentioned at the beginning: the temptation to accept a transcription as given. It is all too easy to take data in the form provided and move on to whatever kind of analysis one favours, being glad not to get one's hands dirty with the processes of collecting and transcribing. But one cannot fully understand data unless one has been in on it from the beginning. While it is impossible for corpus users to share the experience of initial data collection, perhaps the spoken corpora of the future, providing sound as well as sight, should be packaged with a legal requirement that users listen as well as look.

4 Whole-text analyses in computerised spoken discourse

JAMES MONAGHAN

1 Introduction

For several years now, it has been true to say that the information technology currently available to the scholarly community in our area is increasingly able to provide seductively easy-to-use capture, storage, processing and retrieval facilities for speech and natural language data. And the pace is quickening. At first, these facilities were primarily deployed to fulfil what were perceived to be our most obvious current research needs. In other words, the available information technology was seen largely through the spectacles of how pre-computational linguistics had been done before computing came together with linguistics and phonetics.

This explains the bias, which has been observable until very recently within computational linguistics, either towards those methods derived from work on compilers and the like, or towards those derived from work on databases. In fact, there was for a time a rivalry between those espousing the parsing or the statistical corpus-based techniques. The latter dominated the first years of our subject and with the rise of parsing there was some, at times heated, discussion as to what computational linguistics really was. All of us welcome the increasing dialogue between what sometimes were getting close to being two warring camps.

Now the main divergence, though not a hostile one, is between those working in speech and those in language. The present initiative on corpora represents the most important convergence of interests in recent years.

The concerns which dominate a science at any given moment are obviously related to individual talents and the work of gifted teams. On the other hand, the ease of use of a technology subtly shapes the paradigm of what we want. Those of us with a background primarily in linguistics saw the new technology as liberating us from the drudgery associated with traditional problems such as how to handle long stretches of linguistic data and how to compare many examples of potentially patterned linguistic activity. The input from relevant work in computer science had a quick success in solving what had seemed, if not intractable then certainly extremely stubborn, problems, especially in corpus analysis and parsing. On the other hand, those areas of textual study, such as the analysis of whole spoken texts, which did not seem obviously accessible to computational linguistic solutions have tended to be sidelined until recently. This was true of the speech community, which tended to see important features of real conversation such as inaudible segments and hesitations as problems to be filtered out or otherwise overcome. The advances that have been made have, nevertheless, been invaluable and more and more speech work is taking account of areas such as pragmatics. It is therefore doubly important that we are not prevented by decisions which prematurely restrict our possibilities of developing these and similar areas.

When, as now, we concern ourselves with identifying standards, therefore, it is important that they be not developed purely on the basis of current funded research, but also take account of desirable, but not currently implemented work. As well as caution over prematurely restrictive standards, we must also be aware of the new classes of problems inherent in the technology.[1] It always helps to consider not just the most obvious facilities that technology is making available to us and which seem to solve our current wishes, but also to consider the whole range of things we may want to do with the new corpora in the future before we invest time and resources in creating them. To misquote shamelessly, it is a question of 'Ask not what your technology can do for you, but ask what you could do with the technology'.[2]

The present chapter is to be seen as an attempted contribution to this lateral thinking. As part of what I hope is a usefully divergent view, I want to approach the problem from the, in this context, perhaps unusual perspective of an end user whose interest has been for many years in the more extensive structures of whole spoken texts rather than, say, parsing techniques applied to grammatical objects at about the sentence level on the one hand, or statistical aspects of the large written corpora on the other. I am also interested in aspects of speech, but in rather different aspects from the representation of speech at or near what used to be called the segmental level, where most of the most exciting developments of the last years have taken place. I have referred to this area of study as spoken English (Cheepen and Monaghan 1990) to distinguish it from what the speech and language technology community understands by speech research and language research. I want to be able to use information technology to do something that is a mixture of both.

Before looking at some relevant problems of spoken English, I want to make some reference to certain basic concepts of systems analysis and design. Then, taking both of these together, I want to address the problems of encoding high level text features in machine-readable databases, and to put this in the framework of the theoretically non-trivial question of how we leave our encoding maintainable in the systems design sense.

2   The system life cycle

One of the classic statements of systems analysis and design is the System Life Cycle (Davis 1983: 8). This consists of Problem Definition, Feasibility Study,

Analysis, System Design, Detailed Design, Implementation and Maintenance. All the steps are designed to make the design process controlled and repeatable. The steps in the middle of the list – from feasibility study to implementation – are primarily the concern of those involved with the actual setting up of the corpus databases. They involve a checklist of procedures whereby the systems analyst can negotiate with an end user to establish exactly what systems if any are needed to fulfil the user's needs. In the early days of a discipline, as in ours, the end users are usually very computationally sophisticated and can to a large extent specify and design their own system. As larger numbers of naive users get involved the need for skilled systems design and for an understanding of its necessity increase. This is where we are now. I want, therefore, to concentrate in the present account on Davis's first and last features – the problems of definition and implementation and maintenance – as they are the ones which impinge most on the end user, and which are in fact intimately linked.

2.1 Problem Definition

The Problem Definition is a formal description of what the system is designed to solve. We all have our own areas of special interest here, but the present exercise is a salutary attempt to try to describe in some detail the outline of the territory we want to lay claim to, what we want to do there and what we expect the deliverables to be before we start. Changing our plans in the light of experience and increased knowledge and investigatory power must always be possible, but this is no excuse for blundering forward and producing only results that we have not clearly defined in advance. On the whole, such an approach is a waste of our time and resources.

My contribution to the Problem Definition stage of spoken language corpus design would certainly draw attention to the need for access to whole-text structures, with an appeal for a discussion of how the markers of these structures should be tagged. If we look at the definition of this problem from the point of view of the standardization of collections of computerized spoken discourse, we find that it breaks down basically into two different sub-problems, which have often been seen as the domain of different research (sub-)communities.

On the one hand, on the speech side, there is the signal representation problem. This is also an interpretation problem, as we have to make decisions of various sorts. What quality of the reproduction of the sound signal is needed? What if anything do we filter out? How are we to translate and graphically represent the sound signals? How do we link these graphic representations to the signal data? Important features such as overlapping speech which is inaudible to the participants, filled and unfilled pauses, gaps and hesitations are not just acoustic problems to be solved or filtered out, they are the very stuff of real spoken discourse. On the other hand, we have to make the decision as to what additional information to provide in the transcriptions of the texts at levels such as the lexical, grammatical, and phonological where the text structures are signalled.

Obviously, the answers to these questions are mutually dependent, and will be expected to be asked again in the ongoing maintenance process discussed below.

In both speech and written corpora, we are perhaps still at the stage of being grateful that the corpora and the manipulation software are there. It is important, however, that we are prepared to be imaginative and not be deflected by the available from asking about the apparently impossible if that is what we need. The system designers do not know what is needed and to some extent, neither do we. Panini did not see it as a problem that he could not have access to recordings of spoken language. Dionysius Thrax or Appolonius Dyscolus did not miss machine-readable corpora (not to mention printing, photocopying, etc.). We, on the other hand, are in the middle of a revolution and we must think divergently to define all our possible needs and demand the technology to fulfil them. Some solutions will be harder to develop than others, but if enough people want them then they will be produced. Many solutions are already available, but not all are widely known about and some are not thought to be needed – solutions known only to those who do not perceive the problem.[3]

2.2   Maintenance

Maintenance is based on the realization that however well a system is designed to solve a problem or group of problems, the situation will change over the period of the system's use. In fact, the more useful a system is, the more likely it is to generate new demands as new possibilities are revealed by its use. A case in point is the general feature of the linguistic analysis of large text segments that there is always difficulty in attaining a synoptic view of all the examples in a corpus because of their size.[4] Now that text-based work based on naturally occurring corpora is using techniques based on top-down parsing and that parsing systems are achieving very respectable results in the analysis of naturally occurring texts other than those on which they were trained, it is important not to restrict the possibilities for the near future by tying down too closely the type of information made available. This is especially true of dividing spoken texts into those whose overall structure does not signal beginnings and ends and those that do. In the second case, it is important to make available, in machine-readable form, the possibility of tagging for beginning and end markers.

3   Some desiderata

3.1   The Representation of Spoken Language Texts

The analysis of large text structures in spoken language texts involves the storage of the speech data, the graphic representation of the (representable)[5] language tokens this data encodes and the linking of the written realization with the abstract structures it represents. There is a tendency in the computational speech community to concentrate on low level phoneme-size constructs, for lexicologists to spend too much time on individual words and for grammarians to overemphasise the sentence, a construct of doubtful utility in speech (Monaghan 1982). The distinction between the words and higher units that the sound encodes, on the one hand, and the mark-up, on the other, is often blurred, with some mark-up features more obvious than others. For instance, reducing spoken dialogue to machine-readable form immediately requires additional text to make explicit what had previously been signalled phonologically. This is true even in reported dialogue with 'stage directions' such as 'she whispered', 'he roared', etc.

More formal mark-up systems, for all their apparent sophistication, still require the back-up of powerful pragmatic theories to function well in accounting for texts. Homography, especially in deixis, obscures many obvious spoken distinctions between quite different grammatical items, such as *this*, *there*, *the* (compare *There he is!* with *There's only one David Gower*), or lexical items such as *refuse* or *pervert*. Orthographical systems (including most 'transcription' systems) are hopelessly inadequate at representing the richness of prosodic signalling. Current isolated word automatic speech recognition technology also loses stress and intonation signalling as well as important collocational and colligational links, partly because of weaknesses in the linguistic theories underlying them. Certain engineering solutions applied to speech recognition problems seem to have been based too much on brute force and ignorance and these birds are now coming home to roost.

Except for 'continuous states of talk' which may have no structurally determined beginnings and endings, spoken language texts have characteristic structures (Cheepen 1988). This makes it important for their beginnings and endings to be included in the text and marked up so as to distinguish recording beginnings from text beginnings. As has long been recognized, transactional activities such as lessons and interviews, as well as telephone conversations in general, have a greater tendency to be overtly structured than interactional activities like informal chats. It is now becoming clear that these are also structured in ways only visible at a macro level (Cheepen and Monaghan 1990). This makes it more important than ever to describe whole texts to expand our knowledge of text typology, an area acknowledged to be of prime importance at least since the 1960s (Halliday 1975), but neglected mainly because the tools of investigation were not available.

3.2 Annotating the lexical text signal

Because of the above-mentioned tendency to concentrate on small synoptic stretches of language precomputational phoneticians and linguists tended to be very good below the syllable and sentence level respectively. The first temptation with the new computers was to do lots of calculations on the same objects that were of interest before.

Recent work in the analysis of spoken language has revealed text structures such as problem-solution, situation-evaluation and unspecific-specific, logical sequence (Winter 1977) and conversational structures such as story, speech-in-action and scapegoat repairs (Cheepen 1988). An extremely important tool for identifying textual macrostructures such as these is the small, semi-closed set of text signalling lexical items, which I have called 'unfulfilled lexical items' (Monaghan 1987). Unlike grammatically and phonologically signalled categories, such as theme and rheme or given and new, they are not theoretically imposed metalanguage, but are part of the text itself. They are part of the primary data and they survive encoding into machine readable form.

Transactional texts are characterized by the problem-solution relation, while Interactional texts display situation-evaluation. Both these relations are marked by their characteristic vocabulary. In text examples we find 'problem' signalled by words such as *problem, pest, worry* and so on. Solution is frequently marked by being described in the text itself as one. It should also be possible to specify some of the features of mixed mode spoken discourse – where language is spoken in order to be written down, as in dictation, or where language is written in order to be spoken as in formal lectures. Whole text analysis also points up aspects which differentiate from within the texts themselves machine-generated speech addressed to humans and characteristics of human speech addressed to machines.

It is important that such text immanent features be available for coding by standard methods for those who would find this useful. Any coding system should not be a forest of annotations but a facility that individual researchers could take advantage of in terms of their own interests. Each user would be able to select from the coding possibilities rather than be constrained by previous decisions.

Notes

1. One of the first things that anyone dealing with the analysis of real spoken natural language notices is that collecting the data is only the first part of the problem. The older of us in this arcane trade have noted that the development of technology is a two-edged sword. In the 1970s, every student had what we now would call a 'portable dedicated cassette tape recorder', which could still operate successfully to record conversations surreptitiously by being placed under the table in a plastic bag. Ten years later the machines were so overloaded with additional technology that they were not unobtrusive enough. Now the wheel has come full circle, with personal tape recorders designed to be carried in a pocket or a handbag becoming increasingly available. This and the increasing availability of high fidelity recording devices has enhanced the availability of data.
2. A case in point is the situation in the early days of what we now call *radio*. The main perceived problem with the earliest implementations of *wireless* (think about it) technology was the problem of preventing unauthorized users listening in. When the quantum leap of redefining the technology as an opportunity for *broadcasting* was achieved, the old problem was seen to be a new solution.
3. I remember a computer scientist colleague commenting on the *wc* Unix utility, which counts words in a file, and saying he could not imagine why anyone would want to count words in a text!

4. This is a neglected factor in the paradigm shift of the 1950s which replaced text-based work such as Fries (1940), and Harris (1946 and 1951) with the introspection-based linguistics associated with Chomsky. For all the persuasive arguments used afterwards to explain the shift, there is no doubt that early work in the transformational-generative paradigm was also a lot simpler to do than struggling with the complexities of real language.
5. In work with spoken language, we must always remember that we cannot trivially represent the spoken data by writing it down or even by transcribing it using any standard system. How to approximate to this in the areas we want is precisely what we are trying to elucidate in this volume.

5 The Text Encoding Initiative: an overview

LOU BURNARD

This chapter gives a brief introduction to the scope and coverage of the Text Encoding Initiative's *Recommendations for Text Encoding for Interchange*, as published during 1993. Its origins in academic research have made the TEI scheme particularly flexible, involving innovative uses of Standard Generalized Mark-up Language (SGML) and an ambitious modular approach to dtd development. The recommendations for the encoding of spoken language constitute one important instance of this general approach.

1   What is the TEI?

The Text Encoding Initiative (TEI) is a research project sponsored and organized by three leading professional associations in the field of computer-assisted literary and linguistic research: the Association for Computational Linguistics (ACL), the Association for Literary and Linguistic Computing (ALLC) and the Association for Computing and the Humanities (ACH). These societies have a combined membership of several thousand leading scholars, researchers and teachers worldwide. The TEI has been funded throughout its four years of activities on both sides of the Atlantic: primarily by the US National Endowment for the Humanities and by the EU as part of its framework for linguistic research and engineering, but also with grants from the Mellon Foundation and from the Canadian Social Sciences and Humanities Research Council. Most significant, however, has been the donation of time and expertise by the many members of the wider research community who have served on the TEI's Working Committees and Working Groups. These have included representatives of many disciplines beyond the comparatively narrow world of literature and linguistics, notably the librarian and cataloguers serving on the TEI Documentation Committee, the historians serving on the work groups for historical texts and physical description, and leading professionals from the software industry who have served on the TEI Syntax and Metalanguage Committee.

The project aims to deliver a fully specified set of 'Guidelines'[1] which will enable researchers in any discipline to interchange texts in machine readable form, independently of the software or hardware in use, independently of the particular processing application envisaged, and independently of the language, period, or type of textual resource concerned. As the name suggests, these Guidelines are not intended to be binding or prescriptive, but rather to provide impartial guidance for the perplexed.

That is not to say that those whom it is hoped will benefit are in any sense undemanding or unsophisticated. On the contrary, the TEI community is a particularly demanding one: the purpose of research is to discover solutions to problems that have not yet been posed, and any scheme designed to support research must therefore place more emphasis on flexibility and extensibility to cope with the unforeseen than on highly optimized solutions to well-understood problems.

At the same time, academic researchers are likely to be as impatient as anyone else with solutions that require extensive specialist knowledge of little relevance to the problem in hand. The TEI scheme must therefore be simple to grasp in its essentials and of demonstrable benefit in areas that concern researchers as much as they concern other information-handling professionals: above all, the efficient and loss-free interchange of information across different hardware platforms, among different software environments, for the widest possible range of applications. The construction of a major textual or other resource by an academic research project may take years to complete; a scheme designed to support them must thus be future-proof – and this in a world where technology continues to mutate at an alarming rate.

As its title suggests, the TEI community is, of course, strongly interested in electronic versions of written texts, both as a stage in the production of paper documents, and in their own right, whether as a research database or a component in non-paper publications. Transcriptions of spoken language are texts of a very special kind, it cannot be denied, yet their effective handling in electronic form turns out to pose very similar problems, and can thus benefit from very similar solutions, to those derived from a written original. The methodological assumptions and solutions appropriate to the scholar attempting to produce a 'diplomatic' transcript from an illegible medieval manuscript are not so very different from those appropriate to the scholar wishing to share his or her interpretation of an audio tape.

Like the publishing industry, the academic community is rapidly coming to realize that its stock in hand is not words on the page, but information, independent of its physical realization. As technology begins to emerge which is genuinely adequate to the task of integrating text, graphics and audio into a seamless information-bearing vehicle, so the importance of that realization becomes more apparent. By providing a description of information which is independent of realization or media, the TEI scheme, like other SGML-based approaches, enormously facilitates the interchangeability of multimedia. It also places centre-stage the interpretative nature of that description.

The TEI guidelines have a dual focus: being concerned with both *what* should be encoded (i.e. made explicit) in an electronic text, and *how* that encoding should be represented for interchange. The approach taken is a two stage one: first, the identification of those distinctions concerning which there is common agreement; secondly the creation of a uniform encoding system within which those distinctions can be expressed for interchange. Early on in the project, the SGML (ISO 8879) was chosen as the most appropriate vehicle to represent the textual features identified by the scheme, on the purely pragmatic grounds that no other candidate seemed to meet the requirements discussed above. If SGML had proved inadequate to the needs of researchers, we would have abandoned it without a qualm; perhaps fortunately, it did not. On the contrary, it has proved remarkably difficult to find problems for which a solution could not be expressed in SGML.

The prime deliverable of the TEI scheme is a large and integrated collection of SGML tagsets, providing hardware-, software- and application-independent support for the encoding of all kinds of text in all languages and of all times. These tagsets are necessarily based on, but not limited by, existing practice within the research community; they are by design both comprehensive and extensible. They are collectively documented in a substantial reference manual, the *Guidelines for Text Encoding for Interchange*. A first draft of this publication appeared in November 1990, and was widely circulated and discussed.[2] During 1991 and 1992, these initial recommendations were greatly revised and reorganized, largely as a result of work carried out in a number of small specialist work groups, set up following a detailed technical review meeting held in November 1991.

A second draft of the guidelines, known internally as P2, began publication as a series of electronic fascicles in April 1992, and has continued since. Each fascicle is reviewed by both editors and tested carefully for consistency with the remainder before being made available in electronic form. This is greatly facilitated by the use of an SGML-based documentation system developed specifically for the project.[3] Twenty of these electronic 'fascicles' are now available by anonymous file transfer from a number of sites on the Internet, or from the TEI's own Listserv program, in so-called plain ASCII text, Postscript or SGML formats (and shortly in LaTeX as well). The TEI document type definition which these fascicles document is also available from the same sources.

In June of 1993 a draft of P2 including both published and partially drafted fascicles was presented to the project's Advisory Board, which endorsed the work completed so far and the proposed direction of future development. Since then, effort has been devoted to the completion and publication of as many chapters as possible before the Guidelines are published.

In addition to this reference manual – which is a substantial document not intended for casual browsing – the TEI plans to make available a number of smaller introductory tutorials focused on particular application areas. One such, on terminological systems, has already appeared[4] and several others are in the planning stage. Probably of equal importance will be the appearance of demonstration TEI-conformant datasets in particular application areas, for which plans are also in hand.

The TEI guidelines may best be thought of as an enabling standard, from which more focused application-standards may be derived. This process has already begun, for example in the so-called language industries, where researchers in key areas of language technology have now begun a series of detailed evaluations and applications of the TEI proposals for the encoding of language corpora, spoken language and language description, as part of the EAGLES Project. In the remainder of this paper, we attempt to demonstrate the range of facilities supported by the TEI architecture, from which specific application standards may be derived.

2   Organization of the TEI scheme

As an SGML application, the TEI scheme necessarily requires the existence of some kind of document type definition (dtd). However, the TEI scheme describes not one but many possible dtds, which may be tailored to the needs of a particular application in a way difficult or impossible with most other general purpose dtds so far developed.

A TEI dtd (or, more exactly, a view of the TEI dtd) is composed of the *core tagsets*, a single *base tagset* and any number of user selected *additional tagsets* or 'toppings'.

A tagset is simply an ensemble of definitions for SGML elements and their attributes. Every element in the TEI scheme appears in exactly one tagset and elements may be excluded from a TEI dtd or renamed as necessary.

In developing the TEI scheme, a small number of auxiliary tagsets have also been found necessary. These include the 'writing system declaration' which defines the writing system or character-level encodings used within a text and the 'tagset declaration' which provides a tagset for the documentation of SGML tagsets themselves.

At the highest level, all TEI documents conform to a common model: the basic unit is a *text*, by which is meant any single document, or any stretch of natural language regarded as a self-contained unit for processing purposes. The association of such a unit with a *header* describing it as a bibliographic entity (see further section 3.4 below) is regarded as a single < TEI > element.

Two variations on this basic structure are defined: a collection of < TEI > elements is possible (this we call a *corpus*); second, support is also provided for a variety of composite texts. The first solution is most appropriate for large disparate collections of independent texts, for example in language corpora, or collections of unrelated papers in an archive. The second better suits such cases as the complete works of a given author, which might be regarded simultaneously as a single text in its own right and as a series of independent texts.

In the first case, each text is given its own header, with any material common to all texts being factored out to an overall corpus header. In the second case, a special SGML element < GROUP > is used, which can appear as the body of a < TEXT > and which is composed of a sequence of other, nested, groups or texts. This mechanism also allows for the encoding of composite works such as anthologies, in which individual texts may have different structural properties (for example, being composed of both dramatic and prose texts).

2.1 The TEI base tagsets

At the time of writing, eight base tagsets are proposed. Six of these are intended for documents which are predominantly composed of one type of text; the other two are provided for use with texts which combine these basic tagsets. It is possible that other base tagsets will be added in the future. Those currently proposed are as follows:

- prose
- verse
- drama
- transcribed speech
- letters and memoranda
- dictionary entries
- terminological entries

Each TEI base tagset determines the basic structure of all the documents with which it is to be used. More exactly, it defines the constituents of < TEXT > elements, combined as described above. In practice, so far, almost all the TEI bases defined are very similar in their basic structure, though the means exist for them to vary this if necessary. They do, however, differ greatly in their components: the kind of sub-elements likely to appear within the divisions of a dictionary (for example) will be entirely different from those likely to appear within the divisions of a letter, a novel or a transcribed conversation. To cater for this variety, the constituents of all divisions of a TEI < TEXT > element are not defined explicitly, but in terms of *parameter entities*. A parameter entity is an SGML construct which may be thought of in simple terms as like a variable declaration in a programming language: the effect of using them here is that each base tagset can provide its own specific definition for the constituents of texts, which can, moreover, be modified on a document-by-document basis.

2.2 Textual divisions

Some forms of text (notably transcriptions of spoken language) are only notionally divisible into multiple levels of structure. For the majority, however, there is a bewildering and highly application- or culture-specific variety of high level units into which they may be divided. Nevertheless, all objects such as 'chapters', 'sections', 'entries', 'acts' and 'scenes', 'cantos', and so on, seem to behave in the same way: they are incomplete in themselves, and often nest hierarchically. In the

TEI scheme all such objects are therefore regarded as the same kind of element, called here a 'division'; though a distinction is made between divisions whose hierarchic position is seen as being inseparable from their semantics (these are encoded as < DIV1 >, < DIV2 >, etc., down to < DIV7 > elements) and those for which their position in the document tree is regarded as of lesser importance (these are encoded as 'vanilla' < DIVs >). Numbered and un-numbered division elements may not be mixed in the same < FRONT >, < BODY >, or < BACK > element.

A TYPE attribute may be used to distinguish amongst divisions in some respect other than their hierarchic position: the values for this attribute (as for several others in the TEI scheme) are not standardized, precisely because no consensus exists, or is likely to exist, as to a typology. A set of legal values should, however, be defined for a given application, either in the TEI header or by a user-defined modification.

The lower level components of textual divisions are parameterized by means of another mechanism which characterizes the whole TEI scheme: the use of parameter entities whose values are specific to the particular base in use. All divisions are defined in the core dtd with a content model including '%component.seq'; the exact value of this parameter entity will, however, be different in different bases. In this way it is possible for the divisions of a text using the spoken text base (for example) to consist of utterances, kinesics, events, and so on, while those of a text using the dictionary base will consist of lexical entries.

In the normal case, the components of all divisions in a particular base are homogeneous – they all use the same value for '%component.seq'. The scheme also allows for two kinds of heterogeneity. If the *general* base is selected, together with two or more other bases, then different divisions of a text may have different constituents, though each division must itself be homogeneous. A *mixed* base is also defined, in which components from any selection of bases may be combined promiscuously across division boundaries.

At the next level down (below the level of 'components'), there are a number of so-called 'phrase level' elements which can appear in any kind of text. These include features such as names or dates, or (of particular importance for spoken texts) segments of discourse, identified according to syntactic, phonological or prosodic principles. Because these features are common to many base-level components, they are to be found either in the core tagset, or in a special purpose additional tagset.

3 The core tagsets

Two core tagsets are available to all TEI documents without formality, unless explicitly disabled. The first defines a large number of elements which may appear in any kind of document – coinciding more or less with that set of discipline-independent textual features concerning which consensus has been reached. The second defines the *header*, providing something analogous to an electronic title page for the electronic text, as further discussed in section 3.4 below.

3.1 Elements available to all bases

The core tagset common to all TEI bases provides means of encoding with a reasonable degree of sophistication the following list of textual features:

1. paragraphs;
2. passages of verse or drama, distinguishing for example speakers, stage directions, verse lines, stanzaic units, etc.;
3. lists of various kinds, including glossaries and indexes;
4. typographically highlighted phrases, whether unqualified or used to mark linguistic emphasis, foreign words, titles, etc.;
5. quoted phrases, distinguishing direct speech, quotation, terms and glosses, cited phrases, etc.;
6. names, numbers and measures, dates and times, and similar 'data-like' phrases;
7. basic editorial changes (e.g. correction of apparent errors; regularization and normalization; additions, deletions and omissions);
8. simple links and cross references, providing basic hypertextual features;
9. pre-existing or generated annotation and indexing;
10. bibliographic citations, adequate for most commonly used bibliographic packages, in either a free or a tightly structured format;
11. simple or complex referencing systems, not necessarily dependent on the existing SGML structure.

It will be noted that the majority of these features are rarely marked in transcribed speech. Nevertheless, there are few texts which do not exhibit some of these features; and few of these features are particularly restricted to any one kind of text. Of particular use for spoken texts are the elements provided for simple editorial annotation, and linkage. In most cases, additional more specialized tagsets are provided for those wishing to encode aspects of these features in more detail (see further section 4 below), but the elements defined in this core are believed to be adequate for most applications most of the time. Like all others, the particular elements corresponding to these textual features may be renamed, disabled or redefined.

3.2 The TEI class system

Textual features, and hence the elements which encode them, may be categorized or classified in a number of ways. The TEI scheme identifies two kinds of classification scheme: *attribute classes* and *model classes*. The distinction is, however, more formal than semantic; both are used for broadly similar purposes. Members of an attribute class share the same set of attributes. For example, all elements which represent links or associations between one element and another do so using a common set of attributes, and are thus regarded as forming the attribute class *pointer*. In the same way, the attribute class *timed* contains all elements used to represent features which have a duration in time such as utterances or events in transcribed speech. Members of this last class share the attributes DUR (used to specify their duration) START and END (used to identify the point in time at which they begin or end respectively), as further discussed in the paper by Stig Johansson in the present volume. All elements are members of at least one attribute class, the class 'global', which is further discussed below (section 3.3).

Members of a model class share the same structural properties: that is, they may appear at the same position within the SGML document structure. For example, the class *phrase* includes all elements which can appear within paragraphs but not spanning them, while the class *chunk* includes all elements which cannot appear within paragraphs (such as paragraphs, for example). A class *inter* is also defined, for elements such as lists which can appear either within or between chunk elements. Similarly, the class *divtop* contains all elements (headings, epigraphs etc.) which can appear at the start of a textual division.

As well as these general purpose classes, some *functional* or *semantic* classes are defined: for example, all elements used to mark editorial corrections or omissions are all members of the class *edit*; elements marking bibliographic citations, and so on, are all members of the class *bibl*.

Elements may of course be members of more than one class. Classes may have super- and sub-classes, and properties (notably associated attributes) may be inherited. For example, reflecting the needs of many TEI users to treat texts both as documents and as input to databases, a sub-class of phrase called 'data' is defined to include 'data-like' features such as names of persons, places or organizations, numbers and dates, abbreviations and measures. These behave in exactly the same way as phrase elements.

The formal definition of these classes in the SGML syntax used to express the TEI scheme makes it possible for users of the scheme to extend it in a simple and controlled way: new elements may be added into existing classes, and existing elements renamed or undefined, without any need for extensive revision of the TEI document type definitions – though this is perhaps a benefit which only those who have ever tried to modify an existing dtd by hand will truly appreciate.

3.3 The global attributes

One particularly important class is the *global* attribute class to which all elements belong. All elements in the TEI scheme may bear the following attributes:

- id   provides an SGML identifier for an element
- n   provides a possibly non-unique name or number for an element
- lang   specifies the language and hence the writing system used for an element
- rend   provides information about the rendering of an element where this is not otherwise specified

The ID and N attributes allow for the identification of any element occurrence within a TEI-conformant text. Elements carrying an ID attribute value may be the object of a link or cross-reference, or any of the other re-structuring mechanisms proposed by the TEI for circumventing the rigidly hierarchic structure of a simple SGML dtd. The fact that such links are essentially unpredictable is one reason for making this attribute global.

Values on ID attributes must be unique (their declared value is ID). Values on the N attribute, however, need not be; they may be used to carry a TEI canonical reference. A method for defining the structure of such canonical reference schemes is also provided, so that documents using it can be processed automatically.

The LANG attribute indicates both the language and hence the writing system applicable to the element's content, thus providing explicit support for polyglot or multiscript texts. If no value is given, that of the element's direct parent is assumed. (A number of TEI attributes have this characteristic, which is catered for by a TEI-defined keyword.) The value of this element identifies a special purpose <LANGUAGE> element which documents the language in use, optionally associating it with an external entity in which a formal writing system declaration may be given.

The TEI writing system declaration (wsd) attempts to help encoders come to terms with a world in which, for one reason or another, documents may not always use the same universal character set, whether from ignorance, perversity or the sheer impossibility of finding one large enough to represent all the glyphs they comprise. It provides for the systematic documentation of a writing system, in terms of existing international or other standards, public or private entity sets, *ad hoc* transliteration schemes or explicit definitions, as well as combinations of all four.

Finally, the global REND element may be used to give information about the physical presentation of the text in the source, where this is not otherwise given. A default rendition may be specified for all elements of a given type. No specific set of values is defined for this attribute in the current draft, though it is probable that some suitable set of DSSSL primitives will be proposed in a later version.

It should be stressed that the REND element is not intended for use as a means of specifying the desired formatting of an element, except in so far as this may be determined by a desire to mimic the approximate appearance of the original text. Like other SGML applications, the TEI scheme attempts to provide elements for the encoding of those textual features deemed essential to a productive use of the encoded text; however, unlike most other SGML applications, the TEI scheme recognizes that for some, it is precisely the appearance of a text which is the object of research.

3.4 The header

The TEI scheme is perhaps unusual in the stress it lays on documentary or bibliographic information. The header allows for the definition of a full Anglo

American Cataloguing Rules (AACR)2-compatible bibliographic description for the electronic text, covering all of the following:

1. the electronic document itself
2. the sources from which it was derived
3. the encoding system which has been applied
4. its revision history

The header is one of the few mandatory elements in a TEI document, reflecting the importance attached to this kind of information by the research community.

The TEI header allows for the provision of a very large amount of structured or unstructured information under the above headings, including both traditional bibliographic material which can be translated straight into an equivalent Machine Readable Catalogue (MARC) record, as well as a wealth of descriptive information such as the languages it uses and the situation within which it was produced, expansions or formal definitions for any codebooks used in analysing the text, the setting and identity of participants within it. This diversity and richness reflects the diversity of uses to which it is envisaged that electronic texts conforming to these guidelines will be put.

The amount of encoding in a header will depend both on the nature and the intended use of the text. At one extreme, an encoder may provide only a bibliographic identification of the text. At the other, encoders wishing to ensure that their texts can be used for the widest range of applications, will want to provide a level of detailed documentation approximating to the kind most often supplied in the form of a manual. Most texts will lie somewhere between these extremes; textual corpora in particular will tend more to the latter extreme. A collection of TEI headers can also be regarded as a distinct document, and an auxiliary dtd is provided to support interchange of headers alone, for example between libraries or archives.

4   The TEI additional tagsets

A number of optional additional tagsets are defined by the current proposals. These include tagsets for special application areas such as segmentation and alignment of text segments; a wide range of other 'analytic' elements and attributes; a tagset for detailed physical description of manuscript material and another for the recording of an 'electronic variorum' modelled on the traditional critical apparatus; tagsets for the detailed encoding of names and dates; abstractions such as networks, graphs or trees; mathematical formulae and tables etc.

In addition to these application-specific specialized tagsets, a very general purpose tagset is also proposed for the encoding of entirely abstract interpretations of a text, either in parallel with it or embedded within it. This is based on the *feature structure* notation employed in theoretical linguistics, but has applications far beyond linguistic theory.[5] Using this mechanism, encoders are at liberty to define arbitrarily complex bundles or sets of features identified in a text, according to their own methodological bias. The syntax defined by the guidelines not only formalizes the way in which such features are encoded, but also provides for a detailed specification of legal feature value/pair combinations and rules determining, for example, the implication of under-specified or defaulted features. This is known as a *feature system declaration*.

A related set of additional elements is also provided for the encoding of degrees of uncertainty or ambiguity in the encoding of a text. This tagset exhibits in a particularly noticeable form one of the chief strengths of the TEI approach to encoding: it provides the encoder with a well-defined set of tools which can be used to make explicit his or her reading of a text. No claim to absolute authority is made by any encoder, nor ever should be; the TEI scheme merely allows encoders to 'come clean' about what they have perceived in a text, to whatever degree of detail seems appropriate.

A user of the TEI scheme may combine as many or as few additional tagsets as suit his or her needs. The existence of tagsets for particular application areas in the current draft reflects, to some extent, accidents of history: no claim to systematic or encyclopaedic coverage is implied. Indeed, it is confidently expected that new tagsets will be added, and their definition will form an important part of the continued work of this and successor projects.

5 From general to specific

The TEI Guidelines have taken nearly four years to reach their present state, the first at which we feel they can be said to be reasonably complete. In retrospect, it is doubtless true that they could have been created much more quickly with less involvement from the research community, or a clearer statement from it of a set of particular goals. But that statement would have inevitably limited the scope of the resulting scheme, providing exactly the kind of straitjacket which we wished to avoid. Moreover, by prioritizing any one research agenda, however well-articulated, we would have effectively disenfranchized and alienated all others. A little like the early Church fathers then, we have had to provide as broad and as catholic a means of salvation as possible.

The TEI therefore chose to provide general methods wherever possible, by applying rigorously the principle *essentia non sunt multiplicanda praeter necessitatem*. Generally attributed to William of Occam (1300–1349), this recommendation is known as *Occam's Razor*; it may be translated as 'Essences should not be unnecessarily multiplied' and refers properly to the distinction made by the Scholiasts between 'essence' – those properties of an entity which define its type and 'accidents' – those properties specific only to one instance of an entity.

The use of feature structure analysis, referred to above, is one instance of this principle; another is the way in which all kinds of links between document elements, whatever their semantics, are encoded using the same tagset, in just the same way as all kinds of analytic segmentation of elements may be performed using the same basic tagset.

At the same time, there are many situations in which the TEI's desire to exclude no-one has led to a multiplication of distinctions that are at first sight rather bewildering. To say the least, it seems unlikely that anyone will ever encode a document using every possible element defined by the union of every TEI tagset, though such a monster dtd is indeed possible. Even in a relatively small area such as the definition of text classification schemes, the TEI proposes three parallel (and mutually incompatible) methods. In the matter of hypertextual addressing, the TEI syntax permits of 14 different 'location methods'. Names of persons places and organizations may be left unmarked, tagged simply as referring strings, or analysed into subcomponents specific to them. Bibliographic citations may be presented as simple prose, or as assemblages of specific elements, either highly structured or loosely assembled. Temporal alignment and hence overlap in spoken language may be encoded in three different ways.

Some critics may find this richness of choice overwhelming, or indicative of chronic indecisiveness. Given the richness and diversity of the research communities served by the TEI, such criticisms are perhaps inescapable. Certainly, most people confronted by the 800-plus pages of the current printed version are likely to derive less comfort from knowing that somewhere in it exists precisely the general purpose solution they need than they will from a demonstration of the application of that general mechanism to the specific problem currently facing them. Provision of such demonstrations will form the substance of the next, and perhaps most demanding, phase of the TEI's existence.

Standards come into being in many different ways. They may come about as *ad hoc* consequences of market forces; an obvious example is the IBM PC. They may result from pressure applied by well-intentioned groups of experts; much ISO standardization is of this type. Or standards come about as a result of the gradual recognition by all members of a large community that convergence on a common set of principles and practices is in their own best interests. This last method is the most likely to last, but the most difficult to achieve. It cannot be done by fiat but only by experiment. The TEI guidelines aspire to this status, and it is this fact which both explains their peculiar nature and their importance for this audience.

6 For more information ...

A TEI electronic bulletin board is maintained at the University of Illinois at Chicago: this is used to announce availability of TEI drafts and other publications, and to distribute them in electronic form, as well as providing an open forum for comment and discussion of the TEI recommendations. To subscribe to this service, send an electronic mail message in the form SUBSCRIBE TEI-L Your Name to the address listserv@uicvm.uic.edu.

TEI publications are to be found at a number of anonymous FTP archives, notably that maintained by the University of Exeter at sgml.ex.ac.uk in the directory 'tei'.

Notes

1. For more extensive discussion of the project's history, rationale, and design principles see TEI internal documents EDP1 and EDP2 (available from the TEI) and Sperberg-McQueen 1991.
2. Guidelines for electronic text encoding and interchange edited by C.M. Sperberg-McQueen and Lou Burnard (Chicago and Oxford, ALLC-ACH-ACL Text Encoding Initiative, 1990). Brief notices have appeared in *Humanistiske Data* 3–90; *ACH Newsletter* 12 (3–4); *EPSIG News* 3(3); *SGML Users Group Newsletter* 18; *ACLS Newsletter* 2 (4) and elsewhere. More detailed reports include Lou Burnard 1991a, 1992, 1993a, 1993b.
3. This software, the ODD ('One Document Does it all') system, forms the subject of a forthcoming paper by the TEI editors. It follows Donald Knuth's 'Web' system in allowing for the intermingling of code (in this case, SGML document type definitions) and documentation of it within the same document, but benefits greatly from the use of SGML both to enforce consistency and avoid redundancy in describing the complexities of the TEI scheme.
4. Melby et al. 1993.
5. A good introduction to this tagset is provided by Langendoen and Simons 1993; for an extended discussion of an application of the feature structure scheme to the problems of encoding historical source materials, see Burnard in Greenstein 1916.

6 The approach of the Text Encoding Initiative to the encoding of spoken discourse

STIG JOHANSSON

1 The problem

As is amply shown in this book (see also Edwards and Lampert 1993), there is a great deal of variety in the encoding of spoken discourse, both with respect to the features selected for encoding and their representation in written or electronic form. The challenge is to suggest ways of representing speech which are compatible with the general approach of the Text Encoding Initiative (TEI) and express the distinctions needed for research on spoken discourse.

The TEI proposals are presented in Sperberg-McQueen and Burnard (1994); a brief general overview is given in the paper by Lou Burnard in this volume. The TEI proposals for the encoding of spoken discourse, which will be discussed below, should be sufficient for use with a wide variety of transcribed spoken material.[1]

2 Underlying representation vs. display

There is an important distinction in the encoding of electronic texts between underlying representation and display. The TEI approach focuses on an underlying representation, while acknowledging that this can be transformed to a variety of formats for particular processing purposes or for display.

In focusing on an underlying representation it is possible to reduce a great deal of the variety in the transcription of speech. Transcribers have been very much concerned with finding a visual display which eases the (manual) processing of the material. But there is far more variation in display than in the features which the display is intended to represent. For example, most transcribers have ways of indicating pauses:[2]

    Du Bois et al. (1990: 35ff.):
..	short pause
...	longer pause
... (1.5)	timed pause

Jefferson (quoted from Atkinson and Heritage 1984: x–xi):

–	short pause
((pause))	untimed pause
(1.5)	timed pause

MacWhinney (1991: 42):

#	short pause
## ### #long	longer pauses
#1_5	timed pause

Rosta (1990, s. 4.3):

<,>	short pause
<,,>	long pause

Svartvik and Quirk (1980: 22):

.	brief pause
–	unit pause
–. – –.	longer pauses
– – – – –	

etc.

As the examples show, there are differences both as regards the number of distinctions made, whether the pauses are timed or untimed, and with respect to the symbols used. The suggested TEI approach is to define an underlying empty <pause> element, with attributes for 'type' (e.g. long, short, medium) and 'dur[ation]'. In this way it is possible to express all the distinctions made in the examples above in a precise and consistent (albeit less concise) manner, in agreement with general conventions for electronic text representation.

3 Text documentation

It is important to provide documentation on the speakers and the setting as well as on transcription principles and other matters which may affect the interpretation of the text. Information on the setting and the speakers has generally been given in more or less structured form in a header section preceding the text or in a separate printed document or electronic file. Examples:

Du Bois et al. (1990: 173), Corpus of Spoken American English:

$ TRANSCRIPTION TITLE:
$ TAPE TITLE:
$ FILENAME:
$ PRINTOUT DATE:
$ RECORDING DATE:
$ RECORDING TIME:
$ RECORDING LOCATION:
$ RECORDED BY:

84 *Issues and practices*

$ LANGUAGE:
$ DIALECT:
$ GENRE:
$ SETTING:
$ SPEAKER 1:
etc.

Kytö (1990), Helsinki Corpus of English Dialects:
<F SUF3>
<S JW>
<A 68>
<O FISHERMAN 6 BOATSMAN>
<C SUFFOLK>
<V SNAPE>
<D 05–07–72>
etc.

MacWhinney (1991: 108), CHILDES transcription:
@Participants: MAR Mark Child, ROS Ross Child, FAT Brian Father, MOT Mary Mother
@Age of ROS: 7;3.22
@Age of MAR: 5;4.29
@Sex of ROS: male
@Sex of MAR: male
@Birth of ROS: 25–DEC–1977
@Birth of MAR: 19–NOV–1979
@Date: 17–APR–1985
@Coding: CHAT 2–Dec–1987
@Situation: upstairs, getting ready to go to school... etc.

There is a great deal of variety with respect to the types of information recorded and the ways in which the information is expressed. The TEI approach is to use the framework defined for electronic texts in general, with a header containing four main elements:

<fileDesc> giving a bibliographic description of the computer file and its source(s);

<encodingDesc> containing information on the compilation and encoding of the text;

<profileDesc> giving detailed non-bibliographic information on the text (including information on the setting and the participants as well as a description of the text in terms of situational parameters);

<revisionDesc> summarizing the revision history of the electronic text.

The main difference between headers for spoken and written texts is that the source description of the former may require two additional elements: a <recordingStmt> and a <scriptStmt> (for scripted speech).

The advantage of the TEI approach is that the types of information customarily given for spoken texts can be expressed in a non-arbitrary manner. The unified treatment of spoken and written texts facilitates the archiving of texts and the comparison of varieties across speech and writing (for example, as studied by Biber 1988). The main problem with the TEI header is that it may be very extensive, perhaps especially so in the case of spoken texts. Everything does not have to be specified, however. The main thing is that there is a place for each type of information transcribers may want to note. Provision is also made for varying degrees of structuring, as shown by these examples of setting descriptions (quoted from Sperberg-McQueen and Burnard 1994: 657):

```
<settingDesc>
<p>The time is early spring, 1989. P1 and P2 are playing on the rug of a suburban home in Bedford. P3 is doing the washing up at the sink. P4 (a radio announcer) is in a broadcasting studio in London.</p>
</settingDesc>

<settingDesc>
    <setting who='P1 P2'>
        <name type = town>Bedford, UK</name>
        <name type = region>UK: South East</name>
        <date value=1989>early spring, 1989</date>
        <locale>rug of a suburban home</locale>
        <activity>playing</activity>
    </setting>
    <setting who=P3>
        <name type = town>Bedford, UK</name>
        <name type = region>UK: South East</name>
        <date value=1989>early spring, 1989</date>
        <locale>at the sink</locale>
        <activity>washing-up</activity>
    </setting>
    <setting who=P4>
        <name type = city>London, UK</name>
        <time>unknown</time>
        <locale>broadcasting studio</locale>
        <activity>radio performance</activity>
    </setting>
</settingDesc>
```

The extent of detail to be provided and the degree of structuring of the information must be evaluated in the light of the purposes of the individual project.

4 Text units

Although the header remains much the same for spoken and written texts, there is a need for an additional tagset to handle the actual text of speech. Most types of writing in our days are divided into easily recognizable parts, such as chapters, paragraphs and words. Headings, punctuation and a variety of typographical devices further structure the written text. In speech there is basically a continuum, without a clear division into units. Nevertheless, it is necessary to have some sort of segmentation in order to study the text.

Conventional speech transcriptions divide the text up more or less as in writing, using paragraphs, sentences and orthographic words. Linguists often prefer a division based on prosody, for example, the tone units in the London–Lund Corpus (see Svartvik and Quirk 1980) and the intonation units in the scheme set up for the Corpus of Spoken American English (see Du Bois et al. 1990). A different sort of division uses 'macrosyntagms', originally proposed for the analysis of a corpus of spoken Swedish. A macrosyntagm is defined in syntactic terms and corresponds roughly to an orthographic sentence in writing (see Loman and Jörgensen 1971).

Most transcriptions of speech of any considerable length, even those made by linguists, use the orthographic word as the unit below the prosodic or syntactic units mentioned above. A higher-level unit recognized both in conventional and more linguistically orientated transcription is the turn or utterance, which represents the contribution of a single speaker at a particular point in a conversation. Turns may be grouped into speech events or discourse texts which represent some sort of natural unit, but frequently a spoken text is merely a grouping for convenience.

To cater for the various types of segmentation of spoken texts, the TEI scheme includes the following elements (see Fig. 6.1):

    <text>   a transcription of a stretch of speech treated for some purpose as a well-defined unit;

    <div>   a subdivision of a spoken text comprising one or more utterances treated as a unit for analytic purposes;

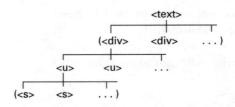

Figure 6.1 The hierarchy of text units in the TEI scheme for the encoding of spoken discourse.

<u> an utterance, i.e. a stretch of speech usually preceded and followed by silence or a change of speaker;[3]
<s> a subdivision of an utterance by prosodic or syntactic criteria.

The basic elements are <text> and <u>; a <text> may simply be divided into a string of <u> elements. The element <div> is an optional layer between <text> and <u>; it may nest, like the TEI element <div> in general, and can then express a hierarchical text structure like that defined by the Birmingham group (Sinclair and Coulthard 1975, Coulthard and Montgomery 1981). The element <s>, like the TEI element <s> in general, does not nest; it provides a means of exhaustively subdividing the text below the level of the utterance. All the elements may have 'n' and 'id' attributes which can be used for reference purposes.

Using the elements proposed above it is possible to express the types of segmentation customarily used in speech transcription. The precise nature of the elements is not defined by the TEI. It is up to the user of the scheme to define each element more exactly and to declare the definitions in the proper section of the <encodingDesc>.

5   Speaker attribution

Most transcriptions take the form of a 'play script', where each utterance is preceded by an indication of speaker identity. Example (from Crowdy 1994: 28, British National Corpus, Longman transcription):

<1>   It's a funny old day isn't it.
<2>   Mm, it's not cold is it?. . .

The exact way in which the speaker prefix is given varies a good deal. The TEI approach is to indicate speaker identity through an attribute of the <u> tag, as shown by a re-coded version of the example above:

<u who=1>It's a funny old day isn't it.</u>
<u who=2>Mm, it's not cold is it?. . . </u>

The value of the 'who' attribute is an identifier which specifies a participant or participant group given in the header of the text (cf. section 3 above). If needed, the TEI notation can easily be converted to a 'play script' format.

6   Other features of spoken texts

Apart from the more narrowly linguistic elements, transcribers have often noted a variety of other features which may be significant for the interpretation of a spoken text: silent and filled pauses, non-lexical backchannels, gestures, background noise, and so on. The types of features included and their representation vary widely. The TEI elements provided for these features are defined below. See also Fig. 6.2; for a more formal definition, see Sperberg-McQueen and Burnard (1994).

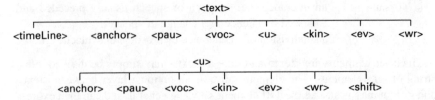

Figure 6.2 The content of <text> and <u> in the TEI scheme for the encoding of spoken discourse (omitting <div> and <s>). As regards <timeLine>, <anchor>, and <shift>, see Sections 8 and 10 below. Abbreviations: pau = pause, voc = vocal, kin = kinesic, ev = event, wr = writing.

6.1 Pauses

The treatment of pauses has already been touched on in passing in section 2 above. It should only be added that the <pause> element may appear within or between utterances. In the former case it is taken to apply to the speaker of the relevant utterance, in the latter case to all participants. If necessary, the attribution of pauses can be specified by a 'who' attribute of the <pause> tag. The <pause> element only applies to silent pauses.

6.2 Vocals

Spontaneous speech contains a good many vocalizations which cannot be broken down into conventional words, for example voiced pauses or non-lexical backchannels. Transcribers customarily deal with these either by giving a description within parentheses (cough, sob, giggle, etc.) or by providing an orthographic form as part of the actual text (*ah, er, um*, etc.). In the latter case transcribers frequently maintain a control list of possible forms. The TEI provides the empty tag <vocal>, with a 'who' attribute for speaker identification and a 'desc' attribute for a description of the phenomenon. A <vocal> can appear within or between utterances. Example (re-coded from Atkinson and Heritage 1984: xiii):

<u who=Tom>I used to <vocal desc=cough> smoke a lot</u>
<u who=Bob><vocal desc=sniff>He thinks he's tough</u>
<vocal who=Ann desc=snorts>

The distinction between vocals and utterances is not always clear, although for analytic purposes it will be convenient to regard them as distinct. Individual scholars may differ in the way the borderline is drawn and may prefer to regard some semi-lexical phenomena as words within the bounds of <u>. This approach is of course only available where it is possible to transcribe, rather than describe, the vocal.

6.3 Kinesics

Where gestures are marked in transcriptions, there is usually a description within parentheses in much the same way as for descriptions of non-lexical vocalizations.

The TEI recommendations provide an empty tag <kinesic>, with a 'who' attribute ascribing the gesture to a particular participant and a 'desc' attribute describing the phenomenon. This is a simple concocted example:

<u who=Jane>Have you read Vanity Fair?</u>
<u who=Stig>Yes.</u>
<kinesic who=Lou desc=nod>

6.4 Events

Utterances, vocals, and kinesics share the characteristic that they are all communicative. On occasion, transcribers have noted non-vocal and non-communicative phenomena which may be of importance for the interpretation of the text. These sorts of features correspond to stage directions in a play and are typically indicated in transcriptions by descriptions within parentheses. In the TEI approach the empty tag <event> is used, with a 'desc' attribute, as in the following example (re-coded from Atkinson and Heritage 1984: xiii):

<u who=Jan>This is just delicious</u><event desc='telephone rings'>
<u who=Kim>I'll get it</u>

If necessary, the event can be associated with a particular participant or participant group, by the use of a 'who' attribute.

The borderline between kinesics and events, like the one between utterances and vocals, is not clear. Individual scholars may differ in the way the borderlines are drawn and should declare their definitions in the file header.

6.5 Writing

Written text may appear as an important element in some speech situations, for example in a lecture or television broadcast. As far as I am aware, speech transcriptions have no special conventions catering for this. The TEI recommendations provide the tag <writing>, with a 'who' attribute identifying the person who reveals or creates the writing and a 'type' attribute categorizing the kind of writing in some way (overhead transparency, subtitle, etc.).

Writing differs from events in that it is communicative and lexical (in other words, it is like <u>). Moreover, the tag <writing> has content, namely the written text displayed, whereas <event> is an empty element. Where it is not essential to record the written text, writing may be treated as an event, e.g.: <event desc='overhead transparency is displayed'>.

7 Duration

Many transcription schemes have ways of indicating the length of pauses (cf. section 2 above). Du Bois et al. (1990: 58) show how the same mechanism can be used more generally, e.g. to indicate the length of a word or a sequence of events.

90   *Issues and practices*

Duration is handled within the TEI scheme by the use of a 'dur' attribute of the following tags: <u>, <pause>, <vocal>, <kinesic>, <event>. Specific indications of length can also be given with reference to the <timeLine> dealt with in the next section.

8   Synchronization

Location in time is generally represented through location in space. In other words, the sequence of words in the written transcription is taken to represent a temporal sequence. The simple analogy breaks down where it is essential to record simultaneous events, as with overlapping speech. Figures 6.3–6.5 illustrate some ways in which speech overlap has been recorded. Overlapping segments are characteristically identified by devices such as pairs of asterisks (Fig. 6.3) or brackets (Fig. 6.4), sometimes combined with co-indexing and vertical alignment to specify more exactly, or show more clearly, what overlaps with what. The scheme illustrated in Fig. 6.5 contains angle brackets enclosing the overlapping segments combined with tags indicating whether the overlap precedes or follows; the latter tags may carry numbers in cases of multiple overlap.

```
A,C   1001 (laugh - - - ) ☆ (laugh - - ) ☆
  C   1002 it ‖really ☆ 'makes 'me SICK■ 1003 I ☆ mean ‖I re△fused to GO to
      'uni'versity■ 1004 ‖point BLANK■ 1005 because the ‖only 'subject I
      'wanted 'do was △FRENCH ■
  A   1006 ‖[m]■.
  C   1007 ‖AND■ 1008 I ‖ felt that I △wouldn't · DO {‖what was RE△QUIRED of me in
      'French {‖ANYWAY■} ■} ■ 1009 I ‖just ☆'wanted ☆ to 'speak it FLUENTLY■ 1010 and
      to
  A   1011 ☆‖YES■☆
> C   1010 ☆☆‖know ☆☆ a 'little ☆'more ☆ A△BOUT it■ –
  A   1012 ☆☆‖[m]■☆☆ 1013 ☆‖[m]■☆
  C   1014 I · ‖probably 'would have 'ended 'up as a ☆'SOCIOLOGIST■☆
  A   1015 ☆<<I ‖must say if>>☆ one △wants to 'be · ‖have a · suc△cess · a
      SUC■‖CESSFUL 'job■ – 1016 and to ‖be suc△cessful in 'what△ever {FIELD}
      △one . . .
```

Figure 6.3   Examples of coding of overlap in the London–Lund Corpus (Svartvik and Quirk 1980: 145).

```
B:    Clint is still screaming about that,
R:    ... [Because he wanted the stamps],
B:        [all those stamps],
      ... Mom let Ted Kenner have.

B:    ... But I thought Mom was raising ... hemp,
          or,
          ... [something] one time.
R:        [What]?
          ...
          [2 Hemp 2].
B:        [2 Hemp 2]
```

Figure 6.4 Examples of coding of overlap in the Corpus of Spoken American English (Du Bois et al. 1990: 25f.).

```
*MOT:   no # Sarah # you have to <stop doing that>
        [>] !
*SAR:   <Mommy I don't like this> [<].
*SAR:   it is nasty.

*SAR:   and the <doggy was> [>1] really cute and it
        <had to go> [>2] into bed.
*MOT:   <why don't you> [<1] ?
*MOT:   <maybe we could> [<2].

*ROS:   well then # four +/.
*MAR:   hey wait.
*MAR:   you were <scared> [>]
*ROS:   +, [//] <five> [<>]
*MAR:   <I> [<] wasn't really scared.
```

Figure 6.5 Examples of coding of overlap in the CHILDES transcription (MacWhinney 1991: 50f.). [>] = overlap follows; [<] = overlap precedes; [<>] = overlap follows and precedes.

The TEI scheme provides a general mechanism for indicating synchronization. The following elements may carry 'start' and 'end' attributes, which define anchor points in the text: <u>, <pause>, <vocal>, <kinesic>, and <event>. Additional anchor points may be specified by empty <anchor> tags inserted within or between utterances. Where it is essential to specify temporal sequence, reference is made to a <timeLine> parallel to the text. The <timeLine> consists of a sequence of points, tagged <when>. Each <when> element has an 'id' (like all other elements) and may have other attributes indicating its position relative to other points in the same <timeLine>. The <timeLine> may have a 'unit' attribute specifying the unit of measurement used in identifying points.

Synchronization is made by connecting anchor points in the text with points in the <timeLine>. This can be done by pointing from the text to the <timeLine>, from the <timeLine> to the text, or by establishing a <linkGrp> consisting of a series of links between the text and the <timeLine>. Only the first of these approaches will be illustrated here. Consider this example (based on Atkinson and Heritage 1984: x):

> Tom: I used to smoke *a lot more than this*
> Bob: *you used to smoke*
> Tom: but I never inhaled the smoke

Notice that the example could just as well be reproduced in this way:

> Tom: I used to smoke *a lot more than this* but I never inhaled the smoke
> Bob: *you used to smoke*

The example can be re-coded according to the TEI scheme as follows:

> <timeLine>
>   <when id=T1>
>   <when id=T2>
> </timeLine>
> ...
> <u who=Tom>I used to smoke <anchor synch=T1>a lot more than this<anchor synch=T2> but I never inhaled the smoke</u>
> <u who=Bob><anchor synch=T1>you used to smoke<anchor synch=T2></u>

As the whole of Bob's utterance is to be aligned, the 'start' and 'end' attributes may be used as an alternative to the second pair of <anchor> elements:

> <u who=Bob start=T1 end=T2>you used to smoke</u>

The <timeLine> can be used to synchronize different types of events, not just overlapping speech. Consider a re-coding of the example given at the end of section 6.3. If we wish to specify that the verbal and kinesic responses are simultaneous, we could do it as follows:

> <timeLine>
>   <when id=T1>
>   <when id=T2>
> </timeLine>
> ...
> <u who=Jane>Have you read Vanity Fair?</u>
> <u who=Stig start=T1 end=T2>Yes.</u>
> <kinesic who=Lou desc=nod start=T1 end=T2>

The use of the <timeLine> has yet to be tested against a wide range of spoken material. There is no doubt, however, that it has the potential for specifying very exactly the temporal sequencing of the variety of elements that make up a spoken text.

Although the use of the <timeLine> is probably the approach of the future, it has the disadvantage that it requires special software which is yet to be developed. A simpler alternative for encoding overlapping speech is suggested by Brodda's (1988) analysis of turns in the London–Lund Corpus. This involves the labelling and cross-referencing of overlap segments and could easily be given a formalization compatible with the TEI guidelines:

<break id= synch= >...</break>
<interrupt id= synch= >...</interrupt>

The <break> is the overlapping segment produced by the first speaker, the <interrupt> the simultaneously occurring segment produced by the second speaker. The example above might then be encoded as follows:

<u who=Tom>I used to smoke <break id=B1 synch=I1>a lot more than this</break> but I never inhaled the smoke</u>
<u who=Bob><interrupt id=I1 synch=B1>you used to smoke</interrupt></u>

This approach would have the advantage that it is closer to traditional marking of speech overlap. The disadvantage would be that its applicability is far more limited than that of the <timeLine> mechanism.[4]

9 Phonological features

The degree of phonetic detail given in speech transcripts varies from none (in journalistic works like Terkel 1975) to a very precise phonetic or phonemic transcription. The latter is rare in extensive transcripts of running speech; an example is the parallel phonetic, phonemic, and orthographic versions of dialect recordings in Melchers (1972).[5] More commonly, the transcription uses ordinary orthography, with the addition of markers of prosody. Prosodic features may be noted by special markers (as in Svartvik and Quirk 1980) or by adaptation of ordinary punctuation combined with special markers (as in Du Bois et al. 1990 and MacWhinney 1991).

The encoding of phonological features has so far not been given much attention in the TEI scheme for spoken texts. Note, however, that a division into prosodic units can be handled by the <s> tag (see section 4 above) and that pauses are represented by the <pause> tag (see sections 2 and 6.1 above). Further prosodic features can be handled by user-defined entity sets, for example defining &lf; for a low fall tone and &lr; for a low rise tone; see Sperberg-McQueen and Burnard (1994). For convenience of reading on the screen, these entity names can be converted to simple markers of the type generally used in prosodic transcriptions. Occasional segmental phonological features can be handled in a corresponding manner. Where there is a great deal of phonetic or phonemic detail, it will be more convenient to define a specialized writing system.[6]

94   *Issues and practices*

Proper treatment of phonological features will require parallel representation rather than the embedding of all information in a single stream. Such parallel representation could be made with reference to the <timeLine> or using the general TEI alignment mechanisms (see Sperberg-McQueen and Burnard 1994).

10   Paralinguistic features

Paralinguistic features (tempo, loudness, voice quality, etc.) have rarely been marked in transcriptions, but fairly elaborate schemes have been devised for this purpose. Perhaps the best one is the Survey of English Usage (SEU) scheme (see Boase 1990, Peppé Chapter 15, this volume), with marginal notation combined with location markers in the main text. The CHILDES transcription of paralinguistic features is superficially quite different, but analogous in combining scope markers in the text and separate descriptors. By contrast, Du Bois et al. (1990) uses labelled brackets embedded in the text, as in (F = forte, increased loudness):

> A: <F It's not the end of Chanukah F>
>   in case you are interested.

It is worth noting that paralinguistic markers were omitted in the London–Lund Corpus, although the texts were originally transcribed according to the SEU conventions. The reasons were 'partly practical and technical' (Svartvik and Quirk 1980: 14), presumably connected with difficulties in devising a practicable electronic representation.

To handle paralinguistic features, the TEI scheme proposes the tag <shift>, with attributes for 'feature' (e.g. loudness) and 'new' (indicating the new state). The example above can be re-coded as follows:

> <u who=A><shift feature=loud new=f>It's not the end of Chanukah <shift> in case you are interested.</u>

The <shift> tag is an empty element specifying a point where there is a marked change in a paralinguistic feature. The feature is assumed to be valid for the same speaker until another state is given for the same feature. An unspecified <shift> tag indicates a return to a normal state. In cases of multiple shifts it is necessary to use attributes consistently to specify the feature and the new state (including the value 'normal', which is taken to mean that the feature ceases to be remarkable for the relevant speaker).

The <shift> mechanism is compatible with the schemes referred to above and has the advantage that it can represent a very wide range of paralinguistic features in a precise and systematic manner.

11   Editorial comment

Transcription schemes regularly propose conventions for editorial comment or, to use the wording of Du Bois et al. (1990), for 'the transcriber's perspective'. These include devices for coding uncertain hearings, unintelligible passages, or editorial comments of other kinds. The conventions used vary widely.

Recognizing the similarity between the encoding of speech and of less than perfect written manuscripts, the TEI scheme proposes general conventions in common for speech and writing. These include mechanisms for marking unclear or unintelligible passages, for expressing regularization, giving alternative readings, indicating certainty of and responsibility for readings, and so on. In addition to the more specialized mechanisms, it is always possible to insert editorial notes using the <note> tag. See Sperberg-McQueen and Burnard (1994).

12   Reference system

If a text is to be used for scholarly purposes, it must be provided with a reference system which makes it possible to identify points or passages in the text. Reference systems for spoken texts have been organized in many different ways (using different types of text codes, identifiers of tone units, etc.). Again the TEI approach is to use general mechanisms available both for speech and writing. A reference system for a spoken text can be defined by the use of 'n' or 'id' attributes for text units (cf. section 4). See further Sperberg-McQueen and Burnard (1994).

13   Linguistic analysis

The analytic categories and their forms of representation vary greatly in spoken as well as written texts. The TEI proposals for the encoding of linguistic analysis apply equally to speech and writing. See Sperberg-McQueen and Burnard (1994).

14   Payne's evaluation

At the Lancaster Workshop on Computerized Spoken Corpora, which gave the impetus to this book, Jonathan Payne compared the TEI Guidelines and the transcription scheme used at COBUILD, Birmingham. The comparison is worked out further in an unpublished paper (Payne 1993). Payne reaches the conclusion that 'the TEI proposals are broadly comparable with current practice in the user community' and states that 'in the majority of cases it will be a straightforward matter to link the machine-friendly TEI codes to more user-friendly encoding systems' (p. 60). Nevertheless, he mentions a number of problematic aspects, some of which will be addressed below.

1.   It is necessary, when using an alignment map, to choose whether the alignment is spatial or temporal (p. 61).

   In the current TEI Guidelines reference is made to a <timeLine> for temporal alignment (cf. section 8 above). A previous proposal was generalized to accommodate both temporal and spatial alignment. Spatial alignment was intended for other purposes than encoding spoken texts, however.

2. A way of relating two points in the text to one another, without reference to an external alignment map, would be a useful addition (p. 43).

A simpler way of marking overlap is indeed included in the current recommendations, although there is no description in the present chapter. The present paper does contain an additional suggestion which would presumably meet Payne's objection (see the end of section 8), but it is not part of the TEI Guidelines.

3. It is not possible to use segments within segments, which makes it difficult to encode grammatical and prosodic information at the same time (p. 61).

It is correct that the <s> tag cannot be used simultaneously to encode grammatical and prosodic information. A choice has to be made by the encoder. If the <s> tag is used for a prosodic segmentation, it is, however, possible to use the general-purpose tools for linguistic analysis to encode grammatical information (cf. section 13).

4. There is no straightforward way of encoding tonics or tones (p. 61).

The current TEI Guidelines contain recommendations for these features (see section 9), though they were presumably not included in the version examined by Payne.

5. There is a need for 'transcriber's comment' codes which can be used for encoding anything that is required (p. 62).

In the scheme which Payne contrasts with the TEI Guidelines there are general codes for transcriber comments, and these can be used for many purposes (divisions, timing of pauses, events, paralinguistic shifts, etc.). The TEI approach has been to propose specific codes for specific features. In addition, there is a general mechanism for editorial notes. (cf. section 11).

6. The treatment of non-verbal elements is too detailed (p. 61).

Payne points out that there exist 'quite detailed procedures for describing silent events which are unlikely to worry the transcriber, who will be working entirely from the speech signal' (p. 61). It is a fact, however, that encoding schemes have included such features, and they must therefore be accommodated within the TEI Guidelines. The user is free to decide whether or not to encode these features.

7. The TEI recommendations err on the side of detail about what should be included in the header (p. 62).

Again the user is free to decide how much information to include (beyond a suggested minimum) and whether it should be given in a structured form or as a description in prose (cf. section 3).

8. There is no clear attempt to balance the requirements of those who need a low-level transcription with those who require more information (p. 62).

Payne is especially concerned with a basic low-level transcription and finds that the TEI Guidelines are more suitable for higher transcription levels (i.e. containing more detail). The fact that very specific recommendations are made for the encoding of particular features does not mean, however, that all these features have to be encoded; cf. the previous two points. Whether the TEI Guidelines will be adequate for different levels of coding can only be shown by further testing.

Some of the problems which Payne draws attention to derive from the fact that he is concerned specifically with the encoding of spoken texts, while the TEI recommendations consider spoken texts within the framework of general guidelines for electronic texts. There seems to be a built-in conflict here; ideally, one would like to satisfy both the requirements of spoken text research and the need for some constancy in the representation of electronic texts.

Payne's scrutiny is very valuable. Further work of this kind will be significant for progress in the development of guidelines for the encoding of electronic texts.

15   Prospects

We can never get away from the fact that the encoding of speech, even the establishment of a basic text, involves a great deal of subjective choice and interpretation. There is no blueprint for a spoken text; there is no one and only encoding. Nevertheless, the TEI scheme has been formulated in such a way that it is compatible with a wide range of encoding schemes.

The generality of the TEI scheme is bought at the expense of a less compact and more complex representation. But the complexity is there for a purpose:

1. to make features of the text explicit;
2. to make it possible to carry out computational searches very precisely.

If the text is to be of real use, however, there is a need for software which connects the underlying representation with a workable format for input and display.

There is no necessary conflict between a representation of the TEI type and transcriptions which aim at a representation which is convenient to read and write. Provided that the necessary software is developed, the underlying representation can be transformed to any form which is convenient for the individual project.

If there is to be some constancy in the electronic representation of spoken discourse – and many would agree that this is a goal worth striving for – it is likely to be found in a representation of the type defined by the Text Encoding Initiative. As the proposals are tested further, they must no doubt be modified and extended to cater adequately for the needs of research on spoken discourse.

Notes

1. The TEI proposals for the encoding of spoken discourse were first worked out by a committee with the following members: Lou Burnard, Jane Edwards, Stig Johansson

(chair) and And Rosta. The initial proposals were presented in Johansson et al. (1991).
2. The examples of timed pauses show how a pause of 1.5 seconds would be represented.
3. Cf. Crystal (1991: 367). The identification of utterances is not straightforward, because of the occurrence of overlapping speech (see section 8 below). The element <u> is perhaps best defined as a stretch of speech attributed to a single speaker or speaker group.
4. For more details on TEI approaches to temporal alignment, see Sperberg-McQueen and Burnard (1994).
5. Melchers' material does not, however, exist in electronic form. Proposals for the encoding of segmental phonological features are given in Du Bois et al. (1990: 52f.) and MacWhinney (1991: 61ff.).
6. On the definition of writing systems, see Sperberg-McQueen and Burnard (1994).

7 From theory to practice

JOHN SINCLAIR
(This chapter was based on John Sinclair's talk, keeping his informal tone)

I want to make three points; they've all been made elsewhere, so the main function I shall perform is to try to consolidate and articulate them. This is already a very useful get-together for me – the important issues seem to be emerging, and I hope I can bring them out.

I've been working with spoken corpora for a while; as far as I know it was my team who produced the first computer-held corpus of spoken language, in the early 1960s – 220,000 words we were very proud of. It was transcribed at Peter French's level one (French 1992), that is to say, no distinction whatever between speakers, no sentence stops, just plain text. We were looking at the vocabulary and so all we needed was the sequence of words. Only one representation for *and* and *an* and absolutely straightforward quick orthographic transcription. Over the years I have been persuaded to add a few frills, but only reluctantly. This work then got absorbed eventually into Cobuild, and we've been accustomed to dealing with millions of words of spoken data since the early 1980s. In parallel with the corpus work, I've been studying spoken discourse analysis since about 1970 (Sinclair and Coulthard 1975). This made me aware of the need for well-transcribed data.

More recently, in work with the European Union, I've been involved with the Network of European Reference Corpora (NERC), and one of my areas of interest there was in the representation of spoken language. The report of that project is with the Union and will be published shortly (Baker et al. 1994). The recommendations of NERC have fed into another group called EAGLES (Expert Advisory Group on Language Engineering Standards). Geoffrey Leech and I are members of a corpus group where our job is to recommend standards for various aspects of corpora. I have some responsibility for the representation of speech and for liaison with the speech community, which is in another group chaired by Roger Moore. The question of standards and standardization is not one I take to readily, but it is highly relevant to this particular meeting.

There are, as I said, three things that I want to draw attention to:

- First of all to pursue the notion of the sound wave and the written record. Students of language may find a new impetus in the technological advances that are reported in this conference.
- Second, I want to look a little bit at corpora. We haven't actually talked about corpora very much, and yet I assume that practically all of us in one way or another are dependent on some kind of corpus or are intent on developing one, or are responsible for one, and so I want to say something about the status of spoken language in corpora.
- Lastly, I want to make my contribution to a discussion that has featured quite a lot in our meeting. That is the relation between transcriptions for humans and those that are suitable for machines.

1 The sound wave and the and the written record

I think we are at an interesting stage in the development of communications, because the spoken language is now in a state where it can begin to go through the same kind of analysis and standardization that the written language has been going through for some considerable time. If you take the initial act of writing, the separation into characters of various kinds in whatever representation, there's some kind of symbolic representation in the very first stages of any kind of written medium. I don't know of a written language medium that doesn't have segmentation. And then of course there are further sophistications like alphabetization, and then a major recent one in the development of printing, which imposed a very rigorous and disciplined standardization. Perhaps there were events like this conference that met and worried about standards at the time. Anyway the standardization of the representation of the written language was perhaps the most important development of that age, one that makes it so easy for us now to handle the written language in machines.

Phonetic representation has come later and is a further sophistication of the printed medium. However, as Guy Cook has pointed out, in Chapter 2, our relation to a written language event is totally different from our relation to a spoken language event, even if that spoken language event is given to us in some kind of written form. We know it's a transcript and there is no integrity in transcription. There is no social acceptance, there is no cultural place, for a transcription.

If we look at the development of the conventions of the written language, we see that they have become very highly disciplined and rigorous. What does a novelist do with speaker overlap? There is no flexibility in the present conventions, no room for experiment. I believe there is a manuscript of the Canterbury Tales which appears to have marks indicating breath pauses in it. It is written out in such a way that you could very easily speak it and it's thought to be a kind of a script for speaking, rather than a kind of written language poem. But of course the development of printing standardized punctuation has established the sentence as a basic unit of the written language.

Today there is an interesting and potentially valuable development, discussed in Johansson et al. 1991. There is now a serious possibility of associating an alphabetic transcription of spoken discourse with the sound wave in a computer environment. Several systems are in prototype form which will accept an ordinary orthographic transcript of a spoken event and which will automatically associate it with the sound wave. So if James Monaghan wants to look at his various *and*s and things, (an example used by Monaghan in discussion) then he writes *a n d* and the machine will search and will give him all the clips of anyone saying *and*. This, if it becomes readily available, will allow a new standard to be set for spoken corpora. It rather sidelines a lot of the debate about transcription levels. It would have to be successful with recordings of reasonable quality, not only those where you need a whole van full of equipment.

At the bottom of the screen, say, there is an orthographic transcription, and at the top of the screen the sound wave in some kind of representation. Then there is room in between for putting in what Jonathan Payne (Chapter 16) was suggesting, such as tonics or other phonological annotations. We can look forward to having a research and description platform which is very much more sophisticated than anything that is currently available. One or two people, of course, have done it individually, as some of my colleagues have made their own platform, but it's been very laborious.

I have an important policy in spoken language collection which may not be shared by everybody here, and that is to put quantity first. Quantity is not here opposed to quality, but rather to detail and specificity. I take the view that there is plenty of spoken language around; there are massive amounts pouring out all day long from all the various media outlets and from all of us, so that if, for example, a stretch of a recorded tape that you have is a little bit indistinct, then it's probably unwise to waste time trying to sort it out. Better to skip on to the next stretch – there's always plenty more. This attitude was adopted for the written language some years ago when demand and supply came together nicely. As my colleagues and I concluded that we needed to go up an order of magnitude from the one-million-word corpora that were then the biggest available, so the spread of electronic typesetting and the invention of the electronic scanner made such targets realistic. Issues of quantity became more important than issues of detail, and we steeled ourselves to work with misprints rather than to spend precious resources correcting them.

The liberation that resulted from this new attitude made us able soon after to move away from trying to preserve and maintain finite collections of written data in machine readable form. Because it became so readily available, the idea of a *monitor corpus* arose, and is the coming state of the art.

Now, the danger is that by not transcribing everything you may be systematically missing something. There may be certain kinds of speech events that only take place when there's three people talking at once, and so if you just skip the indistinct bits on a tape, you may miss those events. It depends on your priorities. Sometimes a total transcription is essential. In the days when I was transcribing classroom discourse, I used several microphones and various kinds of tricks with stereo reproduction in order to try to catch what a pupil said while someone else was moving a desk. It was very laborious, and for the kind of purposes that corpora tend to be used for, the cost-effectiveness of spending time on that is, I think, very doubtful. I'll come back to the question of how you make the decision about whether you are actually losing something that is irrecoverable that you can't find anywhere else.

Having raised the question of cost-effectiveness, I want to stay with it for a moment. For volume transcription of material, anything more elaborate than what Jonathan Payne has illustrated (in Chapter 16) will cost very considerably more. Another order of magnitude will go on the cost even to do the simplest aspects of intonation marking. Cobuild has done reasonably firm estimates of this, tried out various methods and seen how much they cost. When you're talking about millions of words of transcribed data for corpora, then this is a fundamental issue. However, if we can align ordinary transcriptions with the sound wave then most of the problems fall away.

This conjunction of the sound wave and the written record underlines for me the concept of plain text. People should be allowed and encouraged to get on with what they want to do and not try to second-guess the future by putting in lots of annotations that they do not themselves want. In all the experience I've had of corpora for 30 years, we have never once found ourselves with corpus annotations in such a state that another user really wanted them. The next user always wants something slightly different. It is really valuable to pass on or give access to plain text, but there's no way in which I could go ahead and annotate a text in a way that would be exactly suitable for any of your purposes, because what each of you would want is something slightly different. And so, this is where I think that TEI is potentially extremely valuable, because it allows, in principle, this kind of openness. Keeping a strict distinction between the text and the mark-up preserves in principle the notion of the plain text, the readable plain text.

In response to James Monaghan's suggestion at the Conference that speech should be recorded in phonemic transcription, I should say that I too have tried to work with Palmer's *A grammar of spoken English* (1939), and I can't read it. Where I did have to work on a part of it I had to transcribe it into ordinary orthography in order to read a few examples, because it's entirely done in a broad phonemic transcription, and I am not a native reader of a broad phonemic transcription, or indeed of any phonemic transcription.

2   The status of spoken language in corpora

In EAGLES I've been asked to try to establish definitions of different types of corpus, and I find this particularly difficult in the spoken area. The strategy I am adopting is to suggest that the notion of a corpus is associated with a number of other notions by default, and so unless you say 'My corpus is not like this', then it will be assumed that it is like this. Most of the following points are dealt with in a systematic way in a paper that I have drafted for the EAGLES group (see Calzolari and McNaught 1994).

So, for example one of the first problems with the term *corpus* is the question of size. The speech community has been working with samples of spoken language for many years, and uses the term *corpus* for a collection of very carefully planned utterances that have been recorded, perhaps in anechoic chambers. The whole corpus may only be 200 words. When we say that there is associated with the meaning of a corpus the feature that it should be pretty large then a corpus of the type traditionally used in the speech community would have to have a little tag saying 'This one isn't an extensive one, it's one of a very intensive type used for a particular purpose.' As it happens, one of the interesting features over the last three or four years is the way in which the speech community is using much larger sets of texts recorded in a wide variety of conditions. So I don't think this particular problem will necessarily be with us for very much longer.

However, there will always be specialized corpora, and users have to know what they are and how they were produced. The conditions under which speech events are found and recorded vary. In most corpora speech is 'found' data; you go around with your tape recorder and you make recordings in various places where people are talking to each other about a variety of things. But as against that there are collections of spoken data which are produced under various experimental conditions, which I have made and which I know others have made. In task-orientated collections, you get people into a studio and you say 'Do this', and the kind of language that results from that is quite different from that which results under normal conditions. Material of this kind would have to be flagged as saying, 'This is special spoken language; this is studio work, this is something which is the result of intervention, rather than of found data.' Otherwise it might be confused with the real thing.

For example, I have a corpus of recorded conversations which was created for learners of English, and which I use when I feel that it is safe to do so (it is available on tape and in transcription as part of the Collins Cobuild English Course, Willis and Willis (1990)). The recordings are of excellent quality, and the participants are not acting. The artificiality is that they were asked to perform a number of simple communicative tasks in a studio. Over short spells this material seems natural enough, and explicit references to the artificiality can be avoided. However at higher levels of discourse organization the lack of a natural communicative purpose becomes evident in the corpus; Warren (1993) exposes the limitations of this kind of corpus, and the dangers for researchers who do not know its origins.

Nowadays I would not expect many to deny that we associate with a corpus the attribute of it being large. Right from the beginning, when I had 220,000 words of spoken language I thought it was big; I thought it was huge, and so did the computer of the day. This notion of size is obviously conditioned by various factors. So, for example, if the corpus is of a very specialized kind of language, then it would not necessarily have to be as big as it would be if it was of a very general type of language. Something as specific as a sub-language, may well affect the notion of being large. Later on I'll mention audience size as a factor in understanding the dimensions of a corpus.

On sample size, we cannot say there is agreement on what the appropriate size might be. I like a complete record of a speech event, in whatever way it is understood. I know that other people have different ideas about this.

Then there is the question of the definitions of spoken and written language, which one might have thought were non-controversial, but which I find are extremely tricky. When TEI suggests categories of spoken, written, spoken-to-be-written, written-to-be-spoken, spoken perhaps to be spoken or written, and so on, you get the kind of classification made famous by Polonius. Then I feel like getting back to basics, and saying that surely for everything we want to put in a corpus there is a declared medium, that we either take it as spoken or written. If it's spoken, we can always write it down, and if it's written we can always read it out. But who cares? The medium is declared as spoken or written, and the text is devised and constructed on that basis.

This is why I think Guy Cook's (Chapter 2) point about the transcript in relation to the spoken data is very important. There is no such distinction in the written form of the language. The nearest perhaps is the notion of a copy. Nowadays with photocopies you get something almost the same as the original. Previously, of course, text was copied in various ways; you could get, for example, a certified true copy of a document, which didn't look anything like the original document, but in a way bore some sort of transcript-type relation to the original. All the words were there, but aspects of typography and layout may have been quite different.

It seems to me that we ought to go back to the very simplest notions of spoken and written. Criteria such as whether a communication is prepared or impromptu are equally applicable to both. Some spoken events are prepared; I spent some time preparing what I'm saying at the moment. Some events are unprepared. The category of 'scripted' is realized in the spoken medium, but then there is the text of a play, which is a written document, and has its own validity as distinct from any performance of the play. The characteristic of whether or not things are rehearsed is equally applicable to both spoken and written media, and whether or not things are edited is also equally applicable to spoken or written media.

People often assume that spoken language is more impromptu than written; less self-conscious, more natural. That is probably true of some varieties of spoken language, as compared with some varieties of written but I don't know if it is or not. Something more tangible, such as audience size, may be a more useful measure. Consider Fig. 7.1. If you make a chart with *big* at the top and *little* at the bottom and *spoken* on one side and *written* on the other, you can fill in all sorts of categories of material that you will find, related to the audience size. This chart seems to me more useful than trying to assess a quality like impromptuness. After all, what comes out of the radio? It's spoken language. Whether it's somebody solemnly reading out something that he's written or that someone else has

spoken	BIG	written
radio/tv	1,000,000s	newspapers
local radio	100,000s	magazines/books
rallies	1,000s	notices
lectures	100s	local publications
classrooms	10s	workplace records
discussions	5s	circulation lists
interviews	3s	working groups
conversation	2s	private letters
	LITTLE	

Figure 7.1 Audience Size

written doesn't matter. It is spoken language, and it is quite different from written language. The *BBC English Dictionary* (1992) shows how much is distinctive about radio English, from the careful study of a large corpus.

Obviously each of the categories in Fig. 7.1 isn't fixed at a particular number; it covers a broad band. Magazines can be very small circulation or extremely large circulation. But I see no particular reason from this kind of evidence to associate the spoken medium with small audiences. Equally shared between speech and writing are impromptu features, because personal correspondence is usually impromptu; e-mail is often very impromptu and there's lots of that around. The audience size for different kinds of e-mail probably covers all the right-hand groupings of Fig. 7.1. I don't think we should invest the spoken language with any particular set of attributes and then say, 'If it doesn't have these attributes, or if it's heavily rehearsed and scripted, then it's not really spoken language.' I don't think that's a necessary conclusion at all.

Another assumption is the difficulty of acquiring spoken language in machine readable form. In practice spoken language is very easy to get; very large amounts are archived by radio and television companies. On the other hand, intimate written language is extremely difficult to get; it's just as difficult, possibly even more difficult to get than intimate conversations. Last year I asked in the national press for people's love letters. We've had very few, but we got a fair outing on the local radios at the time.

I would like to make one other point, this time about the distinction between internal and external criteria for classifying language, spoken or written. This is an issue which is coming up very strongly in the discussion of corpus typology. I mentioned earlier that if the recording quality of a tape is poor and therefore you don't try to transcribe certain passages, then it could be that you lose certain discourse features. So, for example, if you're in a steel foundry you don't perhaps record what people say when they have their thumb under a piece of machinery that comes down, because there's always a lot of noise at the same time as they lose their thumb. How do we evaluate this kind of situation? It is actually an internal matter, that is to say somebody would have to really go into the detail, use all the very sensitive audio techniques that we have to filter out various types of noise and so on. It would be a serious research project to see whether, by ignoring bits of a tape that are difficult to transcribe, we actually lose anything and if so, what it is that we lose. Until it is done, practical and economic matters help us decide what is the best way to make a useful transcription of a corpus.

Another matter of current concern is the notion of a sub-language. It is possible to select only certain types of people and places and activities, making various restrictions on external criteria, from which we make assumptions that there may be a shrinkage of variety; for example that if we only ever talk to postmen, some restricted kind of language will emerge. Now whether that's true or not I don't know. The theory of sub-languages has to be investigated. Is it true that there exist varieties of language which are so restricted, and so purely disciplined, that the grammars of these languages and the description of these languages are very much simpler than the general language, and yet the texts are selected on *external* criteria? Certainly there are some candidates. I've been working now for several years on a sub-language that does have these characteristics. It is a very highly disciplined and restricted variety. What is not certain is how widespread this feature is – always remembering that we are only interested in authentic language, freely expressed in definable situations. There's a lot of confidence in sub-languages expressed by various people in the corpus community, but how these sub-languages relate to external criteria is another matter. Also, from the evidence so far, the grammar of a sub-language is not necessarily a subset of the grammar of the 'parent' language.

The same kind of issue arises with genre and conformity to genre. If a microbiologist writes a poem to present the results of his research in his academic journal, and if he's got a Nobel Prize, what do you say? Do you say, 'I'm sorry this does not conform to the genre so I will not read it', or do you read it and accept that individual free will is dominant in this case? We have at the moment mainly external criteria to work from; we have the work of people like Douglas Biber (1988) and Junsaku Nakamura (1993) on internal criteria. I think the latter will become more and more important. But in our current work with spoken corpora, I think we are restricted to external criteria and we should make as few assumptions as possible about how they reflect the internal criteria.

3 Machine readability and human readability

At present in spoken language we rely on human transcribers and we probably will for some time to come; the advent of genuine machine help in transcription of the sound wave is still a long way off, and the kind of development that I mentioned at the beginning of my talk is probably going to inaugurate a very substantial new stage in our research methodology. Therefore, because of cost-effectiveness, the task definition of transcription must be biased towards the convenience and the natural tendencies of the transcribers. You've got to give a human transcriber a task to do that they can do readily and easily and that fits in with their view of the job. If they can put in fullstops, let them put in fullstops, so long as they do them in roughly the right places. If they find that too hard, then they can go and work for James Monaghan [*Editors' note*: At the Conference James Monaghan had asserted that transcribers could not identify sentence boundaries.]

Now what we find in SGML and TEI are complex codes. (At the Conference) Tamás Váradi said quite clearly that a code which is convenient for a machine, which may be essential for a machine, may be extremely awkward for humans. For these new conventions to gain acceptance in the research community, there will have to be software interpreters provided, that will allow us to move between human and machine without any expenditure of effort whatever. I can't see any alternative to this, and I doubt if anyone who is managing a large spoken resource would want to dispute it. Humans who are going to use transcribed text will want human conventions as much as the transcribers. They will want to see in front of them something that is reasonably readable.

I think that in the politics of the situation, TEI has done itself and the community a very bad turn by parading in front of us these incomprehensible stretches of mumbo jumbo which we are not supposed to see at all. It's only the machine that is supposed to see this. I've got two printer conventions on my workstation; one is Postscript and the other is something else. Sometimes if somebody has been using the printer for another purpose and has switched it over to this other set of conventions, then I get my Postscript file printed out as a literal file. I don't know if you've ever seen that, a Postscript file where all the codes have been interpreted in ASCII. A short memo goes on for about 20 pages as the machine churns out every last detail; I've no idea how to interpret what it says. But that is what lies behind a tool that normally functions very well; what I normally do is just say 'print' and out comes a small memo, beautifully set out, exactly what I've told it to do.

Now that seems to me to be an analogy with the TEI problem. We have been struggling in a way with SGML and with TEI, because there has been a kind of underlying assumption that we consumers have somehow got to be able to write this stuff. The fact that Lou Burnard can write it is something for the Guinness Book of Records but not necessarily for the rest of us.

I feel very strongly about this, because I'm very much in support of standardization in this area, but I'm also in support of human beings having human-like things to read. I don't think there's any incompatibility; all we need is the software. I think if you look at the difference in Jonathan Payne's examples (Chapter 16), between the ordinary COBUILD conventions, which are easy for humans, and the TEI versions, you will see that although they are in almost every case logically equivalent, and my point is made. Also, we need just one single document type description (dtd) for all spoken text. You may want some minor variations, but just one dtd that specifies your conventions will do.

Hence the last small point that I want to make is that I want to replace the notion of *conformity* to TEI or SGML with *compatibility*. It's not just sophistry to say this. I will certainly be pushing this as hard as I can wherever I'm talking about standards. I want compatibility. I don't want conformity. Now you may find that someone could say 'There is no distinction, because TEI is so flexible, so undemanding, so atheoretical, that you don't need to make a distinction, because it is available for you to write things the way you want to, and then it will all fit in.' But I don't believe that works in practice. I believe that what happens with standardization, is that you won't be free to conform to the actual underlying detailed massive range of options of something like TEI. Instead, what will happen is you will have to conform to somebody's very highly restricted selection of these options.

That is what happens in other areas; it's happening to me at the moment with a formalism for language description in the European Union called the Advanced Language Engineering Platform (ALEP). When you are introduced to ALEP as an abstract idea you have no difficulty in agreeing to conform. It is so simple, so general, there is hardly anything you might object to. But when you encounter ALEP in practice you find that a large number of assumptions about language are already built into the implementation and now form part of the orthodoxy you must embrace. In my case they include most of the assumptions that have kept me away from grammatical formalisms for the last three decades.

I don't want that to happen with TEI. You have to say 'What exactly is it I have to conform to?' Take the contretemps between Jonathan Payne and Lou Burnard (in discussion at the conference) about the transcription of overlap. Now, TEI specifies an utterance. It's a defined concept and there are certain things you can't do, like you can't interrupt it. Now, I believe in life that you can interrupt utterances. I don't have utterances as units in my descriptive system, and indeed many transcription systems don't have a rigorously defined utterance. Maybe somewhere in the bowels of TEI there are conventions with which you can avoid this, to my mind, over-disciplined definition of an utterance. I will personally not accept TEI if it requires me to have an utterance under the definition that Lou Burnard was using, because that is far too rigorous for me and it doesn't represent the world, as far as I'm concerned.

Now if TEI is sufficiently flexible to offer me a way out of this dilemma by translating my indications of overlap into something that fits its internal conventions, then fine. The problem is, will the standardizers of the future recognize that, or will they just say, 'I'm sorry, everybody has to use this utterance thing, as defined in the documentation and you will stick to that.' That's why I think we ought to make a very careful distinction between this kind of regimented conformity and compatibility, which says that I will make sure that everything I do is compatible with TEI, will be renderable in TEI, and is transferable to others, and it's all two-way transferable. If that's the case then I don't think there's any reason to be despondent.

There is one problem, however, and that is the problem of funding. As Wallace Chafe asked, 'So do I go and write everything in TEI notation and then write software which converts it to the way I want it, or do I get my transcribers to do what they've always done and do I write software that will convert it to TEI?' There is a big need for this convertible software and it's not obvious who's going to pay for it, because this is where you're asking someone who is already spending considerable resources on making available research material, to do something else which is of no particular gain, or immediate gain anyway, for the institution concerned. TEI will only be accepted if there is funding with it so that we can carry on doing what is natural to us as humans and make it available in a machine format that is suitable for it.

These, then, are my three points:

1. We can look forward to big improvements in the holding of spoken language corpora in computers, without inordinate extra costs.
2. There is a need for greater clarity in what we mean by 'spoken language', and we must guard against over-specialized and inauthentic material.
3. Attempts to standardize text mark-up must remain user-friendly, add little to overheads and avoid interfering with the plain text.

Part B

Applications and more specialized uses

Introduction

Linguistic corpora, spoken and written, have been developed for a wide range of language studies, for instance in speech science, syntax, semantics, pragmatics, language acquisition, language dysfunction, and conversation analysis. These studies have been put to practical use in designing systems for speech synthesis and recognition and for grammatical tagging and parsing, in writing dictionaries, in analysing style and text types, in translation, in describing language development, and in treating language disorders. In some cases, the corpora were designed for a specific purpose, as, for instance, the COBUILD collection was developed specifically to provide a basis for the development of English dictionaries and learning materials. Others, such as the Brown and LOB corpora, were planned without an immediate project in mind, intending to be open to a wide range of future uses. But in all corpora, needs of users and practical constraints determine crucial decisions that might otherwise be debated indefinitely.

This part includes chapters on a range of applications, from the clinical study of language impairment (Fletcher and Garman, Perkins in Chapters 8 and 9), to the sociolinguistic study of code-switching and of the structure of conversation (Cheepen, Sebba in Chapters 10 and 11), to the tagging of intonation (Roach and Arnfield in Chapter 12) and word class (Garside in Chapter 13), and an experimental study involving a wide range of variables in task-oriented conversation (Thompson, Anderson and Bader in Chapter 14). Reports of these applications are important even for those not immediately concerned with the particular project in the clinic, classroom, or laboratory, because:

1. applications help clarify the implications of the theoretical debates described in the preceding chapters, and
2. applications highlight practical issues of format, medium, and equipment that arise in making corpora useful beyond the immediate purpose for which they were planned.

The chapters are arranged to draw out the range of theoretical and practical issues involved in application. Dealing with corpora of impaired speech, Fletcher and Garman address fundamental issues of units of analysis, while Perkins raises some practical problems of implementation. Cheepen and Sebba both raise issues based on existing analyses of interaction; Cheepen sketches a broad framework for conversational structures, while Sebba deals with ways of marking language shifts. The last three chapters, Roach and Arnfield, Garside, and Thompson, Anderson and Bader, all discuss how a computer readable resource can be made more widely useful. Roach and Arnfield deal with the broad issues raised by competing systems for analysis of intonation. Garside deals with practical difficulties that arose while adapting for spoken data an automatic tagger first developed and tested for written corpus material. Thompson, Anderson, and Bader, as they say, deal with the practical problems that arose in preparing CDs for general distribution. Broadly, this part begins with therapeutic and sociolinguistic applications, and ends with applications to speech and language technology, but some of the same issues arise whatever the application.

When researchers have a particular form of data, and a particular use to which to put it, they can offer insights into long-standing theoretical debates. For instance, Fletcher and Garman focus on issues of segmentation into sentences or other units, issues they say are crucial when dealing with child language or with aphasic speech. Roach and Arnfield address practical implications of the decision between phonetic and phonemic transcription, as a level between orthographic representation and speech signal; they argue that a phonemic transcription functions better in the process of alignment that they describe. Thompson, Anderson, and Bader address the issue of the encoding of pauses and of sounds that are not speech, along with the orthographic representation; they suggest that a mark-up that leaves such notes in text, but indicates their special status with tags, will make automatic searching easier.

Applications also highlight a range of practical issues that will arise with any corpus project:

1. Some *recordings* discussed here were made in highly controlled conditions of broadcast (Roach and Arnfield), or laboratory experiment (Thompson, Anderson and Bader), or clinic (Fletcher and Garman). Others, such as those described by Sebba or Cheepen, could only occur in naturalistic settings in which the recording quality could not be so high.
2. *Confidentiality* arises for Perkins because he is dealing with medical records, but it also arises for Thompson, Anderson, and Bader, because of their ethical relation to experimental subjects.
3. *Transcription* involves in every case an orthographic representation, but there is a wide range of divergence in the treatment of such issues as variant pronunciation, incomplete words, and pauses.
4. Of course, the forms of *coding* and *mark-up* that are added reflect the different purposes. What the writers share is an awareness that any

coding must be easily separable from the transcript. They also point out possibilities for conversion from one system into another, though this conversion may not always be possible without loss of information. Sebba points out that one widely used form of mark-up – involving italics, bold, underline, and other word-processing formats – restrict the data to one wordprocessing system, because they are lost when they are converted to the ASCII (American Standard Code for Information Interchange) form. Several writers touch on the need for software using standard mark-up formats, such as Standard Generalized Mark-up Language (SGML). Thompson, Anderson, and Bader provide a checklist of the kinds of invariants that might be expected to make a text usable, even from those corpora that do not conform to more general standards.

5. Finally, these applications remind us of practical issues of *hardware and medium* that are often glossed over in the more theoretical or visionary treatments of corpora. These issues are most directly addressed by Roach and Arnfield, who mention that very large workstations are needed for their applications in speech science, and by Thompson, Anderson and Bader, who helpfully review the nitty gritty of decisions about hardware, tape format, interfaces, and operating systems. The reader will find these chapters chock full of acronyms, but that is because the writers deal with the specifics of existing equipment. Those unfamiliar with the acronyms can trace them through the Glossary.

Perhaps the most striking aspect of this part, for established researchers in corpus linguistics as for newcomers to the field, is the range of applications implemented or proposed for corpora. These new applications arise now partly because of the more general availability of hardware that can handle large amounts of textual data, and of software for accessing and manipulating such data. But they also arise because of the increasing recognition in many fields that understanding of speech behaviour can benefit from the analysis of the very large ranges of data made possible with machine-readable corpora.

8 Transcription, segmentation and analysis: corpora from the language-impaired

PAUL FLETCHER and MICHAEL GARMAN

1 Introduction

In a series of articles in recent issues of the *Journal of Child Language* (Edwards 1992a, MacWhinney and Snow 1992, Edwards 1993a) Jane Edwards on the one hand, and Brian MacWhinney and Catherine Snow, on the other, swap views about the extent to which the Child Language Data Exchange System (CHILDES) transcripts, encoded in Codes for Human Analysis of Transcripts (CHAT) format, conform to four principles for archive-based language research enumerated by Edwards (1992a) (see also Edwards, Chapter 1). These principles are as set out in (1):

(1)
- Maximum readability and minimum bias
- Consistent encoding for exhaustive retrieval
- Systematic contrastiveness
- Data comparability

It is not our intention here to recapitulate the details or even the essentials of this debate. One of the principles, however, 'consistent encoding for exhaustive retrieval', and the way which it is handled by the protagonists, serves as a convenient introduction for an issue which has been a concern for us since we were first faced with the problem of devising a transcriptional format for a computer database in 1984 (see Johnson 1986 for details of the transcriptional format that was eventually devised). In child language research on normal or impaired individuals, and in research on impaired adult speakers, such as aphasics, transcription is almost always a means to an analytical end that involves at least some automated analysis either of the text directly, as in SALT (Systematic Analysis of Language Transcripts, Miller and Chapman 1985) or in CHILDES, or some coding inserted into the text (SALT again) or on separate lines under the text as in our own SUMLARSP (Johnson 1986), or again CHILDES. In Edwards' discussion of the MacWhinney-Snow system, problems that may make direct automated analysis of text unreliable, and potential difficulties with coding systems, are both addressed.

An example from the first type of problem will suffice. The CHILDES data come from different sources, and transcribers vary in the extent to which they will try to represent immature pronunciations of forms in an orthographic representation. Consequently, even apparently straightforward searches to find specific lexical items, particularly members of grammatical categories that are subject to varying realizations under different stress conditions, can run into problems. Edwards claims, for example, that 'researchers interested in uses of the second person pronoun, you, would need to anticipate at least nine variants of it in a single data set' (1992a: 446). This is no doubt an extreme case, but it serves as an illustration. Under the heading of 'consistent coding for exhaustive retrieval', Edwards cites other examples relating both to automated searches on text and analysis of other markings or codes. However, in Edwards' papers and the responses, in relation to the principle of 'consistent encoding', one fundamental issue in the representation of text from language learners and impaired individuals which is not mentioned is the demarcation of stretches of speech from an individual speaker into individual utterances or rather, analytical units. The point can be illustrated with an extract, from a CHAT-formatted text from the CHILDES corpora (from MacWhinney 1988: 87f), which appears as example (2):

(2) *ROS: because it is so old.
     *MAR: how (a)bout your [!] cat [#] yours is new [!].
     %act: shows Father the cat
     *FAT: that's [#] darling.
     *MAR: no mine [!] isn't old. mine is just um a little [#] dirty.

Here, the symbol [!] marks emphasis on the preceding element, and [#] represents a unfilled pause. The relevant part of the conversation for our purpose is the second line, where no delimiter separates what is arguably one utterance *how (a)bout your [!] cat* from another *yours is new*; and this in spite of the presence of such a division in the last line, between *mine [!] isn't old* and *mine is just um a little [#] dirty*. We have here an exemplification of the persistence of an old problem in language acquisition studies into the relatively new computer databases.

It was recognized fairly early in the modern era of child language studies that age was not a good predictor of grammatical maturity. In Roger Brown's longitudinal study of three children at Harvard in the 1960s (see Brown 1973), one of the children turned out to be an extremely precocious learner. The extent of the variability in rate of development according to age was confirmed on a large sample of 128 children by Gordon Wells in his study of English children in Bristol in the 1970s (see Wells 1985). The alternative grouping metric (alternating to grouping by age) most favoured by researchers from Brown on, in normal language development, has been MLU (mean length of utterance, usually in morphemes, as required by Brown, but sometimes using words). Additionally, comparisons between language-impaired and language normal children have used MLU as a matching measure (see Fletcher and Ingham 1994, table 1, for examples). Brown's tactic was to group children by MLU and then look for grammatical similarities in their output.

As Crystal pointed out (Crystal 1974) in his review of Brown (1973), a significant problem with this approach is that *utterance* is undefined. Investigators fail to provide a set of criteria which would allow replicability of identification of an 'utterance' in any text. This means

1. that the MLU metric may not be consistently used across investigators in grouping children for the purposes of grammatical analysis,

and

2. since the utterances identified by an investigator generally constitute the units for grammatical analysis, the reliability of grammatical characterizations may vary within and across investigations, particularly with older children, who produce more talk in their part of a conversational turn.

Measures such as frequency of omission of grammatical morphemes, or proportion of complex sentences, are going to vary as a function of the definition of utterance which becomes in effect the *analytical unit* for the purposes of computing measures either on intra-sentential categories, or of analytical unit types.

2   Characterizing grammatical impairment in children[1]

The problem of reliable identification of analytical units was one among many that we were immediately faced with in 1984, as we began to develop a transcription format for a computer database of interviews with normal children from 3 to 7 years and with school-age language impaired children. It is important to emphasize that from the outset we were interested in grammatical issues, specifically: what, if any, are the grammatical categories that constitute reliable indices of development for the three- to seven-year-old developmental period? And what, if any, are the grammatical categories that discriminate school-age language impaired children from matched normal children? As we saw it, our transcription therefore had to be geared from the outset to our research questions.

This does not mean that the format itself was not flexible and extensible: Johnson (1986) details how it was designed to transcribe any language (provided it can be represented by alphabetic symbols + numerals), to allow via separate coding lines a range of possible analyses, and to facilitate the representation of a range of phenomena appropriate for naturalistic speech samples – pauses, revisions, repetitions, overlaps and so on (we return to these later in the chapter). However, within the conventions available, a basic decision for us concerned the criteria for segmenting the text into grammatically analysable units which would then entail consistent demarcations across transcribers, normal and impaired children.

We shall now consider a brief extract from a transcript from a seven year-old language impaired child, which we can use to examine the initial solution adopted:

(3)   E: what do you do?
                 what do you do?
         C: we play with this – board game.
                (~5~L~...~)
         E: not games like you play out at break.
         C: no.
                (~6~L~MR~)
         E: what do you do at break?
         C: we play out.
                (~7~L~...~)
         E: have you ever played on that tractor?
         C: yeah.
                (~8~L~...~)
         E: there's a real tractor out there isn't there?
         C: well it used to be – a real^
                (~9~L~I~)
                (it)r it is a real tractor but it used to be – for the farm right down there but the farm gave it to us.
                (~10~L~S(Rp<it>) V(Cop<be,is>) C'(D<a>JN 5c<but> S(Rp<it>)^)
                (^V'(C<used>TCop<be>:VV)   A'(PD<the>N)@o;   A'(Op3)@1; 5c<but>^)
                (^S(D<the>N) V<give,ir> O(Rp<it>) A'(PRp<us>: Op2)@o;^)
                (^:5c,5c,5C1+ ~)
         E: is that where all the horses are?
         C: yeah.
                (~11~L~...~)
         E: oh they're not there now.
         C: still!
                (~12~L~...~)
                they're still there but they inside because it's the weather.
                (~13~L~...~)
         E: have you been on one of them?
         C: yeah.
                (~14~L~...~)

This extract shows both text lines and a separate grammatical coding line. For simplicity, the coding lines have been left empty, apart from those numbered 6 (in which *MR* stands for *Minor Response*), 9 (where *I* stands for *Incomplete*) and 10, which we shall concentrate on here.

120   *Applications and more specialized uses*

In the text lines appear a number of familiar punctuation marks which are used in the transcription to terminate *Analysis units* (*A-units*):

. at the end of l.3, *we play with this – board game*
? at the end of l.1, *what do you do?*
! above unit 12 (coding line identification) *still!*

Each of these symbols has a *readability* function which is similar to that in conventional punctuation: ? indicates an interrogative, and ! is an exclamation mark. (The unfamiliar symbol, ^ , above coding unit 9, indicates an incomplete unit.)

All of them, so far as the transcript convention checking programme is concerned, are alternative ways of defining a complete unit for the purposes of grammatical analysis. Though we do not want to go into specifics of the analysis now, it will be clear from the extract that each unit which is terminated by one of the permitted symbols in the transcript has its own coding line. Units can be relatively simple, as represented in coding line 6, or relatively complex, as represented in coding line 10.

The transcription as exemplified through this short example, and as utilized in our child language project, thus reflects directly some top-down analytical decisions which were driven by the purposes of our analysis. As we shall show later in this chapter, a slightly different set of analytical requirements in a project on adult aphasia, even though the focus of the study was still grammatical analysis, forced different decisions on the analyst which are reflected in somewhat different transcriptional choices. In the initial project we had to provide a consistent set of principles for segmentation of analysis units. The only guidance available to us in the previous literature consisted of rather vague references to the analyst's use of prosodic criteria. We felt that it was unlikely that consistent identification criteria for analytical units for grammar would come by this route: Crystal (1969: 258), for example, found that the best coincidence between tone units and grammatical units in his data from informal discussions and conversations between adults was that between sentences and tone units, where in the sample of adult informal speech studied the boundaries between the two units coincided 37 per cent of the time. A later study of the correlation between clause and tone unit in a corpus of domestic conversational speech samples between adults produced a better fit, but still in only 54 per cent of cases (Crystal 1979: 160).

We took the decision to use as a criterion for segmentation of the child utterances in our database a modified form of Hunt's T-Unit (Hunt 1965), which was originally used to segment written samples. A T-Unit is characterizable generally as *one independent unit of verbal communication, together with any units that are dependent on it*. In our terms *independent unit of verbal communication* is interpreted as *clause* (in the sense of Quirk et al. 1985). Since the sequence coded as 10~L in (3) consists of a main clause and two coordinated clauses (an *independent unit* and two *dependent units*) it is segmented as a single analytic unit. A qualification to the interpretation of Hunt's definition was that we would not regard clauses linked by *and* as *dependent units*, unless there was independent syntactic justification for this in the form of either anaphora or ellipsis between adjacent clauses. The reason for this decision is that *and* is the earliest connective to appear in development, used by children to link sequences of simple clauses which are internally well-formed but which do not show any inter-clausal cohesion. To count these sequences as grammatically coordinated from their first appearance, without the additional requirement for cohesion in terms of anaphora, or ellipsis, would lead to overestimation of grammatical complexity. The effect of this analytical decision on our transcriptional practice is illustrated in the segmentation of (4) below, taken from a conversation with a five year-old normal child:

(4) E: did you get any nice games for Christmas?
     C: yeah.
         (~1~L~MR~)
     E: what did you get?
     C: I got this one.
         (~2~L~S(Rp<i>) V<get,ir> O'(D<this>N)~)
         it's got all sorts of things.
         (~3~L~S(Rp<it>) V'(Ao<have,'aux>V<get,ppi>) O'(Op4)~)
         it's got going to school and got start on home.
         (~4~L~S(Rp<it>) V'(Ao<have,'aux>V<get,ppi>) V<go,ing>^
         A'(P<to>N)@l; 5c<and> V<get,ppi> V<start> A'(P<on>N)@l;^
         :5c, SVO, AX, VO, AX, 5O,50~)
         (and then)r you have to go back home.
         (~5~L~5c<and then> S(Rp<you>) V'(C<have to>TV<go>:VV)^
         A'(Op2)"l;~)

Here two separate analytical units, 4~L and 5~L, segment a sequence which, as in 10~L, consists of three clauses. In (4), however, the clauses are linked by *and/and then*. While the second clause can be regarded as grammatically linked to the first via ellipsis of its co-referential subject, there is no such cohesion between clause three and its predecessors. Hence it is hived off as a separate analytic unit.

These brief examples illustrate how decisions relevant to analysis will inevitably affect the form of a transcription. The form our transcripts take reflect our analytical decisions in respect of the identification of grammatical units. Other researchers interested in grammatical analysis might come to different conclusions on the criteria to be used for segmentation; researchers whose focus of interest lies elsewhere than grammar might not be concerned about segmentation within conversational turns at all. The fact that the transcription itself can change under different research pressures we think raises problems for the goal of transcription convention standardization. We now turn to issues raised for transcription by research into adult aphasia.

2 Characterising grammatical impairment in adults[2]

Turning to the issue of grammatical representation of aphasic speech, we find that there are certain highly developed concepts in the field that need to be addressed, and that some of these are, superficially, at least, distinct from those in child language (impairment): *agrammatism* vs. *paragrammatism*, for instance, and the related notion of *empty speech*; also, the debate regarding whether Broca's aphasics' difficulties with verbs reflect lexical or syntactic disturbance (Caplan 1987). We leave open here whether the differences with child language research issues are more in the minds of the researchers, or whether they reflect real differences in acquired vs. developmental types of language impairment.

In order to illustrate the text coding approach adopted on the Reading aphasia project (see Edwards et al. 1992), we shall begin with a description produced by one of our aphasic speakers concerning how his speech problems began (Example 5):

(5) yes at the beginning I was you know I didn't think I had a stree I thought it was ju- I was ju- you know I had a I had a flu and er I was tired I remember I was tired I thought I'd just want to sleep and I'd be ok and had a good sleep and I felt ok I er you know I'd come back to meet some people and then they decided that it was better for me to come the doctor it was better if I come up back into the hospital and even then I thought I would come back go back home and the first time I the first thing I realized was that we would have to come I would have to come no stay in the hospital I think it was five days six days and th- the main thing about it to me was I couldn't er my words I could not know the words and I couldn't even I couldn't even not even talk

The only linguistic units recognized here are orthographic words and their speech approximations. This representation involves the fewest assumptions about the internal structure of the sample, and serves to illustrate the sorts of issues that arise, and the principles that appear to govern their treatment, in establishing a suitable foundation for grammatical analysis. The issues may be considered under two main headings, formatting and segmentation. As far as formatting is concerned, we recognize the categories set out in (6):

(6) Unintelligible: ... X...
   unintelligible stretches of speech are represented as X for each syllable (with X*X representing a sequence of that is three or more syllables long – see Crystal et al. 1989);
   Pause fillers: ... F...
   since their precise characteristics are not our immediate concern (though their distribution and incidence may be), pause fillers such as *er, erm, ah* etc. are all represented as F (see Fletcher et al. 1986);
   Incomplete forms: ... (... -)...
   incomplete forms of words, such as in *it was ju- I was ju-* and (occurring

as *build-ups*) in *and th- the main thing*, are marked off from subsequent syntactic and lexical analysis by parentheses, although their incidence and distribution may be noted e.g. *it was (ju-) I was (ju-); and (th-) the main thing.*

Paraphasias:
paraphasias such as *stree* in *I had a stree* are bounded by square brackets and tagged, as *I had a [stree][PARA]*;

Non-productive utterances:
minor utterances such as *hello* (see Crystal et al. 1989) are marked off by #; stereotypes have their own boundary symbol $.

Repetitions: ... (W*) W... *
the convention here is to mark only *immediate* and *exact* repetitions, over *word* units (W* indicating any number of words in the sequence); *immediate* allowing for intervention of *X*, *F*, –, and *Minor* forms (since these typically distribute around such points in speech discourse); and *exact* requiring both prosodic and segmental phonological identity (Crystal et al. 1989). Thus the repeated element(s) in such sequences as *I had a I had a flu* are placed in parentheses and play no further role in the analysis (though their incidence and distribution are noted), e.g. *(I had a) I had a flu.*

We now turn to the issue of grammatical characterization of such data. We have already made the point that *segmentation* is a crucial procedure in the delineation of analytical units: it thus stands between transcriptional format and analytical coding, and is therefore sensitive to both demands. In a sense, what we are doing is operationalizing the notion of *utterance*: but it is likely to lead to less confusion if we say that, rather than giving a particular definition to *utterance* we are concerned with defining certain analytical units for the purpose of grammatical representation.

Given the wide range of structural breakdowns manifested in aphasic speech at the grammatical level, and the importance of including control data from normal adult speakers on our aphasia project as well, it seemed most suitable for our purposes to recognize minimally complex units of grammatical organization, with a correspondingly wide range of links holding between them. The segmentation is accordingly in terms of these minimal units, which we call *text units*, and higher-order groupings of these, as established by *immediate grammatical relations* between them (see Garman 1989). (Among such higher-order groupings may be defined the A-Units of the child language project described earlier.) Omitting irrelevant detail, the text units we have to consider are as follows (7):

(7) *Minor* utterances are set out on their own line, except where they occur within the linear domain of some other valid segmentation unit (see also *Unclear* below);

Clausal utterances are set out with just one main verb and its complements per line;

124 Applications and more specialized uses

Phrasal (multi-word) and *lexical* (single-word) utterances may also be recognized, outside these domains, and are set out on their own lines;

Lexical utterances are those single-word types which remain after the preceding have been established;

Unclear utterances (those that have unclear status in terms of grammatical analysis, by virtue of unintelligible syllables, or paraphasias, or because they are incomplete or stereotypic) are set out on their own line, unless doing so would violate the integrity of a larger construction.

The following version of the text illustrates the formatting and segmentation categories we have briefly introduced (8):

(8)

	TU	IGR
#yes#	M	
at the beginning I was	U	
#youknow#	M	
I didn't think	C	
I had a [stree][PARA]	U	T
I thought	C	
it was (ju-)	U	T
I was (ju-)	U	
#youknow#	M	
(I had a) I had a flu	C	
and F I was tired	C	
I remember	C	
I was tired	C	T
I thought	C	
I'd just want to sleep	C	T
and I'd be ok	C	
and had a good sleep	C	
and I felt ok	C	
(I) F #youknow#	M	
I'd come back	C	
to meet some people	C	S
and then they decided	C	
that it was better	C	T
for me to come	U	S
the doctor	P	
it was better	C	
if I come up	C	S
back	L	
nto the hospital	P	A
and even then I thought	C	
I would come back	C	T
go back home	C	

and the first time	P	
I	U	
the first thing	P	
I realised	C	R
was	L	P
that we would have to come	C	T
I would have to come	C	
#no#	M	
stay in the hospital	C	
I think	C	
it was five days	C	T
six days	P	
and (th-) the main thing	P	
about it	P	A
to me	P	A
was	L	P
I couldn't	U	T
F my words	P	
I could not know the words	C	

The first column after the text lines represents the text unit (TU) coding: M = minor, C = clausal, P = phrasal, L = lexical, U = unclear, a total of 51 in all. In the second coding column, we note 18 instances where some of these units are marked for *immediate grammatical relations* (IGRs), that is involving immediately adjacent units. We have nine instances of a *that*- clause (T), as in *I think (that)*..., where the connective that is optional; three cases of other types of subordination (S); two cases where a predicate is linked to a preceding multi-TU subject (P); one instance of a relative clause (R); and three instances where a TU functions as an adjunct (A) of a preceding TU. It should be noted that (as in the child language project) coordination marked by the connectives *and* or *and then/so* is not recognised as an IGR (coordination) unless it is supported by ellipsis or pronominal anaphora across the coordinated clauses.

Once the initial segmentation and coding has been completed, the data is ready for entry into a database, and for further analysis/entry in terms of both syntactic and lexical categories. We shall not pursue these issues here, but conclude with some observations regarding the status of adjuncts (the IGR type A, above). These represent one aspect of a fundamental distinction in grammatical organization of clause elements, namely that between *complements* and *adjuncts* (see Radford 1988). Implementing the distinction has given rise to a number of problems, not least those of specifying more definitively where the boundary lies, and how it may be operationalized in our data. An important theoretical diagnostic is that complements are ordered more internally with respect to their Heads than are adjuncts, as in the following (hypothetical) Example (11), where the adjuncts (A) follow their clause-complement sequences (CCS):

(11) because I was working   CCS
       at that time   A
       but I'm not   CCS
       at the moment   A

However, this canonical ordering is not always respected in our data, as the following (from one of our normal controls) indicates (12):

(12) . . . because I was *then* working but I'm not *now*. . .

The question is, do we wish to recognize four text units in the attested version? If not, are there three? Or two? Appeal here has to be made to a number of principles:

1. one is *linearity*, by virtue of which *then* is taken as being more integrated in its clause-complement sequence than is the case for *at that time* in (11) or *now* in (12);
2. another is the issue of how the complement-requirements of verbs such as *work* may be envisaged to be sensitive to, or supplemented by, their wider grammatical environments. To the extent that this may be so, we could envisage one such requirement for time-specification deriving from an environment where the clause is marked for past tense;
3. further, it may appear that we have to deal with discourse factors too, in that the requirement that is filled by *now* in the second clause sequence of (12) derives from the opposition, in discourse, between that clause sequence and the preceding one, marked by main verb ellipsis, rather than from any inherent (past) tense specification.
4. A further consideration is that *then* and *now* in the attested example are both lexical pro-forms, while *at that time*, *at the moment* are phrasal structures with lexically specified heads.

If we take all these factors into account, then we could argue for linearizing the attested data as follows (13):

(13) because I was *then* working
       but I'm not *now*

4   Conclusion

In conclusion, we may re-state what we believe to be our main points: first, that segmentation is a crucial issue in text-encoding; second, there is no single segmentation unit that all analysts should adhere to, although there may well be shared principles at the grammatical level of analysis that guide and relate the decisions that are made; third, that the choice of unit will inevitably reflect the analysts' purpose(s); and finally, that, in our experience at least, issues of transcriptional formatting, including the crucial segmentation issue, are not merely matters of good housekeeping, but can directly address issues of considerable theoretical importance.

Notes

1. Work reported here was supported by the Medical Research Council (grant No. 68306114N).
2. Work reported in this section was supported by a grant from the University of Reading Endowment Fund, 1990–1993.

9 Corpora of disordered spoken language

MICK PERKINS

1 Introduction

The dramatic progress made in recent years in computational corpus linguistics has important implications for a wide range of areas of language study and applied linguistics, ranging from English language teaching (e.g. Kennedy 1992) to language variation studies (e.g. Biber and Finegan 1991). One area of application, however, which has so far received relatively little attention is clinical linguistics – that is, the application of linguistics to speech and language pathology and therapy. In the move towards the standardization of transcription and mark-up procedures, clinical linguistics is an area which should not be ignored. Disordered spoken discourse has a number of unique characteristics which should be allowed for in the Text Encoding Initiative (TEI) guidelines (see Burnard, Chapter 5 and Johansson, Chapter 6). It is also important that these guidelines be made available in a software format appropriate for clinical linguistics practitioners if the potential of machine-readable corpora of disordered language is to be fully realized.

In this chapter I will give a brief overview of the nature and range of corpora of disordered language in order to make clear the particular challenge they pose for transcription, coding and analysis, and I will also try to justify the need for such corpora and outline what we stand to gain from their development and use.

2 Existing corpora

There are many kinds of language pathology and all levels of language can be affected. Brain damage, however caused, as well as congenital neurological and physiological disability can give rise to impairment of phonetics, phonology, lexis, morphology, syntax, semantics, pragmatics and discourse. There are also disorders such as autism and schizophrenia which are not primarily linguistic in nature but which have a direct effect on communicative ability. The main focus of research and remediation in language pathology is on spoken discourse, but very few corpora of disordered spoken discourse exist. Menn and Obler (1990: 12) note that 'there is absolutely no tradition of publication or even archiving of aphasic texts', and this is equally the case for other acquired language disorders in adults. As for developmental language disorders in children, the situation is little better, although because of the tradition of diary studies of normal child language dating back well over a century (e.g. Darwin 1877) and developed in the 1960s by Roger Brown by using transcriptions of tape-recorded data (Brown 1973) it is at least generally accepted that the best way to study child language disability is through the collection of corpora of either spontaneous or elicited spoken discourse.

An important step forward was taken in the 1970s with the development by David Crystal and colleagues (see Crystal 1982) of the linguistic 'profiling' of both children and adults with impaired speech and language. Profiles of a patient's grammatical system (LARSP), semantics (PRISM), segmental phonology (PROPH) and prosody (PROP) were obtained by collecting, transcribing and coding a short corpus of spontaneous speech. Linguistic profiling has also encouraged the collection of larger corpora for comparative group studies such as that of Penn and Behrmann (1986), who used the LARSP procedure to analyse the syntax of 38 aphasics and Fletcher et al. (1986) who used the same procedure to compare the grammatical development of groups of normal and language-impaired children. These profiling procedures have also been partially automated (Bishop 1984, Long 1987) but still depend heavily on human input.

Despite this progress, most corpora of disordered language remain very small (often amounting to no more than a half-hour sample of an individual patient's language), hard to access (often residing in a patient's confidential case file) and – above all – not in machine-readable format. This latter drawback has begun to be remedied as a result of the CHILDES initiative (MacWhinney 1991) which uses a standard transcription and coding format (CHAT). The CHILDES database currently contains two corpora of aphasic language (Bates et al. 1987, Holland et al. 1988) and six corpora of disordered child language (Bliss 1988, Conti-Ramsden and Dykins 1989, Feldman et al. 1989, Hargrove et al. 1986, Hooshyar 1985 and Rondal 1978). Other notable machine-readable disordered corpora to which access is more restricted are those referred to in Edwards et al. (1993) and in the chapter by Fletcher and Garman in this volume, and the cross-linguistic aphasic corpus of Menn and Obler (1990).

When compared with the corpora of normal language which are currently available, both the paucity and the diminutive size of the disordered corpora referred to above are striking to say the least.

3   The transcription and coding of disordered language

There is little standardization in the transcription and coding of disordered spoken language, though some practices are more common than others. Some progress has been made recently in the area of phonetics with the publication of a set of extensions to the International Phonetic Alphabet specifically designed for the transcription of disordered speech (Duckworth et al. 1990). These include a range of symbols, diacritics and conventions for transcribing both segmental and non-segmental features of abnormal speech. Phonetic transcriptions are sometimes supplemented with instrumental representations of articulatory and acoustic information derived through procedures such as speech spectrography, electropalatography and laryngography.

When the focus of interest is on other linguistic levels some variant of normal orthography is used, though there is considerable inconsistency in the representation of features such as overlapping speech, situational information and non-verbal sounds.

A wide range of procedures exist for identifying and representing the phonological, grammatical, semantic, pragmatic and discourse features of disordered language. The profiles devised by Crystal and colleagues referred to in the previous section all require the transcription and analysis of a corpus of language before profiling can be carried out. For example, a LARSP profile requires sentences to be coded grammatically as follows:

```
            the dog is barking
Clause:       S      V
Phrase:       D  N   Aux v
Word:                3s  ing
Expansions: X+S:NP X+V:VP
```

whereas a PRISM ('profile in semantics') profile requires each word to be lemmatized and allocated a semantic functional category.

There is also considerable variation between procedures on what features of a transcribed corpus they choose to ignore. Both LARSP and PRISM, for example, exclude incomplete utterances and repetitions, whereas both of these would be of primary interest in a dysfluency assessment procedure.

The heterogeneity of transcription and coding practices in clinical linguistics is not a problem as long as interest is restricted to single cases or small group studies. But if there is to be any progress made in the linguistic characterization of language disorders as a whole through the use of machine-readable corpora there is a clear need for standardization. One obvious way of doing this is to ensure the development of software which makes it relatively easy for clinical linguists and speech and language therapists to make use of TEI mark-up formats.

4   Why do we need machine-readable corpora of disordered language?

We need corpora of disordered language for the same reason that we need corpora of normal language: the study of such corpora can provide new insights into how language works, whether it be normal or abnormal – for example, the identification of patterns and regularities which are not impressionistically obvious.

As Fillmore (1992: 35) has observed: 'every corpus that I've had a chance to examine, however small, has taught me facts that I couldn't imagine finding out about in any other way'.

It could also be argued that corpora are even more crucial to the study of impaired language than to the study of normal language. Why should this be so? It is generally assumed by speech and language therapists that a disordered language system is still a rule-governed one, and one of the aims of the therapist is to establish what these rules are – that is what forms are licensed or generated by the patient's impaired linguistic system. Unlike in the study of normal language, one is usually unable to rely on the patient's intuitions in order to do this, and there are no clearly established linguistic norms for specific types of language disorder as there are for normal language. In the study of disordered language, therefore, one has no choice but to analyse corpora. Clinical linguistic descriptions can only be observation-based, as opposed to intuition-based, in the first instance. This does not mean that one should not use corpus data to generate and test hypotheses about a disordered language system – merely that contrary to what Chomsky has for so long maintained for normal language, one cannot do without an initial corpus.

A further reason why we need corpora of disordered language is to enable the description and classification of language disorders according to their linguistic characteristics. In addition to being able to describe linguistic abnormality in terms of its underlying medical causes, it has become increasingly clear over recent years that an alternative account using linguistic criteria is often far more useful for remedial purposes. Linguistic descriptions, however, are still fairly rudimentary and will remain so until far more data has been collected and analysed. Although a fairly small language sample may be sufficient to throw light on individual cases (see, for example, Perkins and Howard 1995), a serious typology of language disability based on linguistic principles will require large amounts of data. The need for such a typology is certainly recognized (see Crystal and Varley 1993), but as yet the collection of the necessary language corpora has hardly begun.

5 Potential and uses of machine-readable corpora of disordered language

Leech (1992) outlines four models of computational corpus processing – (a) the 'information retrieval' model (b) the 'induction' model (c) the 'automatic corpus processing' model and (d) the 'self-organizing' model – which reflect both different stages in the development of the area as well as the degree of human involvement in the process. So far, processing of disordered language corpora has barely reached stages (a) and (b). That is to say, transcription and analysis are carried out manually and the computer merely sorts, counts and arranges the data in such a way as to make possible the testing and generation of hypotheses (i.e. the information retrieval model); and generalizations may be 'induced' automatically from the data via statistical techniques (i.e. the induction model). Stage (c) which involves procedures such as automatic tagging and parsing, and stage (d) in which such procedures are developed and modified independently by the computer are not yet possible in the case of disordered corpora because we do not yet have enough raw data in machine-readable form, nor do we have sufficient normative information. For example, taggers and parsers based or trained on normal language corpora cannot be straightforwardly applied to corpora of, say, agrammatic aphasic language which typically lacks grammatical function words and may include neologisms.[1] In order to develop such procedures that can handle specific types of disordered language we need to collect far more data than is currently available.

In the mean time, however, there is still a great deal of work that can be done on the computational analysis of smaller corpora of disordered language. The multi-feature/multi-dimensional approaches developed by Biber (e.g. Biber 1992, Biber and Finegan 1991) for the analysis of text types and genres are able to represent reliably various linguistic characteristics of a text based only on a thousand-word sample. Procedures such as these hold out great promise for clinical linguistics. For example, the ability to make even a broad diagnosis of a patient's disorder based simply on the computational analysis of a transcribed thousand-word sample would mean an enormous saving in time, money and manpower.

A somewhat less complex yet still potentially fruitful way of exploring and exploiting the disordered corpora that already exist is to carry out simple word and structure frequency counts. The correlation between relative frequency and register in corpus variety studies is well known (e.g. Svartvik 1992). However, frequency generalizations about normal language such as go>walk>stroll; active>passive; positive>negative; declarative>interrogative; the>this/that; simple tenses>compound tenses (as noted by Halliday 1991) are certainly not true for many varieties of disordered language. Very little is known about word and structure frequencies in impaired language, though what is known suggests that this could be a promising area of enquiry. For example, Perkins (1994) has described the lack of productivity and tendency towards stereotypes in a number of language disorders. With regard to specific structures, Nespoulous and Lecours (1990) have noted the relatively high frequency of modal expressions in the discourse of brain-damaged adults, and it is also well known that closed-class words – the most frequent words in normal language – are extremely rare in agrammatism.

Finally, corpus studies have an important role to play in theoretical discussions of language disability. For example, one important insight into the nature of normal language that has received a great deal of support from corpus studies is that in addition to a generative grammar and a lexicon, a speaker's linguistic competence must also incorporate a large number of semi-productive phrases and sentences (cf. Pawley and Syder 1983, Sinclair 1991, Altenberg 1993). Much current linguistic theorizing on aphasia, however, fails to take account of this and characterizes linguistic deficits solely in terms of generative grammatical competence and lexis (e.g. Grodzinsky 1990, Tait and Shillcock 1993). The existence of disordered language corpora large enough to enable the type of collocational study carried out by Sinclair and colleagues (e.g. Sinclair 1991) could have far-reaching implications for theoretical models of language disability.

6 Future developments

If a subdiscipline of 'clinical computational corpus linguistics' is to develop, there is clearly a long way still to go, but I hope the case I have made at least suggests that it may be a worthwhile endeavour. In this final section I will outline a tentative plan for how we might proceed.

It will be clear by now that one of the main obstacles to developing this area is the lack of large machine-readable corpora of disordered language. Another is the relative paucity of impaired language and the fact that its collection and transcription are so labour-intensive. There are no virtually limitless reserves of readily available data, as is now the case with electronic written text, which can be exploited in the form of what Sinclair (1991: 26) terms a 'monitor corpus'. Nevertheless, the outlook is not quite so bleak as this might suggest.

Every day a large number of speech and language therapists as a matter of routine record and transcribe the spoken discourse of their patients as part of the ongoing assessment and remediation process. They are highly skilled transcribers, as is ensured by the rigorous training they receive in applied linguistics and phonetics. The vast majority of transcripts go no further than the patient's case notes and will be seen by no more than a handful of people at most. Although these transcripts play an important role in the treatment of individual patients, it is frustrating to consider the many further uses to which they could be put if only it were possible to incorporate them in some cumulative archive in an electronically readable form.

The current push towards standardization and wider availability in the electronic media – as exemplified in the TEI – suggests a possible way forward. If TEI-conformant software could be developed which was specifically geared towards the needs of speech and language therapists, it should ultimately be possible to create a cumulative online read/write database of disordered language corpora. The software needs of speech and language therapists are:

1. it should make it possible to transcribe in a straightforward way the phonetic, phonological, grammatical, semantic, pragmatic and discourse features found in disordered language systems;
2. it should incorporate a classification system to enable the subcategorization of each transcript according to both linguistic and medical criteria;
3. it should be user-friendly and relatively easy to learn;
4. once learnt, it should take no longer to use than transcription and coding by hand;
5. it should produce hard copy appropriate for inclusion in a patient's case notes.

Linguistic classification of language disorders could be cross-referenced and made compatible with the standardized classification system currently being developed by the British medical establishment (the 'READ' codes – named after Dr Read, the doctor who helped originate the classification). This parallels the classification of corpora of normal language according to 'domain specific' criteria.

In time, such a system could provide a database of sufficient size and flexibility to serve the various needs of speech and language therapists who might wish to enquire about the type of medical condition which may have given rise to a given sample of language; of medical professionals who might want to know what type of linguistic behaviour was typically found in a particular medical condition, and of clinical linguists and researchers who might wish to establish linguistic norms for the whole range of speech and language disorders.

A number of problems would need to be solved in setting up such a system. Even ignoring the many technical and technological difficulties, problems of copyright encountered with corpora of normal language are likely to be more than matched by ethical problems of patient consent and confidentiality in the collection and publication of corpora of disordered language.

On the other hand, the potential benefits to speech and language therapists, to other medical professionals, to theoretical and applied linguists and – most important of all – to people with language disabilities, are too great to let this opportunity slip by.

Note

1. Although it would clearly be inappropriate to regard disordered language simply as normal language with errors (as disordered language should be seen as a system in its own right), programs designed to identify errors in corpora of normal language (e.g. Atwell and Elliott 1987) might have some initial use in quantifying the extent to which a particular disordered corpus could be characterized as 'deviant'.

10 Discourse considerations in transcription and analysis

CHRISTINE CHEEPEN

1 Introduction

In the move towards building a comprehensive and fully functional computer-stored corpus of English, there are, inevitably, a variety of differing opinions about what should be included in the corpus over and above the transcribed text itself. Some sections of the research community have argued for the extreme case that corpora should contain *nothing* but the transcribed text, on the grounds that the transcribed text is the raw data, which, in order to serve the needs of all interested researchers, should be kept separate from any analytical material. This is not, however, a valid argument for a corpus of *spoken* English, as in this case the raw data is clearly the original *speech*, along with the situational features which were in operation at the time of the encounter, so that any transcription is in fact a translation of the data of the speech event. Any transcribed corpus of spoken language is a bank of *pre-processed* data which has already been in some way structured and categorized in order to present it in orthographic form.

It is clear that some descriptive information is required in addition to the actual words spoken, in order to disambiguate and make explicit the range of meaning which, in speech, is signalled phonologically, but in addition to this it is highly desirable (in terms of usefulness in future research) to include also material which is to some extent analytical as well as descriptive. This kind of addition to a stored corpus means that much of the groundwork of textual analysis can be done *as the corpus is built*, so that future research which draws on the corpus does not involve the researcher in unnecessary repetition of the more basic kinds of analysis.

An increasingly widespread example of this kind of analytical addition to stored corpora is grammatical and/or phonological tagging, but these additions, welcomed by and valuable to a range of researchers, are essentially concerned with very low level (in the sense of local) features of texts. Large, computer-stored corpora, while providing excellent opportunities to concentrate on multiple examples of low-level features of language, also open up the potential for work on the higher levels of language – those structures which operate over large sections of text (equivalent, say, to the paragraph and above), and, building on this, structures which operate over the whole discourse, and which characterize different discourse genres.

My aim in this chapter is to focus primarily on a particular kind of spoken discourse – informal conversation – and to make recommendations as to how computer-stored conversational corpora can be augmented so as to include some elements of analysis which are basic to an understanding of this kind of data. Over the following sections I will explain what I mean by conversation as opposed to other kinds of formal and informal talk, identify some of the discourse structures which characterize this particular genre, and specify the lexical features which signal the most common of these structures, using examples from existing corpora. Finally, I will also comment on how a similar approach can be used to deal with more formal kinds of data in order to include in such corpora information about the lexical items used for discourse structuring.

2   Interactional vs. transactional discourse

In the general category of unscripted spoken discourse, there are a variety of different kinds of dialogic encounter – for example, buying/selling, teaching/learning, and doctor–patient interviews. All these, though unscripted, are essentially *transactional* encounters. That is, the participants enter such encounters with the specific aim of achieving some kind of *goal* in terms of the world *outside the encounter*. This predetermined goal means that, whatever structuring is performed dynamically by the participants during the progress of the discourse, this will fit into the framework which is appropriate for that goal. Such transactional encounters are, then, set up at the outset with the general discourse structure(s) which members of the speech community acknowledge as functioning to achieve that goal. In the case of classroom talk between teachers and pupils, for example, although the spoken material is unscripted, it is clearly planned according to a set of structures which are appropriate to teaching and learning, and which are expected by *all the participants* to be in operation for the duration of the discourse.

In the case of *conversation*, however, it is not so easy to identify predetermined structures which characterize the discourse. This is because conversation – or what we might think of as a 'chat' – is dialogue conducted primarily for *interactional*, rather than transactional reasons. A conversation has no overt goal in terms of the world outside the encounter, it serves simply to allow the participants to develop interpersonal ties, so that it is the relationship of the speakers (concretely observable *within the encounter*) which becomes the goal of the talk. Throughout this chapter I am focusing on conversation as a speech *event* – that is, an encounter which has a beginning and an end, and which would normally be described by the participants as a conversation. This may seem a trivial point, but I make it so as to distinguish this kind of encounter from that most difficult and tantalizing of linguistic objects – what Goffman (1967) calls a *continuous state of talk*, which occurs, in an on/off fashion between people who live or work together. This much more random kind of talk is not structured in the same way as *conversation*, and tends not to be described as such by the participants; rather, if asked to report on the subject matter and progress of their talk, participants of a continuous state of talk are usually unable to do so, as it is not normally regarded as an *event*, but as 'just living' or 'just getting on with the work'.

3 Speaker status in spoken discourse

A particularly complicating feature of conversation (for the analyst) is what I would call the *discoursal equality* between the participants. A conversation is a speech event which takes place between equals, unlike many transactional encounters, which operate within clearly identifiable structures which rest on a status difference between the participants (e.g. doctor–patient, teacher–pupil).[1] Where status differences are observable within a discourse they can be seen to be instrumental in much of the discourse structuring. Topic introduction and management is, for instance, always the responsibility of the superior participant, while the inferior participant simply goes along with the agenda set out for him/her, making his contributions in the slots allotted to him. Frequently, the superior produces evaluations of (or judgemental comments on) discourse contributions (turns at talk) by the inferior.[2]

(1) B: you read The Clerk's you read The Clerk's Tale you mean –
     A: [m] .[n] yes . but that was also pre – this is also rather in the mists of antiquity
     a: in other words [er:] you can't remember very much about it
                                                    (Svartvik and Quirk 1980)

At a more 'local' discoursal level of such encounters the same kind of heavily status-based control is observable in features such as question/answer pairs, where the superior participant is usually the questioner and the inferior the answerer. Although many transactional encounters of this kind contain questions asked by the inferior, this is always at the invitation of the superior, as in job interviews where the interviewee is formally invited to ask questions

(2) fine well we've asked you a lot of questions em . I wonder whether there's anything you'd like to ask us
                                                           (Cheepen 1988)

Transactional encounters where these status differences are not adhered to – where the inferior participant does not simply go along with the agenda set by the superior – are liable to break down completely, or to result in serious interactional trouble between the speakers, with the superior insisting upon retaining control by explicitly referring to his/her superior status, e.g. 'who's in charge here?'[3]

Conversations, on the other hand, operate on the basis of speaker equality. This means that, whatever their status outside the encounter, the participants have equal status within it. In a two-party conversation, both speakers have equal rights and responsibilities with regard to discourse management – that is both have equal rights to introduce, change and close topics, both have equal rights to ask and answer questions, and (crucially important for conversational discourse[4]) both have equal rights to make evaluations.

This sharing of rights and responsibilities cannot, of course, take place in parallel, it must be a sequential sharing, so that the participants take turns to select topics, and, within those topics, to talk, listen, evaluate, question and answer. With each changeover, control of the discourse passes from one participant to the other, so that a kind of overall equality is achieved by speakers taking turns to be the superior/inferior partner. This sequential sharing of control does not normally change with each turn at talk, on the contrary a speaker's turn at being superior typically lasts for several utterances, so that it is a phenomenon of conversation which is only properly observable if the analyst considers very large sections of the discourse. A pattern which is observable over a matter of say, two minutes of the conversation, must be seen first in the context of the preceding and succeeding sections, and second in the context of the whole speech event.

Such patterns are rarely explicitly announced in conversation. On the contrary, the changeover points are the result of very complex and delicate negotiations between the participants. Sometimes, certain topics provide an obvious opportunity for one participant to take control of the discourse – e.g. 'what I did at work today', but this is not always the case, and even when it is possible, there are many instances where it is not possible for the speakers to link the appropriate next topic (which will be the 'property' of one particular speaker) smoothly to the ongoing one. Speech participants do, however, have tactics for achieving the changeover, and again these relate to very large-scale structures which operate throughout the whole discourse.

4   Discourse structures in conversation

The main discourse components of conversation have been identified as *introduction*, *speech-in-action*, *story* and *closing* (Cheepen 1988). These categories do not conflict with the features identified by Sacks, Schegloff and others in their work on conversation analysis – for instance, 'turn-taking' mechanisms, adjacency pairs, openings, closings, repairs, and so on. These very local features, which are clearly observable in conversational data, fit within the larger structures which serve to organize the whole discourse, and which allow speakers to exchange roles in terms of their status. In order to take full advantage of the potential provided by computationally accessible conversational corpora, our long-term goal must be to specify these large features in such a way as to make them recognizable by an automatic system, which will then map them onto textual transcriptions. This will allow us to more fully exploit the corpora in terms of description and categorization of whole texts, rather than, as at present, concentrating purely on multiple examples of extremely local features of discourse.

To map large discourse structures onto textual transcriptions we cannot rely solely on intuition. Our evidence for the existence of a particular structure must rest on signals which are made explicit in the speech event, textually or otherwise. The discourse structuring elements of conversation which I have mentioned above are all clearly signalled in the speech event, and in the overwhelming majority of cases the signalling is done by lexical items. While full automation of the recognition of such elements (and eventual automatic mapping onto textual material) is a task which will require considerable time and effort, a start can be made immediately on parts of the overall structure which are signalled by a small, fixed set of lexical items.

5   Story – a major structure in conversation

The bulk of conversation consists of *story*. This should not be confused with what is commonly called *narrative* (following Malinowski's 1923 definition) – which is a monologic event, performed by a 'story teller' for an 'audience'. Although such narratives can and do occur in conversation, they are comparatively rare. The kind of story which characterizes conversation is essentially a collaborative event, where both (all) participants contribute to the telling by guessing what comes next, asking questions to elicit further details, and (typically) contributing evaluations throughout the telling. This kind of collaborative story telling is a major feature of conversation, and it is characterized by a set of lower level features (Cheepen 1988):

- temporal location
- participant specification
- state-event-state sequence
- evaluation

All these features are explicitly signalled in the text, and their recognition can therefore ultimately be automated. At present, however, evaluation is the most difficult because of the very large number of ways in which it can be (and is) signalled. The other features are easier to deal with, and, while it is not yet possible to specify the full range of lexical signals for all of them, sufficient regularities are observable to take the first step of tagging corpora, as a move towards implementing a recognition system which will automatically analyse transcribed material for these signals of discourse structure and assign the appropriate tags.

5.1   Lexical signalling of participant specification

Participant specification, in many cases, is an easy feature to mark out for automatic recognition, although it is not without its problems. Frequently it is signalled by proper names, and though this is a potentially very large set of items, in an automated recognition system this is not a problem, given that we can scan for capital letters which signal such instances. A more difficult case for recognition occurs when the participants in the story are signalled by the use of pronouns, which in any case proliferate throughout conversational discourse. Further work is required in this area, to discover what proportion of conversational stories are signalled (in terms of participant specification) by proper names rather than pronouns. If this is a substantial proportion, then it will be a worthwhile task to automate the recognition of participant specification by proper names, particularly so because, in the examples already identified where this does happen, the names occur *at the beginning* of the story – i.e. within 15 words:

(3) K: yeh I made one for Shirley and one for me

(Cheepen 1988)

(4) a: you were telling us a . a long complicated story about Eileen's sons last night – I hadn't quite got them in order
 B: well she has four boys

(Svartvik and Quirk 1980)

(5) J: now what was I gonna say . oh yes . em . Tom and Myrtle Carter say that they'll be a little bit late

(Cheepen 1988)

5.2 Lexical signalling of state-event-state sequence

As with participant specification, state-event-state sequence can be signalled in a number of different ways, some of which are more immediately and easily identifiable than others.

(6) in a way Eileen has moved into a very sort of --- rather outback kind of place --- and as a result she doesn't em --- expect perhaps the er --- the kind of --- successes I suppose that

(Svartvik and Quirk 1980)[5]

This is a particularly easy example to identify, due to the lexical signal *result*, which indicates a sequential progression from one state to the next. Such text structuring items have been dealt with at some length in the work on written discourse by scholars such as Winter, Hoey and others, and, as Winter points out (1977) these items form a closed, finite set, which is manageable in terms of automation. However, not all examples of state-event-state sequence in stories are signalled by members of this set of what Monaghan (1982) refers to as *lexically unfulfilled items*. This feature can be signalled in a variety of other ways, as in (7):

(7) I went it town I came back Friday it wz late

(Jefferson in Cheepen 1988)

While it is clear that there is a sequential progression here through different states – being 'not in town', being 'in town', being 'back from town' – there is no overt lexical signal for this, instead, the speaker uses simple juxtaposition to indicate the sequence.[6] This kind of tactic in conversation is common, and clearly poses a problem for automatic recognition of the feature. We must remember, however, that these 'low-level' features which signal stories do not occur in isolation, but *in combination* with one another. When considering the practicalities of implementing an automatic tagging system, this means that many potential problems of recognition do not become actual problems, because it is the general combination of features which signals the presence of a particular discourse structure, rather than the identifiability of each individual one. In other words, for a properly functioning recognition and tagging system it is not necessarily essential to identify each and every signal in every example. Two out of three, or three out of four lexical signals clustering together will normally be sufficient to indicate what is happening at the discourse level.

5.3 Lexical signalling of temporal location

Temporal location as a marker of story is, perhaps, the most immediately accessible starting point for automation, as it is signalled by a fixed, very small set of items, e.g. *this morning, last week, on Thursday*.

(8) I went and bought this this morning

(Cheepen 1988)

(9) let's see . Thursday night I went it town

(Jefferson, in Cheepen 1988)

(10) I used to go in (---) and find . Deb was absolute [diza:] ---) into the hospital in the evenings and find her

(Svartvik and Quirk, 1980)

Inspection of a variety of conversational transcriptions shows that this kind of occurrence is to be found *within 20 words* of the beginning of the story, and this makes it an ideal feature for tagging in corpora. As I have already indicated, we must bear in mind that this kind of lexical feature occurs along with the others which signal the presence of stories in conversation. While it is a reliable indicator of story beginnings, its full significance is only clear when it is seen in close proximity to other story-signalling items.

6 Discourse structures in classroom talk

Classroom talk is, like conversation, a potentially ambiguous term. Many kinds of talk occurs in the classroom. In this chapter I am focusing on the primarily *transactional* dialogue which occurs between the teacher and the pupil(s) where the speech event is directed towards teaching and learning, rather than any of the other kinds of discourse which may occur within the classroom. Pupil–pupil talk may, for example, occur within the classroom (even during a lesson) and be properly classified as a conversation.

In their analysis of this kind of teaching discourse, Sinclair and Coulthard (1975) identified a hierarchical structure of *lesson, transaction, exchange, move, act*. These elements function together in a way similar to the interaction between low level features and large discourse structures which I have described operating in conversation, so that, for example, particular kinds of *move* signal certain kinds of *exchange* (which is the next rank in the ascending scale). In this hierarchical system, the lowest rank is the *act*. Some of the acts identified are, at present, unsuitable for inclusion in an automatic tagging system, because they have not yet been specified in terms of their lexical realizations, but can only be identified by their grammatical/situational category (*clue*, for example, is realized by 'statement, question, command, or moodless item'). Others, however, are specified by a closed set of lexical items, and are therefore suitable for tagging without further groundwork.

The act which illustrates this most clearly is the *marker*. It is realized by a small, fixed set of lexical signals, e.g. *well, OK, now, good, right, alright*, and it functions to signal *boundaries* in the discourse, so it plays an important part in structuring the discourse in an overall sense. It is worth noting here that the marker occurs only in the teacher's talk. As I have already indicated earlier, this kind of discourse is essentially an *unequal* speech event, with an acknowledged superior – the teacher. Responsibility for controlling and structuring the discourse lies permanently with that superior, and therefore boundaries in the discourse are signalled in the superior's turn to talk.

(11) Well, what leads you to believe he's like that?

(Sinclair and Coulthard, 1975)

(12) Right. Are you going to colour those?

(Brierley et al. 1992)

As with the temporal location signals in conversational stories, it is a fairly straightforward matter to use a scanning procedure for such items, and so begin the automatic recognition of discourse structures in this kind of transactional speech event.

7   Next steps

The suggestions I have made in the preceding sections are designed to open the way to automatic recognition and tagging of discourse structures in whole texts. As I have pointed out, in conversation and in teaching talk (and, no doubt, in other kinds of spoken discourse) it is not yet possible to specify the lexical realizations of all the structures, but a start can certainly be made on some of the more easily recognizable ones. The automatic recognition and tagging of these will also serve to help with the work needed on the more difficult cases, due to the clustering of features at points in the discourse where one structure is being replaced by another.

Once the initial steps towards partial automation have been taken, then the way will be open for work on other structures. In conversation this will be in the area of *speech-in-action*, which is the next largest discourse structure after *story*, and which functions to allow the speech participants to find new topics for story telling (and status exchange) which have not arisen out of topical links in the preceding story section. In classroom talk, I suggest that the next step should be to deal with a detailed specification of some of the other *acts* identified by Sinclair and Coulthard, concentrating first on those where the set of lexical realisations is likely to be smallest – for example *acknowledge*, which is realized by items such as *yes*, *cor*, *mm*, *wow*, and so on.

As work progresses in these areas, the value of large corpora will become even clearer, as a very large store of computerized data will allow us, in parallel with work on identifying multiple instances of text structuring items, to observe the collocational behaviour of such items. This will inevitably result in adjustments to and improvements on our original hypotheses about the nature and function of the structures which characterize the various discourse genres.

Notes

1. I do not mean to imply that this is true of all transactional encounters. Some, such as certain business meetings, do provide the participants with a basis of equality within the discourse.
2. Similar evaluations of the superior's contribution by the inferior are very rare indeed.
3. This is, no doubt, why it is considered inadvisable to teach one's spouse to drive.
4. See Cheepen and Monaghan 1990.
5. [Editor's note] In this chapter extracts from Svartvik and Quirk (1980) are quoted in a simplified transcription. See Peppé, Chapter 15, for details of the fuller transcription.
6. A case could be made for other kinds of analysis here, focusing on the semantic properties of the verbs *went* and *came back*, but the introduction of such considerations would complicate the implementation of an automatic tagging system to an unacceptable level, and is, in any case, outside the scope of this present chapter.

11 Code switching: a problem for transcription and text encoding

MARK SEBBA

1 The study of code switching

In many bilingual and multilingual communities, it is normal for speakers to use two or more languages in the same interaction – possibly the same utterance – when talking with other bilinguals who share their language repertoire. This phenomenon of language alternation or *code switching* has been attracting attention from researchers for the last few decades. Researchers studying code switching have tended to focus on one of three main areas of interest (see Sebba 1993 for a fuller discussion):

1. The formal linguistic aspects of code switching, in particular the grammatical mechanisms whereby a bilingual individual can produce a sentence (or sentence-like utterance) partly in one language and partly in another without breaking the grammatical rules of either.
2. Pragmatic and discoursal aspects of code switching – in particular, the motivations for speakers' switches and the meanings or symbolic values underlying them.
3. Ethnographic description of code switching, focusing on 'who speaks what language to whom and when' (Fishman 1965), the status of switching within a community and its relation to phenomena such as language maintenance and language death.

Whatever the interests of the individual researcher, code switching raises many questions concerning even the most fundamental linguistic concepts, some of which are of particular relevance at the transcription stage. For example, what is a 'sentence' if it is incomplete in each of two languages? How can we decide where the boundaries between one language and another should be drawn, when both languages appear to be mixed freely and some lexical items could belong to either? Decisions like this have to be made before or during transcription even before the analysis 'proper' can begin.

Code switching: a problem for transcription and text encoding 145

From the earliest studies, which tended to be based on anecdotal evidence and the intuitions of 'native switchers', the field of code switching studies has developed a rich research tradition based on the analysis of large bodies of linguistically mixed data. Because of the strict norms which apply to most standard written languages, code switching is very largely confined to the spoken medium, though there have been a few studies of written code switching, based mainly on personal letters or magazine articles. Researchers tend to work with recordings of conversational data, transcribing utterance by utterance. Transcription of monolingual data is far from a straightforward task; but bi- or multilingual data presents even more complex problems of transcription and encoding.

2 Problems of transcription and encoding

Transcription problems vary, of course, depending on the languages present in the data. (See Martin-Jones and Saxena, in progress, for a discussion of bilingual transcription.) Potential problems presented by code-switching data include:

- how to differentiate in transcription between the codes present in the data (this is a central problem and will be discussed in more detail below);
- whether to use the standard orthographies if they are available for the languages in the data, when this may involve a change of writing system in mid-sentence; or whether to use some form of phonetic transcription, which may make the transcription difficult to read and obscure the points at which switches take place;
- how to mark the differences between two similar codes (closely related languages or varieties, e.g. a standard language and a local variety, or languages with largely shared lexis, such as a Creole language and its lexifier);
- how to transcribe parts of utterances which cannot be reliably assigned to any code: this may include shared lexis, items which happen to have meaning in two codes, interjections, laughter, and so on.

A key problem for all researchers is the first one above: how to represent the languages of the data visually on the page or screen so that readers – including the researcher – can easily distinguish them, where possible preserving their orthographic integrity without obscuring theoretical problems of differentiation between the codes.

Researchers have responded to these needs in different ways. There has never been a 'standard' way of presenting code switching data, but from the beginnings of research in this field, when transcriptions were hand written or typed and underlining was a convenient way of marking one of the codes as different, we have moved into the era of word processors where many more possibilities are available. The problem has thereby evolved into one of finding a way of encoding

146 *Applications and more specialized uses*

the identity of the languages in the data in both a human-readable and a machine-readable form.

The examples in the appendix that follows, show how this ideal has not been met by many of the transcription systems used to date. Devices such as italic, underlining and bold face are convenient ways to distinguish codes on screen or paper but disappear when word processor files are converted to ASCII form and downloaded to a mainframe. Crucial information – without which the research itself becomes pointless – is thus not available except from printouts produced via the researcher's own word processor. Larger-scale processing of the data using corpus tools, and sharing of the data with other researchers, becomes difficult or impossible.

To make the data intelligible to other researchers, interlinear glosses or translations are an integral part of the presentation of more code switching data. Commonly, the typographic devices used to distinguish the codes of the original data are 'echoed' in the translation enabling the reader to follow the switches of code while attending only to the translation. This leads to further complexities of layout and loss of information if the information provided by italics, bold face, and so on is stripped.

3   What researchers need

If researchers are to be able to establish large usable machine-readable corpora of code switching data, then we need:

1. a standard format for encoding the data which is flexible enough to accommodate the needs of researchers in this area but which will allow language labels to be recovered when files are converted to ASCII or similar formats;
2. tools which allow different 'layers' of transcription and interpretation (for example, phonetic transcription, glosses, translations) to be displayed or printed as required, and allow for clear visual marking of the linguistic codes.

The appendix below shows some examples of published transcriptions of code-switching data, with a commentary on the practices they exemplify. From this it is possible to see that no standard ways of presenting the data have emerged, and that all the current practices are dependent on the typographical capabilities of word processors to convey crucial information.

APPENDIX: Examples of transcription practices of different researchers studying mixed-language corpora

1. Researchers commonly employ strategies like using **bold face**, <u>underlining</u> or *italic* to mark one of the codes, leaving the other in normal type. Typographical means must also be found to distinguish the glosses or translations, if any.

(a)
    MR EDER   Dü bekommsch do e Fätze... *Je sais pas dans quelle graisse, avec quoi, avec de, de, de, de, de, was weiss denn de Teifel...*

    What you get from this is scraps.... *In I don't know what fat, with what, with... Goodness knows what...*
                                                          (Gardner-Chloros 1991)

(b)
    V   oh it's a laugh is that one (0.8) watch * *
         <u>watch she a skyank!</u>
         <laughter (3.0)>
    V   did (did you leave) the radio on *? was the radio on?
    ?   yeh
    C   were you dancin' Laverne?
    L   yeah man, see the grooves man
                                                                   (Sebba 1993)

2. Using CAPITALS to mark one of the codes ensures that the code can still be identified if the text is converted to ASCII form, but this is not an option for all languages, and using capital letters may obscure other orthographic conventions.

    'SI TU ERES PUERTORRIQUEÑO (If you're Puerto Rican), your father's a Puerto Rican, you should at least DE VEZ EN CUANDO (sometimes), you know, HABLAR ESPAÑOL (speak Spanish).'
                                                                         (Poplack 1980)

3. Things become more complicated when three different languages are involved, as here in data taken from the kitchen of a Chinese restaurant. Cantonese presents special problems because of the lack of a standard form of transcription. Mandarin is transcribed using the official Pinyin romanisation.

    (Frame: W5 comes into the kitchen and asks for more pancakes.)

    [Can] W5 (Man): *ga sei zang pei!*
                             <four more pan-cakes!>

    [Man] K3 (Can): *si zhang?*
                             <four pieces?>

    [Eng] W5 (Man): **yes, four.**

Applications and more specialized uses

(K3 brings out four pan-cakes and gives them to W5)
(English/*Mandarin* (<u>Cantonese</u>): (Guo 1992))

4. The researchers here have used language-name tags in angle brackets as well as bold and plain face type to distinguish between English and Panjabi. The tags will make the language identities recoverable if the text is converted to ASCII form.

BA: \<P\> ( ) e \<E\> story \<P\> **hegii e** \<E\> banyan tree
This story is about a banyan tree.
{pointing to the tree on the first page}
\<P\> **dii..** \<E\> banyan tree \<P\> **kinoo kende e.**
What is a banyan tree?
vaDDaa saraa drakhat e.
It's a very big tree.
(English/Panjabi (England): (Martin-Jones et al. 1992))

5. An example of transcription similar to (4); here angle-bracket markers have been used to distinguish between English and Welsh.

Customer: **\<W\> modur**
(motor/car)
LW: **\<W\> y modur o'r**   \<E\> lift **\<W\> wedi, wedi**
(the motor from the   **has, has**
\<E\>   what's 'gone wrong'? **\<W\> wedi cael rywbeth** ei
(has had something)
(English/Welsh (Wales): (Jones 1992))

12 Linking prosodic transcription to the time dimension

PETER ROACH and SIMON ARNFIELD

1 Introduction

This chapter is written from the standpoint of researchers using spoken corpora who believe strongly in the value of having the acoustic as well as the textual data in machine-readable form. Having this information allows a number of interesting areas to be explored, as we will explain in the context of the research being done on a joint research project shared between Peter Roach and Gerry Knowles (MARSEC: MAchine-Readable Spoken English Corpus, funded by Economic and Social Research Council Grant No. R000 23 3380).

Something else that we wish to stress here (though the idea is more or less universally accepted) is the importance in a corpus of spoken language of transcribing prosodic and sometimes also paralinguistic information. Deciding exactly what to transcribe, however, and what symbolic conventions to use, is not at all easy. Most prosodic transcription conventions are compromises, and they tend to represent in one or two dimensions information that should properly be regarded as varying on many more dimensions. To give a few examples, it is often assumed that if intonation is represented by tone marks, we can recover from that transcription all the accented syllables in the utterance; most intonation transcription systems have assumed that pauses do not need to be marked with a symbol different from that of tone-unit boundaries; pitch range factors have often been coded simply in terms of 'high' and 'low' varieties of nuclear tones. Many other examples could be cited. In designing a transcription system for corpus use it is necessary to consider very carefully what information users are likely to want to extract, and to plan the coding system accordingly.

The Spoken English Corpus (SEC) was originally devised and compiled from recordings (mainly of radio broadcasts) in the 1980s as a joint project between IBM UK and Lancaster University, and the prosodic transcription was done by Gerry Knowles and Briony Williams (Alderson and Knowles forthcoming, Knowles and Taylor 1988). The transcription system is a variant of what is sometimes known as 'Standard British'. This 'standard' is in fact something of a myth: many recent authors of such systems claim that their system is to some extent based on that of O'Connor and Arnold (1973), but many differences are observable. The O'Connor and Arnold system was too complex for most purposes and many later systems, such as Roach (1991), are considerably simpler. The system used for the SEC dispensed with the conventional British tone-unit structure of Pre-head, Head, Nucleus and Tail and simply assigned one of a set of Tonetic Stress-Marks (TSM) to each accented syllable. The inventory of TSM's comprises High and Low versions of Level, Rise, Fall, Fall-rise and Rise-fall, a total of 10. However, in practice it was found impractical to operate a distinction between High and Low Rise-Fall, since this tone occurs only infrequently.

The corpus has been extensively analysed since its creation, and various annotations have been added to it, including automatic word-tagging (every word of the approximately 53,000 words contained in it has been marked with a grammatical word-class tag) and automatic parsing (the entire corpus has been automatically parsed). Given that the prosodic information has also been added to the text, it is possible to carry out automatic analysis of co-occurrences of prosodic and grammatical features of the corpus (Arnfield and Atwell 1993). In our present project we have added the acoustic signal in digital form, stored on CD-ROM disk, and have carried out a variety of acoustic analyses. The CD-ROM disk contains approximately six hours of recorded speech, digitized at 16kHz in 16-bit samples. In order to make the data manageable on small computers, we have edited the material into 420 one-minute sections.

One of the most important goals of the project was to align the text of the corpus with the acoustic signal, so as to make it possible to locate automatically and rapidly all the acoustic information corresponding to a specific piece of the corpus, down to the size of individual syllables or even, if possible, individual phonemes (see also Sinclair, Chapter 7). This has been the most technically challenging part of the project, and is described in detail in the following section. It is important to bear in mind that the alignment had to be done automatically by computer, since to generate time-references manually for every phoneme in the corpus would have been a task requiring expert work over a very long period.

2   Alignment of text and signal

For our purposes the original text of the Spoken English Corpus can be thought of as a continuous string of characters. One of the most important and difficult tasks on our project has been to provide a link between that string of characters and the sounds in the recorded signal. Our way of doing this was based on the techniques used in various speech database projects to speed up the process of phonetic transcription of corpus data. An example is the CASPAR system used for the transcription of the TIMIT database, described in Leung and Zue (1984).

The task may be likened to that of digging a tunnel, with work starting at each end in the hope of meeting in the middle. Fig. 12.1 shows the two ends: the orthographic text and the acoustic waveform, each of which is a *representation* of the data we are working with, and each of which is available to the computer.

Linking prosodic transcription to the time dimension 151

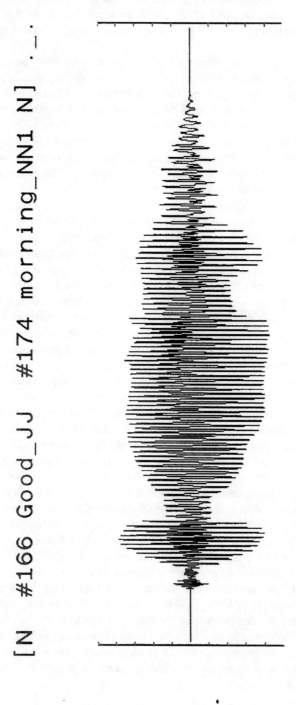

Figure 12.1

To progress to the situation in Fig. 12.2 we must process both of these representations: the text is stripped of all added information such as tonetic stress marks, punctuation and formatting. The speech signal is subjected to spectral analysis.

In Fig. 12.3 we progress further towards linking the two: first, we convert the orthographic representation of the text into a phonemic representation, using computer programs developed by Gerry Knowles and Tamás Váradi. This amounts to a prediction of the sounds that are likely to be detectable in the speech signal. The choice of phonemic rather than phonetic representation is a technical matter which is explained later. Also at this stage we analyse the acoustic signal in such a way that the program outputs a string of phonemic symbols corresponding to the sounds detected in the signal. Thus at this stage of the process we have two approximate phonemic transcriptions, one generated from the text and the other from the acoustic signal. The term 'approximate' should be understood to mean that in neither case is the transcription expected to attain the level of accuracy that would be expected in a transcription carried out by a human expert listening to the recording. At this point our task is to make the best possible match between the two. The program is made to treat the machine-generated transcription as the correct transcription, and to adjust the signal-derived transcription until it matches this as closely as possible. Of course, a better 'correct' transcription would be one carried out by a human expert, but in this project there was not sufficient time for such a task to be undertaken, and the automatic system was felt to be the best solution to the problem of having a very large amount of data to transcribe. An essential part of the output of this process is time-references for the beginning and end of each phoneme; an example of this output is shown in Fig. 12.3. The numbers give starting and finishing time in msec.

The technique used for the analysis was that of Hidden Markov Models (HMM). The software used was HTK, the Hidden Markov Model Tool Kit developed by Dr Steve Young in the Cambridge University Engineering Department, whose advice and assistance we are glad to acknowledge. It would not be practical to attempt to explain here how HMM analysis works, but see Rabiner (1990). It is important to understand that the system has to be trained to recognize the set of sounds that will be found in the data, and that this requires the preparation of a substantial amount of training data consisting of signal files and associated phonemic or phonetic transcriptions which link each symbol to a particular section of the signal file. The data analysis for this material must be done with great care and a considerable amount of phonetic expertise. Sample numbers must be provided manually for the start and end of every segment in the training set. It would have been possible for us to use some existing training data from elsewhere, but since in our case the final step was to be the matching of the output of our HMM recognition with the output of our text-to-phoneme conversion it was crucially important that the same symbols were used for both, and used in the same way. Consequently, having agreed on the symbols to be used, we prepared our own training data.

Linking prosodic transcription to the time dimension 153

[N #166 Good_JJ #174 morning_NN1 N] . _ .

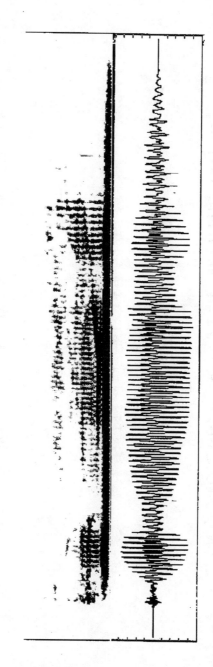

Figure 12.2

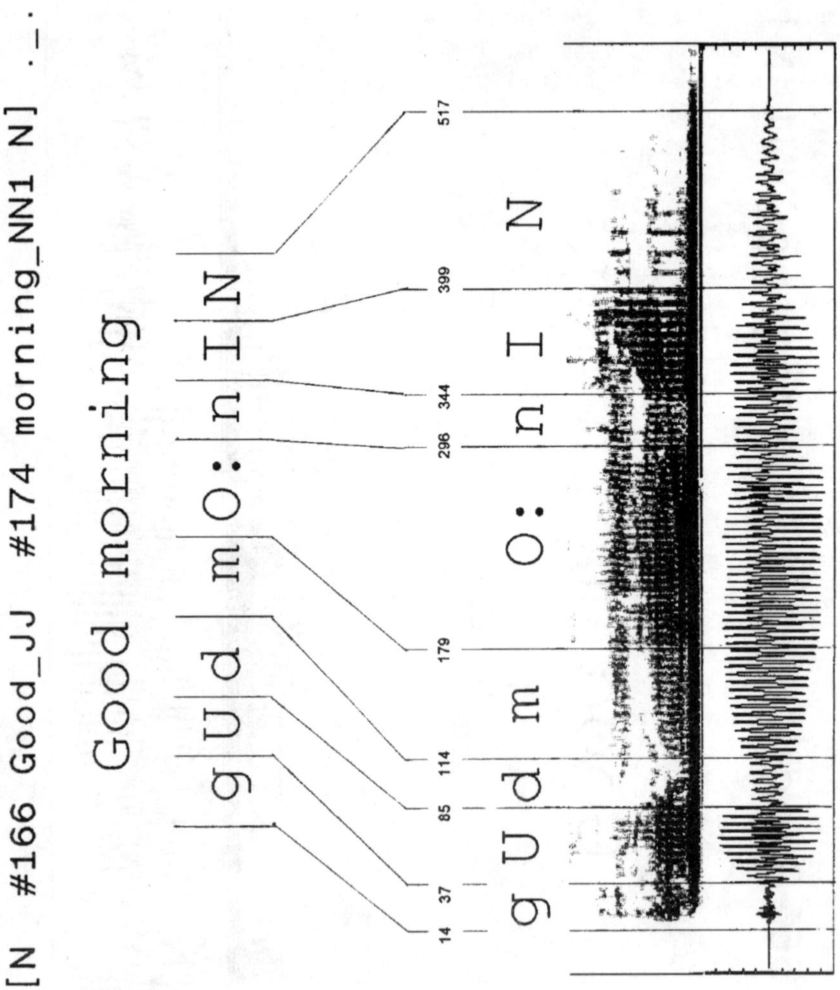
[N #166 Good_JJ #174 morning_NN1 N] ._.
Good morning
g U d m O: n I N
14 37 85 114 179 296 344 399 517
g U d m O: n I N

Figure 12.3

We should explain our reason for using phonemes as the unit for representation at this point: most recent work on labelling of speech database material has been *phonetic*, using a set of symbols which indicate the presence of physically recognizable acoustic segments. *Phonemic* transcription, on the other hand, represents an idealized version of the pronunciation and may well be less accurate in terms of what is physically measurable in a specific utterance. To return to our example, the phrase *good morning* would be represented phonemically, in one widely used transcription, as /gUd mO:nIN/; phonetically speaking, however, the /d/ at the end of the first syllable might well be realized not as /d/ but (through assimilation) as /b/ or even /m/. But such divergences from an idealized standard pronunciation are not completely predictable. Bearing in mind that the output of the text-to-sound conversion program had to guide the search for phonetic elements in the signal, we considered that to have a program which wrongly predicted the occurrence of a phonetic element would probably be no better than one which did not attempt to predict allophonic detail at all. The cost of this decision was in terms of a number of likely one-segment errors, but the benefit was simplicity and the saving of time.

At the end of this process we had a new set of files containing the best-fitting transcription with time-references. It must be pointed out that from the point of view of segmental phonetics this transcription was still not very accurate. Our goal in this short project was to make the time-reference sufficiently accurate to enable us to locate automatically any prosodic event in the recordings with a high probability of finding the syllable or syllables over which it was manifested. This cross-referencing from text to time-aligned transcription file can be laborious, and one of the objectives of the project has been to find an effective way of 'navigating' automatically through the various annotations in order to find a particular point in one file that corresponds to a point in another file. Our preliminary design for this was published in Ghali et al. (1992), and a working system for use in the UNIX environment has now been completed. Having achieved the goal of aligning our text with its speech signal, we are in a position to compare the prosodic information in our corpus with other ways of coding such information in similar corpora. The most interesting from our point of view is the ToBI system, which has been developed in the USA specifically for computer-based prosodic transcription for speech corpora.

3   The ToBI system

Prosodic transcription systems in the past have tended to be the work of one or two specialists writing for a specific audience. But if one wished to devise a system which would be suitable for use as a widely used standard it would obviously be preferable to involve as many people as possible in the planning stages. This has been done with ToBI: three workshops have been held at which experts worked together on refining the theory, testing the usability of the system and examining inter-transcriber agreement. The first was hosted by Victor Zue at MIT in 1991, and the second by Kim Silverman at Nynex (New York) in 1992. At the last of these workshops, held at Ohio State University in July 1993 and organized by Mary Beckman and Gayle Ayers, the question of the applicability of ToBI to non-American dialects of English was considered, and intonation specialists from Australia and Britain (including the first author of this chapter) took part. Another important feature of ToBI is that accessibility of training and explanatory material has been given a high priority, and most ToBI material can be copied free of charge by anonymous ftp from a file-server in the USA. While little of this material has yet appeared in print, a preliminary paper about ToBI appeared in the Proceedings of the 1992 International Conference on Spoken Language Processing, which was held in Banff (Silverman et al. 1992).

The ToBI system is unusual in a number of ways, and it is difficult to know where to start in describing it. One of its most individual characteristics is that it is explicitly designed to be used in interactive labelling on a speech workstation, and does not depend entirely on the intuitions of the trained transcriber working auditorily. The preferred computing environment is the xwaves package running on a UNIX workstation, and software designed to speed up the transcription process is available to researchers working with this system. While it is undoubtedly important to listen analytically while labelling speech with a ToBI transcription, this should always be done while visually observing a fundamental frequency track that is time-aligned with the words of the utterance being analysed. A proper ToBI transcription embodies not only the prosodic marks, but also the digitized acoustic record. The question of the reliability of the trained transcriber of intonation is, of course, controversial. A much-cited study by Philip Lieberman (Lieberman 1965) established to the satisfaction of many linguists that the claimed objectivity of auditory analysts was in fact spurious, their judgement being heavily influenced by their knowledge of the structure and content of what they heard (though the 'experiment' that Lieberman carried out could scarcely be considered a properly controlled scientific one and its conclusions should be treated with some scepticism). Crystal (1969) carried out somewhat better-controlled tests, but with rather inconclusive results.

The name ToBI gives a good indication of the nature of the system. It is, of course, an acronym. The 'To' stands for Tones, and 'BI' for Break Indices. ToBI does not only mark intonation, but also the nature of the breaks between words – what in an earlier age was known as 'juncture' (Trager and Smith 1951, O'Connor and Tooley 1964). Where words are so closely linked that no phonetic indication of separation exists (e.g. 'didja' for 'did you'), a break of Level 0 is assigned. A major break such as a silent pause would be marked with a Level 4 break. The inclusion of break indices adds considerably to the effort of doing transcriptions, since every word boundary must be assigned one or other of the break index numbers.

Let us now look at the treatment of tonal phenomena. When one looks at the ToBI system it is immediately obvious that it bears a strong resemblance to the work on intonational phonology of Janet Pierrehumbert (e.g. Pierrehumbert

1980); this work itself was not produced in a theoretical vacuum but had strong links to autosegmental and metrical phonology. One consequence of this is that a ToBI transcription is multi-tiered: tones are on one level and break indices on another, for example; association of tones with lexical material is ensured by asterisks identifying accent placement in relation to the orthographic tier. Another consequence is that the system resembles autosegmental accounts of African tone languages: the basic inventory of tones for English consists simply of H (high) and L (low), which may, with certain restrictions, be combined into bitonal accents. All other intonational variation is explained in terms of contextual influences such as downstep, tone-spreading and boundary effects. It has to be said, I think, that this approach, though undoubtedly appealing to theoretical phonologists, looks rather unpromising from the point of view of workaday transcribers toiling over their daily quota of corpus material. However, although those responsible for the development of ToBI have no difficulty in dealing with theoretical issues in phonology, they have worked hard to make the system comprehensible to non-phonologists, and to free it from some of its less accessible underpinnings.

In looking at how intonation is transcribed using ToBI conventions, it is obviously helpful to be able to see and hear examples, and here it is very valuable to have access to the ToBI training material. There is a wealth of illustrations (some admittedly rather contrived) to show how particular patterns are to be represented, and a brief outline of the system such as this is not adequate to convey this information. One very important point to make is that tones are not assigned only to accented syllables: they are also placed at the end of intonational phrases. Here we find a hierarchy such as has been suggested in many earlier works on intonation, where major intonational phrases (tone-units, sense-groups, etc.) contain one or more lesser phrases. Consequently each major intonational phrase boundary is also a boundary of a lower-order phrase, and each of these must be assigned a tone. 'Boundary tones' (major boundaries) are marked with H or L followed by the % sign; intermediate phrase boundary tones have H or L followed by the − sign. Accented syllables have H or L (or a combination) with no additional sign other than the * which links them to a particular syllable on the orthographic tier. It is worth recalling that the older American tradition of the Trager and Smith system (Trager and Smith 1951) used 'terminal juncture' tones in a similar way.

Thus a full intonational phrase boundary will be marked with two tones, which may combine as follows: L-L% (low ending); L-H% ('continuation rise'); H-H% (high-rising ending, as in yes-no questions) or H-L% (falling; the H tone raises the final L to mid). Accented syllables are marked somewhat differently: they may be H* (non-low accented syllable); L* (accented, but using lowest pitch of speaker's range); L*+H ('scooped accent', low tone followed immediately by sharp rise to high peak); L+H* ('rising peak accent', a high peak target on the accented syllable which is immediately preceded by a sharp rise from a valley in the lowest part of the pitch range); H+!H* (the ! mark indicates downstep; this

Will you have marmalade, or jam?
L*　H−　　L*H− H%

Figure 12.4

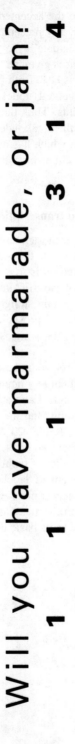

Figure 12.5

pitch accent is a clear step down onto the accented syllable from a high pitch which cannot itself be accounted for by any preceding accent).

The first example in the ToBI training data is the 'marmalade' file. The text is 'Will you have marmalade, or jam'. This is given an 'open listing' intonation with a final rise, so the final boundary tone is H%. Both the word *marmalade* and the word *jam* are phrase-final, and both receive H-tones. Finally, the rising tones on both nouns begin with L* pitch accents. Thus the full tonal-tier transcription looks like that shown in Fig. 12.4. On the break index tier, the transcription is as shown in Fig. 12.5. An additional tier, which has not been mentioned so far, is the miscellaneous tier, on which annotations of such things as disfluencies, gestures, and so on, may be made.

4 Future work on time-aligned transcription

We feel that it is important to increase the amount of spoken corpus material available with machine-readable text linked to time-aligned acoustic records. One small initial step currently being worked on is to experiment with ways of converting the British-style transcription of the SEC into a ToBI-like transcription. This cannot be a full conversion, but certain straightforward conversion operations can be carried out automatically. The prosodic transcription of the whole corpus has been converted in this way; the work is described in Roach (forthcoming).

The material in the SEC is suitable for grammatical and lexical study, but in terms of its emotional content is almost entirely neutral. Work is in progress on a project shared by the Speech Research Laboratory in the Department of Linguistic Science, University of Reading, and the Department of Psychology, University of Leeds (ESRC grant no. R 000 23 5285) which is collecting a corpus of emotional speech. The intention is to transcribe the basic intonation patterns with the ToBI system, but to add a lot of paralinguistic and prosodic detail in the Miscellaneous tier using a system of labels based on the conventions developed by Crystal (1969). In this way a novel collection of data should be added to the existing stock of spoken corpus material, while the ToBI system can be broadened without any modification to its basic design.

13 Grammatical tagging of the spoken part of the British National Corpus: a progress report[1]

ROGER GARSIDE

1 Introduction

The British National Corpus (BNC) will contain 100 million words of varied types of modern British English. It is designed to provide an unparalleled resource for the construction of dictionaries, for linguistics research, for the implementation of natural language processing systems of various kinds, and so on. This chapter is concerned with the grammatical tagging of one part of the BNC, that devoted to spoken language, and discusses how tagging software originally developed for the written language has had to be adapted.

The BNC has been constructed over the period 1991 to 1994 by a consortium led by Oxford University Press, where the partners have the following tasks:

1. The texts have been collected by Oxford University Press, Longman UK Ltd and Chambers.
2. They have been processed, checked and stored by Oxford University Computing Services.
3. Linguistic (part-of-speech) annotation has been inserted by UCREL (Unit for Computer Research on the English Language) at the University of Lancaster.

The corpus is being encoded using SGML (Standard Generalized Markup Language) in conformance with TEI (the Text Encoding Initiative), an international project to lay down guidelines for a clearly defined format for machine-readable text interchange (see Burnard, Chapter 5 and Johansson, Chapter 6).

The whole of the 100 million words is being assigned part-of-speech markers from a tagset of 61 tags, which we call the c5 tagset; this is listed in the Appendix to this chapter. A selected core sub-corpus is being tagged with a more detailed tagset of about 170 tags, which we call the c6 tagset.

This part-of-speech assignment or tagging is being carried out by the Claws4 tagging system. An earlier version of this is described in detail in Garside et al. (1987), but in general there is:

161

1. An initial part-of-speech assignment from a lexicon, supplemented by rules for unknown items, involving for instance word-endings, capitalization, hyphenation, and so on. The result of this is a set of possible part-of-speech tags for each word, considered in isolation.
2. Disambiguation by a Hidden Markov Model (HMM) procedure (see Rabiner 1990). This makes use of the Viterbi alignment procedure (see for example Jelinek 1976) to select the sequence of part-of-speech tags with the highest probability, taking account of the transitional probability from one part-of-speech to the next, and the probability of any word being a particular part-of-speech.
3. Supplementary disambiguation by means of a library of patterns. These patterns are sequences of specifications (either full or partial) of words and parts-of-speech, the latter assigned by earlier phases of the program. A matched pattern, or the highest scoring pattern if there are several matches, specifies a new set of part-of-speech tags for some or all of the matched items. One recent innovation in the Claws system is to have several sets of such patterns, each to be matched on a separate pass, so that later passes can make use of the results of earlier passes.

After the Claws tagging system has been run, there is a manual post-editing phase where linguistic analysts can correct the part-of-speech assignment preferred by Claws. Obviously, in a project of this size, it has not been possible to post-edit all the texts; we have post-edited a sample of each new text type we encountered, and then we have continued to post-edit selected samples of the text. The whole of the core sub-corpus is being post-edited.

Finally, there is a set of further automatic procedures which reformat the text into the format in which it is sent back to Oxford University Computing Services, and in the process check the text for a number of possible error conditions (including ill-formed SGML structure).

2   The spoken part of the BNC

The spoken part of the BNC will be up to ten million words in size. It is divided into:

1. A *context-dependent* section, collected from various business, leisure and other events (sales demonstrations, after-dinner speeches, etc.).
2. A *demographic* section, where volunteers (selected to cover the main regions of the country) record all their conversations over a period.

This is described in more detail in Crowdy (Chapter 19).

Most of what we have received is reasonably straight-forward to tag, as the transcription does not attempt to reproduce tricks of speech. This is unlike some of the written material: a notorious example in the written part of the BNC is a 'Captain Pugwash' story, which contains such phenomena as *m-m-must* to represent hesitation.

Grammatical tagging of the spoken part of the British National Corpus 163

An example of the type of material received by UCREL is the following, from the demographic section, where Dorothy (from Hereford) is talking to her three-year-old son Tim. [For interpretation of TEI mark-up, see Johansson, Chapter 6.]

> <u id=D0009 who=W0001><vocal desc=laugh> <pause> Hallo Bertie. How are you? <ptr t=P1> <unclear> <ptr t=P2></u>
> <u id=D0010 who=W0003><ptr t=P1> Mum, do fish like <ptr t=P2> people?</u>
> <u id=D0011 who=W0001>Do fishes like people? Don't know, what do you think?</u>
> <u id=D0012 who=W0002>Mummy.</u>
> <u id=D0013 who=W0001>Hallo Bertie Edward. <ptr t=P3> Do you like us? <ptr t=P4></u>

Here utterances are delimited with the pair of SGML tags <u> and </u>. An indication of the speaker is given by the *who* attribute, which refers to details held earlier in the text file. Overlapped passages are indicated with SGML <ptr> tags, but each utterance is represented as consecutive text, which makes part-of-speech assignment easier. Various phenomena, including here laughs and pauses, are indicated with an appropriate SGML tag, the complete set of possible tags and entities being specified in the document type description (dtd).

After processing by UCREL this becomes:

> <u id=D0009 who=W0001>
> <s c="0000379 002" n=00041>
> <vocal desc=laugh> <pause> Hallo&ITJ; Bertie&NP0;.&PUN;
> <s c="0000379 022" n=00042>
> How&AVQ; are&VBB; you&PNP;?&PUN; <ptr t=P1> <unclear> <ptr t=P2> </u>
> <u id=D0010 who=W0003>
> <s c="0000381 002" n=00043>
> <ptr t=P1> Mum&NP0;,&PUN; do&VDB; fish&NN2; like&VVI; <ptr t=P2> people&NN0;?&PUN; </u>
> <u id=D0011 who=W0001>
> <s c="0000382 002" n=00044>
> Do&VDB; fishes&NN2; like&VVI; people&NN0;?&PUN;
> <s c="0000382 042" n=00045>
> Do&VDB;n't&XX0; know&VVI;,&PUN; what&DTQ; do&VDB; you&PNP; think&VVI;?&PUN; </u>
> <u id=D0012 who=W0002>
> <s c="0000384 002" n=00046>
> Mummy&NN1-NP0;.&PUN; </u>
> <u id=D0013 who=W0001>
> <s c="0000385 002" n=00047>

Hallo&ITJ; Bertie&NP0; Edward&NP0;.&PUN;
<s c="0000385 032" n=00048>
<ptr t=P3> Do&VDB; you&PNP; like&VVI; us&PNP;?&PUN; <ptr t=P4> </u>

Here the text has been split into 's-units' (essentially functional sentences), each given an identifying code number. Each word is assigned a part-of-speech marker, which is an SGML entity constructed from the list given in the appendix, such as '&NN2;' for a plural common noun (e.g. *fishes*). Notice that a contracted word like *don't* has two parts-of-speech indicated, *do* tagged as base part of the verb DO and *n't* tagged NOT.

3 Tagging the spoken part of the BNC

Our strategy has been to use the same version of Claws for assignment of part-of-speech markings to both the written and spoken parts of the corpus. Our reason for this is that there are many examples in the written parts of the BNC where spoken data are recorded; since these are not marked sufficiently explicitly for Claws to be able to distinguish the two modes, we have attempted to provide a 'general-purpose' tagging system which covers both.

Thus most of the modifications for spoken data mentioned below are also in place for tagging written texts as well. Claws has a 'spoken data' flag for those few procedures which we did not want to take effect on written data, and this flag is automatically switched on by the processing script which recognizes where the input data is taken from (and therefore, whether it is written or spoken data). We have generally arranged the additional resources for spoken data, such as lexicons and pattern lists, as separate files which can be merged with the main lexicons or not, as appropriate for processing any particular type of input data. Currently the transitional probability figures from one part-of-speech to the next are based on general, mainly written, data; when sufficient spoken data has been processed in the BNC, we plan to produce a set of transition probability figures specifically for spoken data.

The main modifications we have made to the Claws system to deal with spoken data are as follows:

1. Additions to the lexicon (from lists supplied by Longman). There are about such 250 words at present:

    - interjections of various sorts (*ah, blah, grrr, mhm, oi, okey-dokey,* etc.)
    - various taboo words
    - slang words (*jim-jams, lughole, nowt,* etc.)

    We have also constructed by hand a small list of words which are used very differently in written and spoken English. This list contains words where the possible parts-of-speech, or the frequency with which they are used, in the general-purpose model (which is biased towards written data) needs to be modified for spoken data. The main examples of this are interjections like *well* and *right*. This list then replaces the appropriate parts of the main lexicon when spoken data is being processed.

2. Additions to the contractions recognized by Claws. Claws originally had a rather short list of common contractions, such as *don't* and *won't*, together with an indication of how the word should be split and what part-of-speech marker should be assigned to each part. This list has been extended to between 30 and 40 items; examples are *d'ya* tagged VDB+PNP (i.e. base form of DO + pronoun) and *gotta* tagged VVN+TO0 (i.e. past participle + infinitival TO).

   Claws also now includes a check for words in the lexicon which appear in the text with a dropped initial *-h* or final *-g*; thus, for example, the word *'avin'* in the text would receive the part-of-speech markings associated with *having* in the lexicon. Similarly in the word-ending list, *-in'* is treated as a variant of *-ing*.

3. Special treatment of truncated words and some interjections. Truncated words are already indicated by SGML mark-up in the data received by UCREL – Claws simply marks such words UNC (unclassified). Certain interjections (at present only *er* and *erm*) are treated in all pattern matching and the Viterbi alignment as if they were not present. Suppose, for example, that Claws is attempting to choose between the tags VVD and VVN (i.e. past tense and past participle) for a word ending in *-ed*, on the basis of the presence or absence of an auxiliary verb preceding it. Then the intervention of *er* or *erm* between the two words would be ignored, and not affect the decision about which is the correct tag for the verb.

4. Recognition of repetition. The version of Claws which deals with spoken data looks for repetitions of sequences of words in the input text, perhaps with various separators (commas, ellipsis, interjections), and processes the text as if the repetition were removed.

Thus if Claws reads a sentence:

oh, not very well, we erm, we stopped going after Christmas

it recognizes the repetition of the word *we*, together with the intervening interjection *erm* and comma, and treats the sentence from the point of view of the disambiguation procedures as if it were:

oh, not very well, we stopped going after Christmas

Once Claws has made decisions about what part-of-speech each item should have in this form of the text, the original form of the text is recovered, and part-of-speech tags inserted for the repeated items; thus in the above example both instances of the word *we* receive the same tag.

Sequences of repeated words (to a maximum length of five words) and multiple repetitions are allowed, but we have limited the possible intervening items to those indicated above. Further we do not use this procedure on the written data, because of potential problems with sequences like *had had* and *you, you*; such sequences could of course also occur in spoken data, but we feel that in this case the advantages in the checking for repetition outweigh the dangers.

4   Conclusions

We have now processed some 250,000 words of the demographic section of the spoken data and looked in detail at selected output from the Claws system, to establish the problems encountered and how well Claws is dealing with them. We are now moving over to the production phase, with manual checking only of selected samples.

APPENDIX: The c5 part-of-speech tagset

AJ0	adjective (unmarked) (e.g. GOOD, OLD)
AJC	comparative adjective (e.g. BETTER, OLDER)
AJS	superlative adjective (e.g. BEST, OLDEST)
AT0	article (e.g. THE, A, AN)
AV0	adverb (unmarked) (e.g. OFTEN, WELL, LONGER, FURTHEST)
AVP	adverb particle (e.g. UP, OFF, OUT)
AVQ	wh-adverb (e.g. WHEN, HOW, WHY)
CJC	coordinating conjunction (e.g. AND, OR)
CJS	subordinating conjunction (e.g. ALTHOUGH, WHEN)
CJT	the conjunction THAT
CRD	cardinal numeral (e.g. 3, FIFTY-FIVE, 6609) (excluding ONE)
DPS	possessive determiner form (e.g. YOUR, THEIR)
DT0	general determiner (e.g. THESE, SOME)
DTQ	wh-determiner (e.g. WHOSE, WHICH)
EX0	existential THERE
ITJ	interjection or other isolate (e.g. OH, YES, MHM)
NN0	noun (neutral for number) (e.g. AIRCRAFT, DATA)
NN1	singular noun (e.g. PENCIL, GOOSE)
NN2	plural noun (e.g. PENCILS, GEESE)
NP0	proper noun (e.g. LONDON, MICHAEL, MARS)
ORD	ordinal (e.g. SIXTH, 77TH, LAST)
PNI	indefinite pronoun (e.g. NONE, EVERYTHING)
PNP	personal pronoun (e.g. YOU, THEM, OURS)
PNQ	wh-pronoun (e.g. WHO, WHOEVER)
PNX	reflexive pronoun (e.g. ITSELF, OURSELVES)
POS	the possessive (or genitive morpheme) 'S or '
PRF	the preposition OF
PRP	preposition (except for OF) (e.g. FOR, ABOVE, TO)

PUL	punctuation – left bracket (i.e. (or [ )	
PUN	punctuation – general mark (i.e. . . ! , : ; – ? . . .)	
PUQ	punctuation – quotation mark (i.e. ` ")	
PUR	punctuation – right bracket (i.e.) or])	
TO0	infinitive marker TO	
UNC	'unclassified' items which are not words of the English lexicon	
VBB	the 'base forms' of the verb 'BE' (except the infinitive), i.e. AM, ARE	
VBD	past form of the verb 'BE', i.e. WAS, WERE	
VBG	-*ing* form of the verb 'BE', i.e. BEING	
VBI	infinitive of the verb 'BE'	
VBN	past participle of the verb 'BE', i.e. BEEN	
VBZ	-*s* form of the verb 'BE', i.e. IS, 'S	
VDB/D/G/I/N/Z	forms of the verb 'DO'	
VHB/D/G/I/N/Z	forms of the verb 'HAVE'	
VM0	modal auxiliary verb (e.g. CAN, COULD, WILL, 'LL)	
VVB	base form of lexical verb (except the infinitive) (e.g. TAKE, LIVE)	
VVD	past tense form of lexical verb (e.g. TOOK, LIVED)	
VVG	-*ing* form of lexical verb (e.g. TAKING, LIVING)	
VVI	infinitive of lexical verb	
VVN	past participle form of lexical verb (e.g. TAKEN, LIVED)	
VVZ	-*s* form of lexical verb (e.g. TAKES, LIVES)	
XX0	the negative NOT or N'T	
ZZ0	alphabetical symbol (e.g. A, B, c, d)	

Note

1. This chapter describes the state of BNC tagging as of September 1993.

14 Publishing a spoken and written corpus on CD-ROM: the HCRC Map Task experience*

HENRY S. THOMPSON, ANNE H. ANDERSON and MILES BADER

The HCRC Map Task Corpus comprises over 16 hours of spoken dialogue, recorded in acoustically controlled conditions, together with careful orthographic transcriptions. A digitally sampled form of the dialogues, the transcripts and a substantial amount of ancillary material has been published for distribution to the research and development communities on eight CD-ROMs. In this chapter we discuss the problems we faced, the lessons learned and the issues which remain for enterprises of this sort, in the hope that those who come after can benefit from our experience.

1   Introduction

The HCRC Map Task corpus has recently been collected and transcribed in Glasgow and Edinburgh, and has been published on CD-ROM. This effort was made possible by funding from the Economic and Social Research Council, with crucial assistance from the US Linguistic Data Consortium for the CD-ROM publication effort.

Using an elaboration of a design developed over a number of years, we recorded 128 two-person conversations (each talker in four conversations), employing 64 talkers (32 male, 32 female). High quality recordings were made using Shure SM10A close-talking microphones in a recording booth, one talker per channel on stereo DAT (Sony DTC1000ES). Each participant has a schematic map in front of them, not visible to the other. Each map is comprised of an outline and roughly a dozen labelled features (e.g. 'white cottage', 'Green Bay', 'oak forest'). Most features are common to the two maps, but not all. One map has a route drawn in, the other does not. The task is for the participant without the route to draw one on the basis of discussion with the participant with the route. Figure 14.1 shows a sample map.

* HCRC is supported by the Economic and Social Research Council

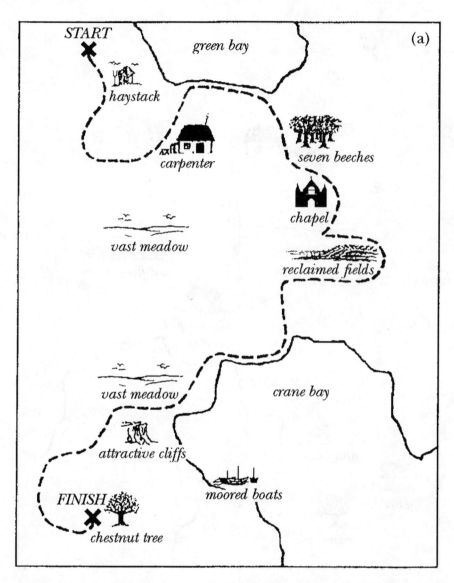

Figure 14.1a Samples of maps used in the Map Task: Instruction Giver's map

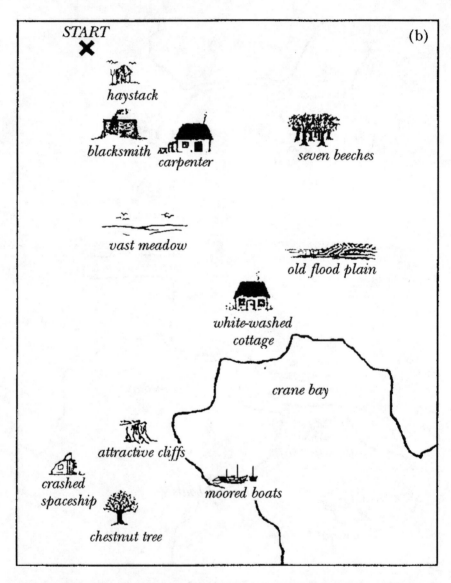

Figure 14.1b Samples of maps used in the Map Task: Instruction Follower's map

The experimental design is quite detailed and complex, allowing a number of different phonemic, syntactico-semantic and pragmatic contrasts to be explored in a controlled way. In particular, maps and feature names were designed to allow for controlled exploration of phonological reductions of various kinds in a number of different referential contexts, and to provide, via varying patterns of matches and mis-matches between the two maps, a range of different stimuli for referent negotiation. Also the conditions of the conversations were carefully balanced: in half of them the talkers were strangers, in half friends; in half of them the talkers could see each other's faces, in half they could not.

Our research purposes in collecting such a corpus were varied and quite wide ranging. We were interested in exploring issues in speech production/perception such as how the clarity with which words were spoken was influenced by dialogue context, the role of phonological reductions in such differences, and how intonational 'tunes' were used to signal different pragmatic functions. We were also interested in investigating aspects of the syntactic structure of dialogues as well as examining how the different strategies speakers adopt influence their chances of achieving successful communication. We therefore needed a large number of comparable unscripted dialogues where the communicative goals of the speakers were known to the researchers, and where the quality of the recordings was adequate for detailed acoustic analysis.

Sixty-four undergraduates at the University of Glasgow (32 male 32 female) were recorded in the corpus. Subjects' ages ranged from 17 to 30 with a mean of 20 years. Sixty-one of the 64 subjects were Scottish, 56 of them from within a 30-mile radius of Glasgow.

Subjects accommodated easily to the task and experimental setting, and produced evidently unselfconscious and fluent speech. The syntax is largely clausal rather than sentential; showing good turn-taking, with relatively little overlap/interruption. The total corpus runs about 18 hours of speech, yielding ~150,000 word tokens drawn from ~2,000 word form types. Word lists containing all the feature names were also elicited from all speakers, along with a number of 'dialect diagnosis' utterances.

The design and collection of the corpus are addressed in detail in Anderson et al. 1991. Here we will focus on issues which arose from the decision to make the corpus public, and to do so using the CD-ROM medium. It must be said that we seriously underestimated the scale of the task, which required on the order of one and a half person-years' effort over a 16-month period.

Why have we gone to this trouble, instead of simply making the transcriptions available via anonymous FTP and copying the DATs for the few who would want them? Basically because we are convinced that when a particular body of high-quality data is widely available, a community of effort naturally arises, from which the scientific benefit is enormous, to us and to the research community as a whole.

We think the time is right for a revolution in the way linguistics research above the level of phonetics is done, the same way phonetics has been revolutionized, by shifting from an idealization-orientated stance to a data-orientated stance. Doing this requires large amounts of real language, both written (already increasingly well provided for by, for example, the ACL Data Collection Initiative and European Corpus Initiative and the Linguistic Data Consortium) *and spoken*. We believe that spoken language is interestingly different from written language, and that the best way of fostering its investigation is by making large amounts of it available in as accessible a form as possible. Accordingly we see the Map Task Corpus as our contribution to what we hope will be a rapidly expanding provision of similar material.

Of particular relevance to this volume, is the fact that a systematically annotated corpus which has its corresponding acoustic material readily accessible will allow users to finesse many of the controversies about the appropriate formats for presenting transcriptions, transcription conventions, coding and so on. Fairly simple computations will allow users to transform to their own preferred formats, any of the annotations or display formats which they find cumbersome or inappropriate. More importantly ready access to the original acoustic signal allows users to customize and code the transcriptions for any linguistic features of interest at the grain of detail suitable for their own research purposes. The details of the transcription scheme which are provided in the CD documentation will allow researchers to search rapidly for contexts such as overlapping speech, filled pauses, disfluencies which they may wish to analyse in more detail than is provided in an orthographic transcription.

Our aim in this chapter is to describe the stages involved in the production of the HCRC Map Task CD-ROMs. We hope that other corpus researchers who wish to make their data available in this format will benefit from our experiences and so accomplish their task more efficiently. We trust that the technical detail that this description involves will not bore the general reader nor dissuade others from embarking on such a project. These details should allow other researchers to estimate the time and resources which they will require, more accurately than we were able to do in 1990 when we began.

2 The sampled speech

2.1 Digital capture

Although we originally recorded on Digital Audio Tape (DAT), moving the resulting vast amount of data (around 15 Gigabytes spread out over 24 DATs) onto computer-accessible media and managing it thereafter was a considerable chore. We might have undertaken this work eventually anyway, but using the original DATs and/or cassette copies for transcription and coding of transcripts was reasonably satisfactory. This was probably the area where we most seriously underestimated the work and time involved.

As we only wanted to transfer a direct sample-for-sample image from DAT to a format readable by a typical computer, the problem at first seemed relatively easy. In fact many technical and resource problems had to be overcome.

There exist interfaces which allow the digital output of (audio from) a DAT player to be directly accessed as a tape device by a host computer, but the one we knew of was relatively expensive. We eventually bought a much less expensive digital audio interface board intended to be used with a DSP card in a PC. This turned out to be a real problem; even though PC hardware is plentiful and cheap, there is no automatic way of resolving the various resource conflicts that arise from using several different non-standard pieces of hardware. As we needed a SCSI disk driver (see later) and a Ethernet interface in addition to the DSP board and DAT interface, getting the system to boot, much less work, was a long and frustrating process of trial and error.

The board we bought came with some sample software to do a DAT-to-disk transfer; although it worked relatively painlessly, the fact that it was on a PC, which does not have a standard development environment, meant that we couldn't easily modify it, which caused some inefficiencies.

We originally planned to use a PC version of NFS to mount a large disk on a UNIX™ system, from which we could easily write a tape, but NFS turns out to be so slow in writing (and a large part of this seemed to be the protocol itself, not just the fact that we were running it on a PC), that it could not keep up with even the relatively slow pace of the 48KHz audio. We had to move the disk onto the PC itself, capture the DAT image onto the disk and then write the tape over the network using FTP (into a FIFO which was being read by a program doing large page-aligned transfers to the tape).

If we had simply bought the expensive interface (which we subsequently used, and which proved to be almost totally trouble-free) and had it hooked up to a UNIX™ machine (on which it is both easy to write new code and hook together existing code), we could have streamlined the process considerably, and simply transferred the data directly from DAT to tape, probably in much less time.

2.2   Rate conversion and compression (NOT)

The original data was sampled by the DAT recorder at 48KHz, much higher than required for speech research. We eventually settled on 20KHz for distribution, following the *de facto* European standard established by the SAM ESPRIT project. This then required careful rate conversion and filtering. Despite the resulting 60% reduction in size, the sampled audio still takes up over 95% of the CD-ROMS, but in the absence of a standard for compression, we decided *not* to compress the audio. Compression would also have interfered with the simplicity of our intended usage, and compromised the wide distribution we envisage, in that it would have limited the on-line use of the CD-ROMs to systems fast enough to run the decompression in real-time.

To do the rate conversion, we were advised that a simple FIR filter between interpolation (upsampling, by inserting zeros) and decimation (downsampling, by dropping samples) steps was an accepted standard for our application. Technical problems with the available optimized rate converters forced us to write our own. A copy of this converter is included in the distribution.

Although the conversion algorithm is quite simple, and the filter design software well-known and available, finding usable implementations, and, in particular, convincing ourselves of the validity of the result, was much harder than we had anticipated.

2.3   'Filleting' and timestamping

The raw data was recorded on 24 DATs, and the raw 48KHz DAT images occupied 15×10^9 bytes, representing 22 hours of running time for 16-bit stereo. Of this, slightly less than 20 hours actually ended up on the CDs, 15 hours of stereo conversations and five hours of wordlists and diagnostics.

We created a set of 8KHz DAT mono images for use in extracting the relevant sub-parts, using the built-in 8-bit µ-law digital audio output facility available on Sun SPARC-stations.

```
<text id=q3ec1>
<!--      Conversation: Quad 3, eye contact, conversation 1, -->
<!--                unfamiliar talkers, duration 10606393 -->
<!--        Giver: q3eta1 -->
<!--                Philip, age 18, birth.place Glasgow, male -->
<!--        Follower: q3etb1 -->
<!--                Ross, age 20, birth.place Glasgow, male -->
<!--        Map: m14, +giver contrast, +follower match, reduction type 3 -->
<!-- Copyright 1992, Human Communication Research Centre -->
<u who=G n=1>
<sfo samp=350>
The route . . . starting at the beginning, head due south.
You'll see a diamond mine, on your map
<u who=F n=2>
<sfo samp=160913>
{gglMmhmm}.
<u who=G n=3>
<sfo samp=178013>
<bo id=o17a>
Avoid the diamond mine
<u who=F n=4>
<sfo samp=242788>
Due south?
<u who=G n=5>
going due south
<u who=F n=6>
To the left of the diamond mine?
<u who=G n=7>
followed by east.
<eo id=o17a>
<u who=F n=8>
<sfo samp=314473>
To the west?
```

Figure 14.2a   Extract 1 from a Map Task Dialogue Transcript

Once the sampled speech was available on-line as a set of DAT images, we built a graphical interface to a 'digital tape recorder' which enabled us to easily construct a map of each image, separating out the interesting bits from the rest, associating each interesting region with the identity of the transcript, wordlist or diagnostic passage involved and its position in the experimental design (which *inter alia* identified the talker(s) involved).

In the process we also timestamped the transcripts every few seconds with pointers into the sampled audio, using a semi-automated procedure built around a simple parameterized silence detector. This enabled the postgraduate students we employed for the purpose to listen to each conversation while editing the transcript with a restricted interface which would play a short section of speech, up until the next 'silence', at which point if this was actually at a turn boundary they would indicate in the transcript using mouse or keyboard where the boundary was, and the timestamp would automatically be inserted and the speech up to the next 'silence' would be played. When non-boundary 'silences' were offered, a single keystroke would play the next segment without inserting a timestamp. Figure 14.2 shows a section of transcript with timestamps, which use the SGML tag sfo, for speech file offset.

```
text id=q4ec1>
<!— Conversation: Quad 4, eye contact, conversation 1, —>
<!—         unfamiliar talkers, duration 4249874 —>
<!—       Giver: q4eta1 —>
<!—         Sandra, age 19, birth.place Aberdeen, female —>
<!—       Follower: q4etb1 —>
<!—         Bryan, age 19, birth.place Glasgow, male —>
<!—       Map: m13, +giver contrast, +follower match, reduction type 2 —>
<!— Copyright 1992, Human Communication Research Centre —>
<u who=G n=1>
<sfo samp=1942>
Start at the extinct volcano,
<sfo samp=62694>
and go down round the tribal settlement.
<sfo samp=152564>
And then
<u who=F n=2>
Whereabouts is the tribal settlement?
<u who=G n=3>
It's at the bottom.
<sfo samp=212652>
It's to the left of the {able} extinct volcano.
<u who=F n=4>
<sfo samp=268104>
Right.
<sfo samp=304354>
How far?
<u who=G n=5>
<sfo samp=329327>
{fp|Ehm}, at the opposite side.
```

Figure 14.2b Extract 2 from a Map Task Dialogue Transcript

176   Applications and more specialized uses

This proved quite a congenial process for people to use, and took only around two or three times the running time of a conversation to carry out. Feedback was immediate enough from the process itself that the students had little difficulty adjusting the parameters of the silence detector (via the graphical interface) when persistent rate and/or volume changes made this necessary.

2.4   File formats

There are competing international 'standards' for the format of sampled audio. We compromised by providing raw files with no header at all, along with several alternative headers, for each sample file. The situation here is in a considerable state of flux, and this non-solution is unlikely to have pleased everyone, but as both the header formats we chose, the NIST SPHERE format and the SAM format, are structured ASCII text, they at least serve as easily interpreted definitions of what the sample files look like, even for those who cannot utilize them directly.

3   The transcriptions

The transcriptions are at the orthographic level, quite detailed, including filled pauses, false starts and repetitions, broken words, and so on. Considerable care has been taken to ensure consistency of notation, which is thoroughly documented. Figure 14.2 illustrates a number of aspects of the transcription (see section 3.2 below for a discussion of the use of SGML for markup). The transcript begins with information about where its conversation sits in the experimental design. The balance of the transcript is a sequence of turns, separated by blank lines. Each turn begins with a u tag identifying the talker (Giver or Follower and the turn number). This may be followed by an sfo tag connecting the transcript to the sampled audio (see section 2.3 above). Although the full complexity of overlapping speech has not been reflected in the transcriptions, regions where overlaps occur *are* clearly set off from the rest of the transcripts, using paired bo (beginning of overlap) and eo (end of overlap) tags (see Fig. 14.2a for an example).

3.1   Transcription conventions

In order for the transcripts to be useful, we needed to guarantee that they observed a range of invariants (use of punctuation, spelling, notation for non-words of various sorts, etc.). A lengthy process of proofreading and semi-automatic filtering was required. No matter how explicit the instructions given to transcribers are, the complexity of the data is almost certain to provide the opportunity for individual variation in their interpretation, and of course with the best will in the world some mistakes will also be made.

In the final version of the transcripts, we used a single, consistent annotation style which we called microtags, to identify everything other than ordinary words. Anything out of the ordinary was annotated with one of these, that is bracketed with curly braces and a two-letter code. There were a dozen or so types, some of which, ab for abandoned word and fp for filled pause, gg for grunt, as well as overlap marking and file header information, are shown in Fig. 14.2.

Without going into detail, here are some examples of normalization issues we confronted, drawn from the logs we kept of the normalization process:

1. Spacing and low-level punctuation (e.g. no line-final spaces, two spaces following sentence-final punctuation).
2. Hyphens. We kept hard hyphens only, with every case checked and standardized (e.g. transcribers had used both 'bypassing' and 'by-passing'; 'jutty-out' and 'jutty out'; 'right-angle' and 'right angle'). Note that in the last case, the choice of which is correct is context dependent – 'make a right angle' versus 'a right-angle turn'.
3. Use versus mention of the feature names written on the map, e.g. 'go towards the missionary camp' versus 'turn at the {le|m} in the word {cil|missionary}'.
4. Capitalization. Proper names, sentence start, interaction with microtags and false starts/corrections.
5. Name/noise ambiguity. Does 'ha ha' mean the talker laughed, or said 'ha ha [sic]'? A similar problem arises with quotation marks.
6. Phonetic distinctions without a difference. Does e.g. 'd'you' reliably indicate something different from 'do you'? What about 'gonna' and 'going to' or 'Yep' and 'Yeah'?
7. Elided initial syllables. We retained only 'til' for 'until' and 'cause' for 'because', using the ip microtag, but e.g. normalized 'bout' to 'about'.
8. Filled pauses and their relatives. We distinguished three categories, namely filled pauses, which almost always occur in mid-utterance, e.g. 'uh', 'erm'; grunts, which almost always stand as complete utterances or adjuncts, e.g. 'uh-huh', 'mmhmm', 'oops'; mixed cases, ambivalent between filled pauses and grunts, e.g. 'ah', 'um'. Note that what we have called grunts pattern pretty much like 'yes', 'no' or 'okay', but lack official status, as it were.
9. Phonetic spelling of various sorts. These were used for expressive pronunciation, e.g. 'rrrright', slips of the tongue, e.g. 'spaceslip' and miscellaneous noises, e.g. 'shh', 'bddllpp'.
10. Non-speech sounds. Laughter, snorts, sighs, throat-clearing, etc. are all separately marked as being to some extent out of the speech stream.
11. Unfilled pauses and disjuncture. Getting this exactly right would have taken much more transcriber time than we had available. Transcribers used '. . .' to indicate noticeable pauses and/or disjuncture, but probably not consistently.

For ordinary misspellings we used UNIX™ spell, which of course also threw up a range of typographical errors, dialect words, gaps in spell's wordlist, and so on. Documenting the latter, and providing a wordlist of additions needed to make spell happy, proved a good discipline, and useful for regression testing. Given that there were only a bit more than 2000 word form types, near the end of the normalization process we actually looked at the whole list, and spotted a few things spell had missed.

Of course for invisible misspellings, such as 'it's' for 'its' and 'you're' for 'your', spell is no use. We found that constructing tables of preceding and/or following bigram types was very helpful in spotting at least some of these errors. For example, 'you're left/right' is probably (although not always!) an error, as is 'its above [or any other preposition]'. 'They're/their/there' proved harder to diagnose in this manner.

Lest some of the above examples be taken as excuses for sloppy practice, it should be emphasized that the transcriptions were meant to serve at least two distinct purposes. On the one hand, they should allow a relatively superficial reading to give a rough impression of what was said, and of *how* it was said. It is for this goal that '...' and indeed the use of standard orthographic punctuation of the material into clauses and sentences is included. On the other hand, the transcripts are an indication of the words uttered and an index into the sampled audio. For these purposes, and for any serious linguistic investigation, all punctuation and case-shifting in the transcripts should be removed or ignored, and even lexical identity taken with a grain of salt. The easy accessibility of the corresponding acoustic signal allows the user to overcome such unavoidable limitations of a written transcription of an extract of spoken language.

3.2   Use of Text Encoding Initiative recommendations

We used pre-publication versions of the Text Encoding Initiative (TEI) recommendations for SGML mark-up of corpora and spoken transcriptions. Although valuable for enforcing discipline at various levels, we often had to modify the TEI suggestions in detail. In fact as far as the transcripts themselves, we ended up using very few of the tags suggested for the transcription of spoken material in fascicle 34 of the 2nd draft standards. The main reason for this is that although by and large we agree with the taxonomy of *what* needs to be tagged (e.g. filled pauses, non-speech vocalisations, non-talker-produced noises, editorial comments), we disagree on *how* they should be tagged.

In many cases, fascicle 34 provides tags for things that were said in which what was said is the value of an attribute in an empty tag, for example filled pauses. In principle we prefer an approach which leaves such things as text, but with their special status indicated with surrounding tags. In practice, we also wanted something which was much lighter weight visually, as we anticipate that most users of our materials will *not* be using them via SGML-based tools.

For this reason we have also made it particularly easy to extract the raw transcription from the mark-up: all lines in the transcript files either begin with the character '<', in which case they contain only mark-up, or else, if they begin with any other character, they are transcription lines containing nothing but transcribed speech.

We strongly support the efforts of the TEI to promulgate a set of guide-lines for the interchange of electronic texts, and accept that despite its failings SGML is the best available vehicle for this effort. Time will tell whether the detailed proposals for specific text types, such as that contained in fascicle 34, will be accepted as *de facto* standards, or will simply stand as one example of possible practice.

4 The CDs themselves

4.1 Formats: ISO-9660

Producing CD-ROMs which will be readable *and* useful on a range of systems (at least UNIX™, PC and Macintosh™) causes a number of difficulties. The ISO-9660 standard provides a lowest common denominator approach, which at a minimum guarantees that data will be available and directory hierarchy preserved on all three systems. Since PCs impose the most serious restrictions (e.g. eight-character names, three-character extensions, etc.) this means observing those restrictions across the board.

4.2 Structuring across and within disks

Laying out the audio, transcriptions and other material across the eight disks required to hold them all so as to maximize utility when not all can be mounted simultaneously was extremely difficult.

Since the sampled speech takes up 95 per cent of the space on the CD-ROMs, the layout of the corpus was essentially laying out the speech and verifying that the rest fits in the resulting cracks. The design naturally divides the corpus into sixteen 'quads' (a quad being the set of eight conversations produced by a group of four talkers), and coincidentally, the sampled speech at 20KHz is slightly less than eight CD-ROMs worth, so two quads per CD was the obvious layout.

The material is divided into a per-quad-pair portion, which is different on each CD, and contains speech files, transcripts, and maps for that quad-pair, and a common portion which is duplicated on every CD. There is a unique sub-directory for each quad, to maintain the invariant that different contents are under different pathnames, so the CDs are simply slices of one giant directory tree. Thus if you just happen to have eight CD-ROM drives and a driver that can overlay the contents, you can access the whole corpus at once without problems. A file containing a mapping from each filename to the CD-ROM(s) on which it occurs is also provided.

4.3 Fiddly details: pre-mastering, labels and inserts

Choice of firm to do the pressing has a big impact on cost. Label artwork has to be produced, decisions have to be made on whether to use a paper insert, and on how to package the set. These are tedious but important details.

We did do two test-pressings, since the pre-mastering was being done for us by the LDC at the University of Pennsylvania, but it is not clear this was really necessary, since the pre-mastering process involves the creation of a complete CD image, which can be mounted as a UNIX™ file system and tested as such.

Not surprisingly, the amount of work required to produce a high quality and useful product was much greater than we had expected, but we hope others will be able to do better for having observed our efforts.

Part C

Samples and systems of transcription

Introduction

Part C will be concerned with the practical description of existing corpora. Each chapter aims to describe a particular corpus project, including its rationale, its special features, the principles of transcription and the system of mark-up employed. This final part of the book will therefore, we hope, be a valuable reference source, enabling readers to compare the various systems and solutions adopted.

It must be acknowledged that Part B and Part C are not so distinct as they were in our minds when we planned the book. On the one hand, relatively detailed descriptions of corpora can be found in some contributions to Part B – for example, that of the Edinburgh Map Task Corpus in Chapter 14 (Thompson et al.). These have not been repeated in Part C. On the other hand, some of the contributions to this part are far from being purely descriptive: the rationale for the corpus, and the principles underlying the format adopted, may be the major focus of the chapter. An example is in Knowles's Chapter 17, which justifies the reasons for adopting, as a plan for a spoken corpus, a relational database. Ultimately, it is a matter of degree of emphasis whether explanation (as in Part B), or description (as in Part C) is uppermost. We should also note that this part cannot be seen as a survey of all the computerized spoken English corpora in existence. There are some, such as the Corpus of Spoken American English (CSAE) and the Child Language Data Exchange System (CHILDES) database of children's language, which are not included here, although they are referred to elsewhere in the book.[1] Such is the variety of corpora already becoming available, that we cannot claim to present more than a selection of corpora in this part. However, there is no doubt that the corpora dealt with here are important enough and varied enough to provide a good representation of the types of transcription and mark-up currently employed.

The order in which the chapters are placed owes a lot to chronology: the earliest of the corpora to be made available (the SEU, Survey of English Usage and the LLC, London–Lund Corpus) come first, and the latest to begin, the COLT corpus, comes last. But there is a great deal of chronological overlap between the various projects, and so a strict historical order of presentation cannot be maintained. There is a thematic, rather than temporal, link between some of the chapters.

Since computer corpora of spoken discourse developed out of transcriptions on paper, a fitting starting point is provided by Susan Peppé's contribution (Chapter 15): it compares the original transcription scheme of the SEU, begun by Randolph Quirk in 1959, with the simplified version of that scheme which was adopted for the first extensive and widely available computer corpus of spoken English, the LLC developed by Jan Svartvik and his team at Lund (begun in 1975). The details of the transcription scheme are interesting enough, since it is richer, even in the stripped-down version for computer, than any transcription employed in any other sizeable English corpus since that time. However, another major interest of this chapter lies in the changes and simplifications that had to be made, at that time, in order to represent the transcribed data on computer, and the advantages which accrued from this conversion. Because of its general availability through the International Computer Archive of Modern English (ICAME), the Oxford Text Archive, and on CD-ROM (Compact disk–read only memory),[2] the LLC has been the spoken corpus most widely used for linguistic research,[3] but it also suffers from a considerable drawback: the original sound recording has not been released.[4]

Another contribution which occurs early in the sequence of chapters is that of Jonathan Payne (Chapter 16), presenting the transcription and mark-up scheme of the Collins/Birmingham University International Learners' Dictionary (COBUILD) spoken corpus material (Birmingham). John Sinclair, in Chapter 7, comments that he and his colleagues were early, if not earliest, in the game of collecting spoken texts on computer. Also, the COBUILD project at Birmingham began the collecting of spoken materials early in the 1980s, and has now built up a long experience in transcription. However, there is a contrast with the preceding case of the SEU and LLC corpora: the aim has been to transcribe by an adaptation of orthographic conventions. By this means, a large quantity of data can be transcribed within a relatively short time, as is required for the primarily lexicographical function of the COBUILD project. Up to now, dictionaries (even modern ones) have been dominated by the written word, and this trend is now being corrected, to an increasing extent, through the sheer quantity of spoken data that is now being collected and transcribed.

In Chapter 17, Gerry Knowles presents the Machine Readable Spoken English Corpus (MARSEC) project (Lancaster and Leeds), by which the original IBM/Lancaster Spoken English Corpus, a corpus of formal speech compiled in 1984–7 (Knowles and Alderson 1994), has been converted into a relational database. The argument here is that it is misleading to think of a transcribed discourse as a linear sequence of written symbols, on the superficial analogy with a written text. Rather, the trancription and annotation of a spoken corpus form a multi-levelled structure, and hence are more suitably stored and searched as a database rather than as one or more text-files. The MARSEC database, now on CD-ROM, provides, in addition the levels of transcription and annotation available for the SEC, phonetic transcription, digitized sound, and alignment between the different levels, so that they can be investigated in parallel.

Another corpus initiative of growing significance is that of the International Corpus of English (ICE), coordinated by Sidney Greenbaum, and represented in this book by Gerald Nelson's Chapter 18. The goal of the ICE project is to develop a whole set of comparable corpora of different national varieties of English – including corpora from countries where English is a second or foreign language (e.g. India, Nigeria, Singapore), as well as countries where English is primarily a native language (e.g. Australia, the Caribbean, the USA). The British corpus, including half a million words of spoken English, is already complete and grammatically tagged, and this chapter presents the scheme of transcription and mark-up employed for its spoken half.

In Chapter 19, Steve Crowdy reports on the collection and transcription of approximately 10 million words of speech, as part of the 100-million-word British National Corpus, reaching completion in the spring of 1994. As with the COBUILD corpus, the requirement here of collecting, transcribing, and marking up millions of words within little more than three years has meant the adoption of relatively simple, orthography-based transcription practices. The collection and transcription have been undertaken by Longman, who, as publishers, share with COBUILD the goal of using spoken corpora as an input to better dictionaries. But the whole British National Corpus (BNC) corpus is marked up in conformity with the Text Encoding Initiative (TEI) (see Burnard Chapter 5 and Johansson Chapter 6), and this is a first example of a large spoken corpus developed in accordance with these relatively exacting encoding standards.

In the final chapter, Chapter 20, Vibecke Haslerud and Anna-Brita Stenström report on a corpus which is being incorporated in the BNC, and which supplements the above corpus in the age groups 13–17. The COLT corpus, compiled at the University of Bergen, Norway, employs the same basic methods of collection, transcription and mark-up, as have been used for the rest of the spoken data of the BNC.

Developments in corpus compilation are taking place so quickly that it is difficult to take stock of what is happening at a given time, or to predict what will be the state of play in one, two, or three years' time. In this shifting situation, considerable comfort can be gained from the experience of the past 20 or 30 years: corpora, although they begin to date almost before they are completed, become obsolete slowly, and perhaps never. Hence there is a value in making a snap-shot record, as has been done here, of current practices in spoken corpus development. These practices will almost certainly lead to greater and more collaborative achievements in the future, and the existing corpora shown here may well undergo future transformations (as the SEC has already been transformed into the MARSEC database). But it is almost certain that the present resources will remain valuable and widely used. Corpora do not necessarily depreciate rapidly, as cars tend to do in our rust-inducing climate; they may, like musical instruments, be valued records of their time, and find new uses as time passes.

Notes

1. See the Subject Index for references. In fact, electronic collections of American English spoken discourse have been slow to develop, and are poorly represented in this volume. Another such collection is Switchboard, announced as a 'large corpus of conversational speech by many talkers over long distance telephone lines ... collected by Texas Instruments and produced on CD-ROMs' (*Linguistic Data Consortium*, Newsletter, 1.2, February 1993). The Linguistic Data Consortium, based at the University of Pennsylvania, makes available a wide variety of electronic language data. The LDC's E-mail address is: ldc@unagi.cis.upenn.edu
2. The CD-ROM, containing a number of different corpora of written English, as well as the LLC, is available from the Norwegian Computing Centre for the Humanities, N-5007, Bergen-University, Norway. E-mail: icame@hd.uib.no
3. See the extensive listing of publications making use of the LLC, in Altenberg's bibliography (1991).
4. But it is possible to consult the original sound recordings by special arrangement with the SEU, University College London.

15 The Survey of English Usage and the London–Lund Corpus: computerising manual prosodic transcription

SUE PEPPÉ

1 The SEU

The pioneering aspect of the Survey of English Usage corpus (SEU) was the inclusion of informal conversational material: with the advent of the tape–recorder it had become possible to record and thus to study comprehensively 'the most natural form of language and the one that is most overwhelmingly dominant for any individual in whatever walk of life' (Svartvik and Quirk 1980: 9) as had not been the case for earlier grammarians such as Poutsma, Kruisinga and Jespersen. The SEU was set up to collect a million words of English as used by adult educated native speakers of British English in as complete a variety of registers as could be conceived when the project was begun at the University of Durham in 1959: material includes love letters and scientific lectures, sermons and coffee-break chat. The SEU moved to University College London in 1960, and the collection of data was finally completed nearly 30 years later. During that time it provided a fund of authentic language-data from which examples could be drawn to support language-theories: much of the research subsequently based on it[1] can truly be said to have been data-driven.

2 The original transcription

Recording is an advantage in obtaining authentic data, but the practice of studying the language requires (as yet, given current technology) that the material should be retrievable in small sections in a visual (printable) form: hence the need for transcription. This leads to choices about departing from the conventionally-punctuated format for conversational material, and to the problem that inevitably arises in translating material from one medium to another: that some form of selectivity and interpretation is bound to be involved. The 'total accountability' principle of corpus-based study, requiring the material to be subjected to total description, was a fundamental tenet for the SEU. This led to the development of an analysis sensitive to a wide range of the prosodic and paralinguistic

Samples and systems of transcription

features to be heard in the recordings: the basic principles informing the design of this analysis can be found in *Prosodic Systems and Intonation in English* (Crystal 1969). All the material was transcribed by phoneticians working in pairs: the work of one was comprehensively checked by another. The SEU takes the form of texts, each of 5000 words, in booklets and on slips: each slip contains an example of a syntactic structure taken from a live language-situation and reproduced with its surrounding context. These are housed at University College London, under the auspices of the SEU's successor, the International Corpus of English (ICE).

3   The LLC

In 1975 it was decided that in order to make the SEU corpus accessible to interested scholars in any part of the world, a machine-readable as well as printed form of the SEU should be made available by the Survey of Spoken English at Lund University: the result became known as the London–Lund Corpus (LLC). The computerization of corpora is a bigger innovative step than tape-recording was, and the possibilities offered by word-processing packages, still being developed, are increasingly relevant to transcription. In 1975 it was necessary to simplify and reduce the transcription for ease of computerization: in the intervening 20 years this need has decreased so much that it seems likely that future considerations will be concerned less with reduction than with augmentation. For this reason it is difficult to project transcription policies with regard to computerization. In the meantime, the practice of transcription makes uneasy compromises between totality and selectivity, between phonetics and phonology, between opacity and readability, and between saving time and wasting it (no longer a trivial consideration). In Lund in 1975, as at the ICE in London in 1994, it was recognized that in practice scholars consulting the transcribed corpus might need access to the original tapes or other sources from which the transcriptions were made. This suggests that the role of transcription in language study is perhaps best seen as a staging-post: a convenient way of gaining an impression (if not always an accurate one) of the material.

4   Comparison of the manual (SEU) and computerized (LLC) transcriptions

Transcription symbols as they appear in the SEU are shown in the margin; where different, LLC variations are shown in braces: { }; where a feature is omitted, {0} shows there is nothing in LLC for this feature. Examples are taken from both corpora. For students unfamiliar with it, the description is detailed enough to serve as an adequate guide for deciphering all aspects of the transcription; by no means all of these aspects are relevant to the larger questions of the role of transcription.

4.1 Physical format

The SEU typewritten slips (size A6) each contain a dozen lines of text with a running overlap of two lines top and bottom to ensure adequate contextualization for any material to be examined: an example appears in Fig. 15.1. The LLC is available either in printed form (as shown in Fig. 15.2) or in electronic form.

Texts in both SEU and LLC have a *main body* and a *margin*. The margins show speaker identification and, in the SEU, abbreviations for features covering several syllables in the text: these are described below in section 4.3 on *marginal glosses*. The main body of the text carries the dialogue with prosodic analysis, a description of which follows, with the symbols used to indicate features on the left.

		S.1.12.8
	* D	⁺ə f̲/ Ī ə / Ī f̲/ # ⁺.
	. * B	you / âpplied to go dídn't *you#m̲#*
	D	*1̲ I* / found ;N̲ òut# - - - p̲ that / ðL: 1̲# .
?non-nuc		!Royal N̲?Àir Force# . m̲/ did 1̲ re!search on
m̲:nar		plàstics#m̲# in [?òne ?place]1̲# and ŏne
?xN̲y̌		place ˙ only# . and / that was ma!terials
		de'partment 'R A ;È#p̲# - - - f̲/non
		me,tàllic#f̲# . in / L̲bràckets# . and I / wrote
		'up to the !chief gáffer# – 1̲/ and I °says
?non-nuc		I !want to ?Ncŏm̄e#1̲# – aa m̲ to do m̲#aa#
m̲:lax		re/seărch on 'plastics# – / ānd# . / this is
q̲:lau	*	the plàce# . q̲/ and he said W̲ éh# q̲' / HW ís
q̲':fal		it#q̲'#q̲# . * – * ¯ and m̲/he 'didn't knŏw#m̲#
m̲:scan,	*	
wide		

Figure 15.1

D	
B	⁷⁰ you ‖A͡PPLIED to go DIDN'T↗ ☆ you ■ ☆
D	⁷¹ ☆ I ☆ ‖found OUT ■ - - - ⁷² that ‖[ði:] · ΔRoyal AI̯R Force ■ · ⁷³ ‖did reΔsearch on PLA̯STICS ■ ⁷⁴ in ‖{ONE place} and ONE place ▷only ■ · ⁷⁵ and ‖that was maΔterials de'partment 'RAE ■ - - - ⁷⁶ ‖NON-METALLIC ■ . ⁷⁷ in ‖BRA̯CKETS ■ · ⁷⁸ and I ‖wrote 'up to the Δchief GAFFER ■ – ⁷⁹ ‖and I ▷says I Δwant to COME ■ – ⁸⁰ to do RE‖SEARCH on 'plastics ■ – ⁸¹ ‖AND ■ · ⁸² ‖this is the PLA̯CE ■ · ⁸³ ‖and he said EH ■ ⁸⁴ ‖Is it ■ · ⁸⁵ ☆ – ☆ and ‖he 'didn't KNO̯W■ – –

Figure 15.2

190   *Samples and systems of transcription*

4.2   Main body

4.2.1   Scripts

The words of the text are written orthographically, in lower case; {LLC small capitals for some words, see below at Nuclear Tones}. No rules of conventional punctuation apply. There are no abbreviations for the reductions and slurrings of normal speech apart from the conventional ones (*n't*, etc.). Where words are left unfinished the fragment is transcribed phonemically, within square brackets. Occasionally a word is spelled phonemically, when its pronunciation is thought to be significantly irregular; this applies particularly to the 'strong' forms of *the* and *a* when they occur before consonants instead of before vowels: they then appear as ði and eɪ (inside square brackets in LLC but not in SEU). If they are also lengthened they have length-marks as follows:

>ði˙ and eɪ˙ {[ði˙]} and {[eɪ˙]} for slight lengthening, and
>ði : and eɪ: {[ði:]} and {[eɪ:]} for decided lengthening.

Other occurrences of phonemic script are:

>ʔ denoting a glottal stop
>ʔ̱ denoting vocal creak
>{LLC: both appear as ʔ}

4.2.2   Transcriber doubt

Where there was some doubt about what words were said, they appear in double round brackets; where the words were not at all recoverable, the estimated number of syllables uttered appears also in double round brackets, for example:

>((are 2sylls people actually)).

(See also section 4.4.)

4.2.3   Sound-intrusions

In single round brackets are noted events (such as laughing) which are non-linguistic or paralinguistic and intrude into the conversation but are relevant for communication. The length of time they take is noted as for silent pauses (see 4.2.4), for example:

>(- - laughs)

For paralinguistic features such as voice quality, see section 4.3.

4.2.4   Pauses

Where there are no words or sound-intrusions, there are gaps or pauses marked thus:

.	the briefest possible silence
-	silence of one 'beat'
-.	silence a little longer than one beat
--	silence for two beats
--.	silence for three beats or a little less
---	silence for upwards of three beats

A 'beat' is a measure of the current speaker's stress-timing, at the current speech-tempo.

These pauses may be 'voiced' or 'filled' with an *er*-sound, which appears as ə {[ə]} with length-marks as for ði and e1. It is worth noting the difference between *m* {LLC: [m]}, a word, usually carrying a tone and having the meaning 'yes' or 'what' depending on the direction of the pitch-movement, and *əm* {LLC: [əm]}, a 'voiced pause' ending in /m/.

4.2.5 Overlapping talk

This is denoted by a system of asterisks and plus signs: anything between single asterisks (be it talk or sound-intrusions) occurs simultaneously with other material between single asterisks; the same applies to material between double asterisks and plus signs, thus:

```
            I ‖really 'could have 'gone on the △whole ✭△TIME■ 105 and it
            ‖would have △been all △RIGHT■ 106 ‖YOU know■✭
    B       107 ✭(laughs – – )✭
    a       108 (laughs · )
    A       109 ‖then he ‖then ✭✭he 'started ✭✭
    a       110 ✭✭verbal ✭✭diarrhoea in +fact . (laughs – – )+
    A       111 +‖YEAH■ 112 ‖verbal DIARRHOEA■+ well ‖no it △WASN'T
            REALLY■
```
[S.2.9]

(The text numbers follow the reference system for both the SEU and the LLC; the letter S indicating that the text is spoken (i.e. spontaneous conversational) material, not written-to-be-spoken.)

4.2.6 Syllabification

Most of the prosodic indications are inserted 'before syllables'. The division of words into syllables is at morphological junctures, for example 'un/stressed', but if necessary this defers to a requirement to start a syllable with a consonant , for example 'su/bordinate'; note also 'wi/thout'.

4.2.7 Tone units

The dialogue is all divided into *tone units*, which are bounded by:

192   Samples and systems of transcription

/		the *onset*, placed immediately before the first stressed syllable
{‖}		of a tone unit, (for 'stressed' see *Stresses*, section 4.2.9) and
#		the *close*, placed after the end of the last syllable of a tone
{■}		unit.

Between these markers there may be some unstressed syllables which syntactically belong to the start of an utterance and are therefore designated 'pre-onset syllables'.

For a full description of the notion of the tone unit see Crystal (1969). It also appears in the work of Halliday (1967), O'Connor and Arnold (1973) and others. Briefly, the tone unit is an intonational unit of speech, which sometimes coincides with a grammatical sentence but is usually much shorter: coterminous more often with phrases and clauses. Both the syntax of an utterance and its phonetic features combine to give the sense of a complete tone unit. Where the syntax suggests a completeness but the phonetic markers of completeness are absent, no intonational boundaries are assigned. Where the transcriber hears the phonetic indications of completeness but the syntax is incomplete, the intonation-marks show subordinate tone units (see Subordination, section 4.2.10). Where the syntax is broken off and the intonation is also incomplete, this is deemed to be an 'incomplete tone unit' ('itu' is marked in the margin in cases where the feature is not necessarily clear). In the LLC, all tone units, whether complete or not, are numbered in superscript. Sources of examples within the corpus are referred to by text-number (e.g. S.2.10) and by slip number for the SEU, by TU (tone unit) number for the LLC.

Onsets may be marked:

H̲	high or
{0}	
L̲	low, according to whether they are relatively high or low for that speaker.
{0}	

4.2.8   Nuclear tones

The presence of a *nuclear tone* is the sine qua non of a tone unit: this is the criterial phonetic indication of completeness, though it may occur well before the end of the tone unit. A tone is an occurrence of pitch-movement on the word which is regarded as the nucleus of the phrase. (Although level pitch cannot be described as pitch movement it is regarded as a nuclear tone when prolonged and on the most prominent syllable.) The tone usually combines with other features of accent such as a pitch-jump (most often upwards, but sometimes down) at the start of the targeted syllable, an increase or decrease in the duration of the syllable (according to the phonological length of its main vowel: increase in the case of long vowels, decrease in short) and sometimes increased loudness. The location of the tone and the direction of its pitch-movement are combined in one marker, an accent placed on the most prominent syllable. Five kinds of pitch-movement are identified in this system:

\	{↓}	falling
/	{↗}	rising
V	{∨}	fall-rise
ʌ	{∧}	rise-fall
−	{→}	level

They are placed over the vowel of the tonic syllable (where this consists of more than one vowel (e.g. 'meat', 'fear') over the first. Consistency on this point may vary for some words where this is counter-intuitive, e.g. 'guess'). In LLC the word containing the tonic syllable is in small capital letters.

Syntactically and semantically the nucleus often co-occurs with the focus of an utterance, and some conflation (or confusion) of systems in the transcription of this corpus means that the tone is always marked as occurring on the syllable that phonologically 'takes main stress', although its phonetic markers (pitch-movement, etc.) are often heard among the following syllables, known as 'the tail', as well or instead. A classic example of this is the oft-recurring

((/thánk)) you#

where the tone is located on *thank*, although the word may be inaudible, because it is the 'stressed' element of *thank you*; the pitch-direction of the tone is determined by the movement heard on *you*, the tail. For further elucidation of nuclear tones, see Crystal (1969).

Tones may be marked:

<u>W</u>	wide, or
{0}	
<u>N</u>	narrow, to show the amount of movement:
{0}	'wide' covers a big section of the speaker's pitch-range, 'narrow' a small section.

4.2.9 Stresses

Syllables which are designated onset-syllables and tonic syllables are deemed to be stressed; in addition, there is the marking of 'ordinary stress' which indicates a syllable which carries phonological or word accent. In this system, the marking of stressed syllables indicates both the location of stress and the pitch relative to other syllables in the tone unit (this is known as the 'booster system'):

'	ordinary stress: on (before) an accented syllable which is
{'}	slightly lower than the preceding syllable(s), accented or unaccented
·	level booster: on an accented syllable at the same pitch as the
{▷}	previous accented syllable
:	single booster: on an accented syllable higher than the previous
{△}	syllable

194   *Samples and systems of transcription*

!	high booster: on an accented syllable higher than the onset or
{△}	than the preceding boosted (! or : or ·) syllable

All boosters are relative to the pitch of adjacent syllables or stressed syllables within the tone unit, apart from the following:

!!	double-high booster: this marks a syllable that is specially high
{△}	for that speaker;
,	low booster and
{0}	
;	very low booster mark syllables that are specially low for that
{0}	speaker;
¯	marks an unstressed syllable that is noticeably high,
{0}	
_	marks an unstressed syllable that is noticeably low.
{0}	

There is one feature to mark extra loudness:

"	occurs before any accented syllable that is heard as especially
{■}	loud

and some features to indicate unusual length:

·	over a vowel or consonant means that it is 'clipped' (short).
{0}	With plosive consonants, this usually means they are exploded where they would otherwise be expected to be run into the next sound)
=	over a vowel or continuant means that it is 'drawled' (long)
{0}	
=	under a plosive consonant means that it is held longer than usual.
{0}	

4.2.10 *Subordination*

Square brackets, [ ], with roman script inside them mark a subordinate tone unit {{ }}. This covers the phenomenon of intonational 'afterthought', where the speaker sounds as though, while speaking, he has changed his mind as to which of two items is to carry the greater emphasis. Both items carry similar nuclear tones (fall-rises are deemed to be (wider) exponents of rise, and rise-falls (wider) exponents of fall); the fact that one has a wider tone indicates that the speaker has decided to place the main emphasis on this item. The one carrying the narrower tone is therefore subordinate and placed, with its most closely related syllables/ words, within square brackets:

/ this ˈ!nèar ˈside [of the /field#]#

(S.10.2 slip 12)

If it comes after, as in the example above, it is post-subordinate, and has its own onset and close within:

[of the /field#]

If it comes before the main tone it is pre-subordinate, with the onset or booster (whichever is relevant) outside:

/all of them _have a :multiple ![chòice] as !wèll#

(S.2.9 slip 6)

The tone in the subordinate tone unit usually starts lower than the main tone (this is the unmarked form, as in the two examples above):

H shows that it starts higher than the start of the main tone:
{0}

and I /knew I'd done ⁻you /knów# a '/[Hlòt better than] :average#

(S.2.9 slip 9)

E shows that it starts and ends higher (extra-high):
{0}

/ [Eòn] that Wfirst 'half 'John#

(S.10.2 slip 2)

L shows that it starts and ends lower than the whole of the main
{0} tone:

and I thought / òh# . I'll/rèad a'bout [/ Lthàt#]#

(S.2.9 slip 2)

4.2.11 Tempo and loudness

These are marked with abbreviations for Italian musical terms. There are no markings for tempo and loudness in LLC.

a	fast (allegro)
aa	very fast (allegrissimo)
ac	getting faster (accelerando)
l	slow (lento)
ll	very slow (lentissimo)
ral	getting slower (rallentando)
f	loud (forte)
ff	very loud (fortissimo)
cr	getting louder (crescendo)
p	soft (piano)
pp	very soft (pianissimo)
dim	getting softer (diminuendo)

Such passages start with the appropriate letter(s) underlined and end with that letter plus #, both underlined, for example:

{0} aaI /mean it !sounds as _thoughaa#.

196   *Samples and systems of transcription*

Occasionally one feature will develop into another, eg. 'soft' will become 'very soft': in this case, instead of finding

p . . . p#pp . . . pp#

you will see

p . . .=pp . . . pp#, or *dim* . . . =pp . . . pp#

Other markings which appear in the main text are glossed in the margin and are therefore described as:

4.3   Marginal Glosses

The marginal notes are reserved for features which span more than one syllable, as do the tempo and loudness markings, but which are in general more complicated to describe and judged to be more peripheral to the meaning than such features as tone-units, tones and pitch-patterns. These are 'modifying' features and 'qualitative' features; the place of their beginnings and endings in the main body are marked respectively:

m . . . m# and q . . . q#.

Where more than one of these occur simultaneously, they are marked m', m", q', q", and so on, which can produce sequences such as the following:

m m 'm" . . . m#m '#m"# . . . m 'q' . . . m '#q '#

4.3.1   Modifying features, or modes of speech

(Omitted from LLC.) These cover:

1.   Overall pitch-range:

        m: high   all syllables high for that speaker
        m: low   all syllables low for that speaker
        m: wide   big pitch-jumps between syllables, but not necessarily wide tones
        m: nar   narrow: very small pitch-jumps between syllables and all tones narrow
        m: asc   ascending: each succeeding tone unit higher than the last
        m: desc   descending: each succeeding tone unit lower than the last

2.   Other features of pitch-patterning which affect the relation of pitch between one syllable and another:

        m: mon   monotonous: each syllable is at the same pitch as the previous one
        m: scan   scandent: each succeeding syllable is higher than the last, ending in a falling tone.

3. Features which combine syllable-related pitch-patterning with a feature of rhythmicality:

    m: sp/   spiky rising: unstressed syllables noticeably higher than intervening rhythmically stressed ones

    m: sp\   spiky falling: unstressed syllables noticeably lower than intervening rhythmically stressed ones

    m: gl /   glissando rising: similar to spiky rising but where the unstressed syllables also rise in pitch relative to each other;

    m: gl \   glissando falling: similar to spiky falling but with the unstressed syllables also falling in pitch relative to each other. The glissando feature therefore occurs over stretches where there are several unstressed syllables between stresses, as opposed to the spiky feature where there is only one syllable between stresses.

4. Features relating to rhythmicality only:

    m: rh   rhythmic: stresses occur in beatable rhythm
    m: arh   arhythmic: the speech is particularly halting

5. Features relating to accentual patterns:

    m: st   staccato: every stressed syllable doubly stressed
    m: leg   legato: every syllable receiving more or less equal stress.

6. Features of tension of articulation, on a four-valued scale. Unusually tense speech manifests itself as clipped, well-defined vowels and consonants; lack of usual tension results in consonants elided or mumbled, vowels drawled. These features are not noted if they are part of the speaker's habitual speech: they are noted only where they occur unusually for that speaker, and are likely to indicate a particular mood or attitude.

    m: ten   tense speech
    m: pr   precise, i.e. very tense speech
    m: lax   lax, i.e. rather mumbled, slack articulation
    m: sl   slurred, i.e. very lax speech

4.3.2 Qualities of voice

(Omitted from LLC.) These concern phonatory and articulatory settings and vocal events:

    q: wh   whisper   q: gig   giggle (unvoiced laugh)
    q: br   breathy   q: lau   voiced laugh
    q: hsk   husky   q: sob   sobbing

198 *Samples and systems of transcription*

q: crk	creaky	q: cry	crying
q: fal	falsetto	q: yaw	yawning
q: res	resonant	q: sigh	sighing
q: trm	tremulous	q: spr	lips spread, as if smiling

4.3.3 Exceptional features

In the margin, α may refer either to a single α in the main text, or {0} to a stretch starting α and ending α#. It refers to some phenomenon such as foreign pronunciation or anacoluthon not covered by the m and q features, and will be briefly but (with luck) intelligibly glossed in the margin (e.g. α: anac). Notes of any complicated or systematic use of this mark are kept at the ICE at University College, London.

4.3.4 Speaker identification

A,B   denote different speakers. Some notes about the speakers (age,
{A,B} occupation, regional/educational background) were taken at the
      time of recording and are kept in London.
NSA   NS (non-surreptitious) before a capital initial shows that the
{a}   speaker knew the recording was happening, so is not
      transcribed.

Where capital initials are in round brackets {preceded by <} the speaker is continuing a tone unit begun in a previous utterance but interrupted by another speaker (with or without overlap):

A   ²⁸² ☆ ‖if it had ˈbeen the ☆ ˈ△SUN∎ ²⁸³I ‖mean the △sailors
     ˈwouldn't have △GOT it △{‖WOULD they∎}∎.
a   ²⁸⁴ but I thought ☆ ☆that [ə ə:] ☆ ☆
>A   ²⁸⁵ ☆☆cos there's ‖plenty of SUN∎ ☆ ☆
>a   ²⁸⁴ the vitamin that [ə:] – oranges supplied you with – was the
     vitamin that the sun supplied you with

                                                          (S.2.9 TU 282–4)

4.4 Queries

? Any part of the text, segmental or suprasegmental, may be marked {0} in the main body with a question mark: the question mark appears in the margin beside it with an alternative interpretation, thus:

      ?collect /Curry :fails to ?cónnect#

                                                          (S.10.2 slip 16)

The Survey of English Usage and the London–Lund Corpus

Perhaps the most common query on words concerned whether *the* or *a* was heard. Most of the queries concerned types of tone as in the example below:

{0}   ?\   /these wartime eN?mérgencies# are a/màzing Náctually#

(S.2.3 slip 53)

Queried features can be linked, as queries **x** and **y**: if an alternative interpretation is applied to feature **x**, feature **y** is interpreted differently, as in the following example:

?x ˋy   well /?that's ?nò ((good# /thăt one#))

(S.2.10 slip 170)

where if the preferred interpretation is that the fall occurs on *that's*, then *no* is merely stressed, not tonic.

Summary of the differences

Omissions from LLC include:

- all queried material
- all exceptional pronunciation (α-markings). This implies a loss of some attitude-indicators; however, the feature was not very common
- all tension features
- all loudness features
- all tempo features except for length-marks on filled pauses
- all features of rhythmical and emphatic speech apart from the double-stress
- all features concerned with overall pitch-range; this has implications not only for attitude but also for transcriber doubt, see section 4.2.2
- all voice quality features except for intrusions such as a laugh or a sigh, and instances of creak and glottal stops (which are indistinguishable in LLC).

What is retained in LLC therefore gives:

- words, phonemes where necessary, some doubt about words
- sound-intrusions
- turns and overlap
- tone units, main and subordinate (information groupings)
- pauses
- nuclearity/tonicity (focus)
- tone direction
- an impression of pitch-patterning, but see section 4.5.3.

200   Samples and systems of transcription

4.5   Implications of changes

The omission of queries means that virtually anything in the transcription might have an alternative reading. There are not many queries – elements of perhaps one word in 50 are in doubt – but this possibility should be taken into account when doing, for example, a feature count. Queries occurred in the SEU when the interpretation given in the margin was a strong contender and no other interpretation was likely. In this case the interpretation in the main body was not in double round brackets, because it was not a matter of doubt, but a question of one of two given alternatives. Since there are no queried features in LLC, no doubt at all is shown at this point. Queried pitch-patterns usually occurred where pitch-movement and range was very narrow: all indications of narrowness are, however, also omitted from LLC.

4.5.1   Length

The retention of the length marks in filled pauses implies an attention to length which is otherwise lacking, and similarly the instancing of creak and glottal stop suggests that some account is taken of voice quality, which is not the case.

4.5.2   Loudness

The retention of the double-stress-mark similarly implies (erroneously) that some systematic attention is paid to loudness in LLC, but this feature is more problematic. In the SEU, where a number of successive accented syllables were doubly stressed, such a stretch would have been marked m: st(accato) in the margin and the double-stress-marks would have been omitted from the main body of the text, on the principle of avoiding the inclusion of redundant information wherever possible. In the LLC those stress-marks would not be given since the **m: st** feature would have been removed. Isolated instances of double-stress-marks would remain in both the SEU and the LLC, however. This would suggest that instances of extra-heavy stress were noted consistently in LLC.

4.5.3   Pitch-patterning

This systematic error is repeated in matters of *pitch-patterning*, as shown below. The inclusion of most of the SEU boosters in LLC implies the retention of pitch-patterning, and since this is a fairly major feature of the transcription (unlike loudness) it is more serious that erroneous impressions can be gained from it:

1.   The omission of m: *asc*ending and m: *desc*ending means that where successive tone units were higher or lower than the last respectively, this relation will not be shown: this could have implications for discourse organization.
2.   The omission of low boosters (, and ;) and of high and low unstressed syllables means that occasionally nuclei which were low-boosted in

SEU are not so marked in LLC, and that a few unstressed syllables which were unusually high or low also go unnoticed. This means that any pitch-contour which appears to be smooth in LLC may in fact have some excursions.

3. The omission of pitch-markings on subordinate tone units is likely to give an erroneous indication of their pitch relative to the main tone unit.
4. The omission of *m: scan*dent (where each successive syllable is higher than the last) and of *m: mono*tonous (where each successive syllable is at the same level) means that these will appear as ordinary declination, the boosters having been omitted from the SEU as redundant; and the same will be true for the pitch-patterns of the *m: sp*iky and *m: gli*ssando: features will produce similar results, except in some of the later texts where a few transcribers re-inserted boosters to compensate for this.
5. The retention of the extra-high booster, like the retention of the double stress, creak/glottal stop and length-marks, is anomalous in view of what has been omitted.

5   Computerizing manual transcription

The comparison of manual (SEU) and computerized (LLC) transcriptions points out some of the inconsistencies in the reduction: some features have been removed apparently systematically but occasionally one small exponent of a system remains. However unimportant these discrepancies may be to the researcher, it is worth finding out whether they point to any real drawback to computerizing manual transcription, and whether there are any other problems associated with the process.

The discrepancies entered the system when the transcription was pruned for computerization. The reasons advanced for reducing the number of features were:

> partly practical and technical, partly linguistic. While we do not want to minimise the importance of paralinguistic features, it is clear that they are less central than the basic distinctions (such as tone units, types of tone, place of nucleus) for most prosodic and grammatical studies of spoken English.
>
> (Svartvik and Quirk 1980: 14).

While one might demur over the linguistic reasons given here (the current notion of 'basic distinctions' is probably different), the main concern is that 'practical and technical reasons' (unspecified) are also advanced. In 1975, the paralinguistic comments in the margin were difficult to reproduce in the regular computer format, and this probably led to the decision to omit marginal glosses (apart from speaker-identification). Some pre-editing of the texts before they were pruned would have ensured that it was done consistently, but another argument could have been that the process of putting everything on computer was a lengthy enough business without adding a pre-editing exercise.

The computerized version of the SEU is more misleading than it need be, and may have also given the impression that computerization involves constraints that are not present in manual transcription, which is very unlikely to be the case. In the early years of word-processing it was difficult to organize text in two columns: this is now less of a problem. The objection that computerizing transcription is time-consuming is still valid; it has been said that, contrary to hopes and expectations, computers do not save time, they only raise standards.

Supposing the time-input factor for computerized transcription to be not greatly different from the manual process, it must be considered that is possible to produce a very high standard of transcription using sophisticated software. The LLC demonstrates the advantages of varied typefaces – the use of small capital letters makes the nuclei very easy to spot – and of a range of symbols far more varied and eye-catching than anything a typewriter could manage; not to mention the obvious advantage of its reproduceability.

It may be, however, that there is a tendency to adopt a transcription-policy as though all possible word processing facilities had already been made available. It is understandable that there is no point in waiting until they are, but it should be feasible to take into account a few likely technological developments and to make some allowances for the possibility of upgrading. For instance, with the increase of researchers working from disks and screens, there may soon be the facility of visually superimposing transcription – and different levels of transcription – on a text at will. This would do away with the objection that the more mark-up there is, the harder it is to read the words and this step would bring about a near-revolution in the process and aims of transcription. It might also be possible to establish a simple way of indicating gaze-direction and gestures; with that we might have a more realistic notion of total description and total accountability.

Note

1. Record of all published research making use of SEU resources are kept at the International Corpus of English in the Department of English, University College, Gower Street, London WC1E 6BT.

16 The COBUILD spoken corpus: transcription conventions

JONATHAN PAYNE

1 Introduction

The conventions below are the result of over 30 years experience in transcribing spoken language for computer analysis, and have been developed jointly since 1991 by COBUILD and JP French Associates.

The COBUILD spoken corpus, of over ten million words (November 1994), consists of a wide variety of spoken English. Informal conversation, as exemplified in the above extract, has always been a crucial element of the corpus and the collection of spontaneous spoken discourse continues to be a priority for the future.

The corpus forms part of the Bank of English, a very large corpus of spoken and written English, which is used for linguistic research, lexicography and the study of grammar.

2 Transcription and transcribers

The transcription conventions are designed to provide a level of detail that meets the requirements of corpus users without needing trained phoneticians and linguists as transcribers, which would add considerably to the cost, and hence limit the size of the corpus.

Transcribers have secretarial experience, and are therefore used to representing speech in writing in various ways, whether through the medium of dictation, or in the taking of minutes. More particularly, they are familiar with applying punctuation to transcriptions of speech. It is logical, then, to employ punctuation-based conventions; these have the further advantage of being easily readable by users. It is a simple matter to convert these into a standard computer-readable format as recommended by the Text Encoding Initiative (TEI) (Payne 1993, Sperberg-McQueen and Burnard 1994) if required.

204 *Samples and systems of transcription*

3 Turns and sentences

Using punctuation does not imply treating the transcript as if it were written English. Grammatical completeness is only one of a number of factors which can, severally or in combination, mark the end of a speaker turn. In arriving at a basic unit of spoken interaction, then, intonational and pragmatic factors have also been taken into account. The resulting 'functional sentence' is perhaps difficult to define precisely in linguistic terms, but as an essentially practical unit creates few problems for transcribers, as it is using their intuitions about when speakers are starting, continuing and completing what they are saying on the one hand, and when they are abandoning incomplete utterances on the other.

The following excerpts from the instructions for transcribers (French 1992a: 14) give a good impression of what is concerned:

Try to be guided by intonation – the rises and falls in the voice – as well as by the words themselves. If it sounds as though someone has finished a sentence and gone on to another (their voice drops, they take a breath and start on a higher note) then it's probably fairly safe to start a new sentence.

In the sample in Fig. 16.1, for example, the transcriber has distinguished between 'Yes I'm gonna. .' at the beginning of line 10 and 'Yeah. 'Cos we got her. . .' at the beginning of line 43. The same grammatical pattern has distinct prosodic features in each case. It should be noted that *gonna* and *'cos* are both normalized forms from an allowed list. Question marks are used to indicate things that function as real requests – requests for information not already known.

At line 30, for example, a grammatical interrogative has not been interpreted as a functional question, while at line 33 a grammatical declarative has been interpreted as a functional question.

Exclamation marks, commas, semi-colons and colons are not employed. The absence of either a full stop or a question mark implies incompletion:

When a speaker doesn't finish what they're saying (if they're interrupted or they tail off), don't put a full stop.

A substantial proportion of the speaker turns above do not end in full stops or question marks, and can therefore be interpreted as incomplete utterances. This implies either that they continue further down in the transcription, as is usually the case here, or as at line 6, that a speaker has abandoned her utterance. *Erm* is a standardized spelling for the filler/hesitation marker that is pronounced on a level tone by speakers to continue their turn. This can be compared with the standardized back-channel *Mm*, at line 20 and elsewhere, which encourages another speaker to continue.

Non-verbal speaker inputs, and utterances which are unintelligible, are similarly represented with reference to their role in the turn-taking, as at lines 47 and 49, for example.

The COBUILD spoken corpus: transcription conventions   205

1   <M01> [laughs] [pause] <ZZ1> 058–063 <ZZ0>
    <F01> Oh there's a lovely recipe here for "Asparagus
    quills with parmesan and walnuts" FX.
    <F02> Ooh.
5   <F01> [laughs]
    <F02> Oh <ZGY> [pause] <ZGY> have it now. [pause] Erm
    <F01> It involves large quantities of double cream
    <F02> [gasps] ZG1 Oh no <ZG0>
    <F01> and butter.
10 <F02> Yes I'm gonna have to do all those meals and have a
    four-course meal with cream in every course.
    [laughter]
    <F01> FX <ZG1> used to like <ZG0> <ZGY>
    <F02> Mm. Cream. I thought she lost weight here.
15 <F01> Yeah.
    <F02> She did. She didn't <ZGY>
    <F01> But she ate proper food instead of
    <F02> <ZGY>
    <F01> crisps and chocolate all the time
20 <F02> Mm.
    <F01> and you know puddings and stuff like that and 'cos
    she used to eat six bags of crips you see at one
    sitting.
    <F02> <ZG1> Bloody hell <ZG0>
25 <F01> Six one of those bumper packs <ZGY>
    <F02> [laughs]
    <F01> and chocolate you know.
    <F02> Oh I feel sick.
    <F01> And erm
30 <F02> Do you like snacky things <ZGY>
    <F01> cream and stuff like that will really make you fat.
    <F02> Mm.
    <F01> I'm sorry?
    <F02> <ZGY> like snacky things but in excess.
35 <F01> Yeah.
    <F02> <ZGY>
    <F01> Well she ate an excessive amount of snacky things
    <F02> Mm.
    <F01> <ZF1> as well as [pause] <ZF0>
40 <F02> Having a meal.
    <F01> as well as having a meal.
    <F02> But it was the drink as well <ZGY>
    <F01> Yeah. 'Cos we got her off beer and got her onto
    wine.
45 <F02> Yeah. Right.
    <F01> And she'd drink twelve pints of lager at lunchtime
    <F02> [laughs]
    <F01> and go back to work.
    <F02> <ZGY>
50 <M01> Is this FX?
    <F01> Yeah.
    <F02> Mm. She was incredible.

Figure 16.1 COBUILD spoken corpus

206 *Samples and systems of transcription*

4 Interruption and Overlap

When there is an overlap between the end of one turn and the beginning of another, this is not shown explicitly as it does not affect the turntaking. However, if a speaker's utterance overlaps with that of another speaker entirely, so that she starts speaking after the other speaker, and finishes speaking before her, use is made of the familiar conventions of the playscript. Lines 29 and 31 represent one complete utterance by <F01> during which there is an interruption/overlap by <F02>. The lower case letter at the beginning of line 31 clearly marks a continuation in a system in which upper case letters mark a new functional unit. It might be argued that dividing up utterances in this way is artificial and disrupts the syntax. The TEI recommendations in this area prefer transcribing <F02>'s turn after <F01>'s turn with SGML tags indicating the position and extent of the overlap, for instance. This will be equally artificial and will disrupt the turntaking. In either case it is possible to clarify exactly what is happening by referring to a timeline; it is just that in the second case the transcription could not be interpreted without a timeline, which has important cost implications.

<F01>	First female speaker
<F02>	Second female speaker
<M01>	First male speaker
FX	Replaces female name
MX	Replaces male name

Text Codes:

<ZF1> *text* <ZF0>	Enclose false start repetition
<ZG1> *text* <ZG0>	Enclose guess at unclear utterance
<ZGY>	Replaces wholly unintelligible section
<ZZ1> *text* <ZZ0>	Enclose comment from transcriber: used here to show duration of long pauses
[*text*]	Enclose representation of non-verbal speaker input
[pause]	Unexpected pause

Punctuation:

capital letter		Indicates beginning of functional sentence
full stop	.	Indicates end of functional sentence
question mark	?	Indicates end of functional question
quotation marks	" "	Enclose direct quotation from written source
single apostrophe	'	Used for contracted words (and possessives)

A full statement of the codes employed can be found in French (1992a).

Figure 16.2 Key to symbols used

5 Summary

To summarize, the conventions are designed to reflect the particular characteristics of informal conversation as opposed to more formal varieties of spoken English and to written English generally. At the same time, they exploit familiar conventions for representing speech, making the transcriptions easy to interpret for users, and making it possible for non-specialist transcribers to be employed. Third, by means of a simple conversion programme it is a straightforward matter to link these user-friendly codes to a standard machine-friendly system, such as that proposed by the TEI [see Johansson, Chapter 6].

17 Converting a corpus into a relational database: SEC becomes MARSEC

GERRY KNOWLES

1 Introduction

One of the unseen revolutions currently taking place as a result of the development of large linguistic corpora and databases concerns the way linguists have to think about data. Until very recently, it was desirable when representing the spoken language to compress as much information as possible into the simplest possible symbol. The virtues of this approach include readability and economy in printing, as can be seen in conventional phonemic and prosodic transcriptions, but it is not in principle a matter of linguistic theory. There is no reason in the 1990s to continue to solve the problems of paper-and-pencil technology.

The new opportunities are not yet being fully recognized and exploited by linguists (see Edwards and Lampert 1993 and Knowles 1994). Texts are still seen as objects in book format, with words running in horizontal lines from left to right. Annotations are added to these horizontal lines. But book format is an attribute not of speech, but of Western writing systems. There is no reason beyond established custom and practice to present speech in this way. On the contrary, since there are often several annotations relating to the same piece of data, book format is in many cases inappropriate. The use of book format without consideration of other possibilities is based on a confusion between the organization of the data itself, and the presentation of the data on the printed page.

If we are to use computer-based technology to represent speech, we have to radically re-think what we are trying to do. What is the nature of the data we are trying to represent? What are the relationships among items of data? What data structures will best handle these relationships? How can the data and the relationships be presented to the human user of the technology? This paper will seek to show how computer-based data structures can handle speech data much more effectively than book format.

2 SEC and MARSEC

The SEC is the Spoken English Corpus which was compiled between 1984 and 1987 in a collaborative venture between Lancaster University and the former IBM UK Scientific Centre. The aim was to collect suitable materials to use as models for speech synthesis, and for this reason the corpus consists of about 53000 words of naturally produced speech in a range of styles, but mostly of prepared or semi-prepared speech, in British English which broadly comes within the category of Received Pronunciation. The orthographic transcripts of the texts were processed in the same way as written texts, being grammatically tagged and manually parsed. Unpunctuated versions were transcribed prosodically by two phoneticians working independently but overlapping for about 9 per cent of the total corpus. Figure 17.1 gives a sample of the original prosodic transcription of the SEC, showing the use of tonetic stress marks (tsms), based broadly on the O'Connor and Arnold transcription system.

MARSEC is a relational database which was generated from the SEC between 1992 and 1994 in a collaborative project at the Universities of Lancaster and Leeds (ESRC grant No. R000 23 3380). Researchers at Leeds, led by Peter Roach, digitised the audio recordings and made them available on CD-ROM, so that the waveforms and annotations can be searched using a speech workstation. Researchers at Lancaster, Gerry Knowles and Tamás Váradi, converted the original corpus files, most of which were in horizontal format, into tables which can be handled by a standard database management package, such as the Windows-based Access or FoxPro. The design and development of the database was undertaken by Tamás Váradi. This chapter will concentrate on work carried out at Lancaster.

3 Constructing a flatfile

The original SEC contained different kinds of information in separate files: orthographic transcription, prosodic transcription, grammatical tags, parse trees, and so on. The researcher had to find corresponding information in the different files, and then locate the relevant portion of the audio tapes. The first stage was to bring linked pieces of information together in the form of a flatfile.

Take for example the phrase *the gratitude that millions feel towards him*, which occurs towards the end of file M06. In the orthographic, tagged and prosodic versions this appears as follows:

>the gratitude that millions feel towards him.
>
>the_ATI gratitude_NN that_CS milllions_ NNS feel_VB towards_IN him_PP3O ._.
>
>the /gratitude | that ⁻millions · feel to \wards him ||

Figure 17.1

210 *Samples and systems of transcription*

The prosodic transcription used specially designed non-standard symbols, several of which are not available even in extended character sets. For this reason it was necessary to replace the non-standard symbols with ASCII characters:

the ,gratitude | that ~millions *feel to'wards him ||

The ASCII transcription is the one used in this chapter. A key to the symbols used is given in Fig. 17.2.

Category	Symbol
low rise	,
high level	~
stressed but not accented	*
low fall	'
minor tone group boundary		
major tone group boundary	||

Figure 17.2

The first task for the design of the database concerned punctuation. When the files were tagged, punctuation marks were treated as separate words, but if records were based either on words or on punctuation marks, this would create records of different kinds and having different sets of fields. If the space between words is treated as a punctuation mark too, then every word can be said to have an associated punctuation mark. Although the mark indicates a boundary between groups of words, in practice it is joined to the preceding word. Following this practice, we can treat punctuation as a field of the preceding word. In the same way we can treat tone group boundary markers '|' and '||' along with spaces as fields belonging to the preceding word.

The information in the separate files can be aligned and presented in the form of a single table of the kind reproduced below in Fig. 17.3. Every record has a unique identifier, here called *phon_id*. This is in fact a much simplified version of the actual table that was constructed at this stage.

phon_id	orthog	punct	tag	prosody	boundary
525400	the		AT	the	
525410	gratitude		NN	,gratitude		
525420	that		CS	that	
525430	millions		NNS	~millions	
525440	feel		VB	*feel	
525450	towards		IN	to'wards	
525460	him		PP3O	him	||

Figure 17.3

It is taken for granted that the obvious unit on which to base the record is the orthographic word. This was the unit used by the grammatical tagger, by the parsers, and by the prosodic transcribers. The corresponding information about each word is presented in the different fields on the same line.

The flatfile makes a significant move away from book format by presenting the data in vertical format instead of the more familiar horizontal format. More importantly, it enforces a more rigorous definition of the data, and separates the problems of data organization and data presentation. In order to construct the flatfile, it is necessary to identify precisely the kind of data to be associated with any record, and which record any piece of data belongs to. This is a matter of data organization. Once the data is properly organized, it is a trivial matter to present it in any desired format. The orthographic forms of the above table can be written out as a standard text using the word and punctuation fields, and these can be linked by an underscore to the corresponding grammatical tag. Similarly, the prosodic transcription can be generated using the *prosody* and *boundary* fields.

The information in the flatfile is exactly the same as the information in the original corpus files, but it is much more usable, because the links between pieces of information are made explicit, instead of being left to the researcher to establish. But the flatfile also has serious shortcomings. It is far too big and cumbersome, and most users will need only a small subset of the information available for most of the time. Most applications will require further fields to be generated, and records will have to be split or joined, all of which uses even more space. The answer is to move from a flatfile format to a relational format.

4 Excursus: flatfiles, relational databases and mark sheets

The categories of speech data are extremely complex. To illustrate some basic points of data handling let us consider the simpler case of a mark sheet, as presented in Fig. 17.4.

Name	cw	exam	unit
John	60	42	51
Mary	55	55	55
Max	35	50	43
Belinda	68	0	34

Figure 17.4

The name given here is just a rough mnemonic. If for some reason tutors need to identify the student more precisely, they have to consult separate student records containing fuller details. These might be as presented in Fig. 17.5.

It would of course be most inefficient to include all this information in the mark sheet, especially as it would have to be reproduced for every course that the student takes. However, whereas in the mark sheet students are identified by their

Samples and systems of transcription

Student _Number	First_name	Surname	Sex	Year	Address
193868	John	Smith	M	2	38 Chorley Street
193779	Mary	Jones	F	3	93 Lancaster Road
193842	Max	Pettigrew	M	3	20 Corporation Ave
193791	Belinda	Langthwaite	F	3	14 Fellside Crescent

Figure 17.5

first name – and there may be several Johns and Marys, and the tutor has to know which one to look for – every student is identified by a unique number in student records. If the student were to be identified by this number also in the mark sheet, it would be possible to look up the details automatically by finding the corresponding record with the same number. Figure 17.6 presents a revised mark sheet in which the student is identified by number.

Student _Number	cw	exam	unit
193868	60	42	51
193779	55	55	55
193842	35	50	43
193791	68	0	34

Figure 17.6

This process of looking up is not one that has to be done by a human being: it is precisely the kind of task performed efficiently by the database management system. When the mark sheet is displayed on the screen or printed out, the number can be replaced by any of the information in the student record. The mark sheet displayed can in fact look exactly like the original table above. In this way the organization of the data is treated as a separate problem from its presentation.

Names are more convenient for humans, but the unique identifiers are essential for computer processing. The use of student numbers rather than first names is significant and opens up new possibilities of data manipulation. The original mark sheet and the student records are unconnected *flatfiles*. The revised mark sheet is explicitly linked to the student records, and together these tables form a simple *relational database*.

The coursework and exam marks are *primary data*, which we cannot derive from anything else, and which therefore have to be included in the database. The unit mark, on the other hand, is a *calculated field*, which means that it can be calculated by formula from the coursework and exam marks. It is therefore not necessary to store the result in the database. Given the relational structure, it is still possible to make this calculation, but in addition a wide range of calculations are made possible, for example the average exam mark for female students.

We have so far considered the organization of the data, how students' marks relate to personal information about them. It may seem that the information contained in the tables is purely factual, and therefore independent of any particular theoretical perspective. Even so, in order to make sense of the data, we have to know what coursework is, what exams are, what marks are for, and what a student means by giving a local address. If we understand these things, we also understand why fields and records are set up as they are, and why information is placed in different tables. This knowledge corresponds in the linguistic database to linguistic theory, the general knowledge about language which the linguist uses to make sense of the data. While we can try to set up structures which will receive the assent of a large number of linguists, we cannot do this in a way which is independent of theory. To that extent the structure of the database implements a theory.

5 A relational database of spoken language

Apart from identifiers, which are necessarily unique, the data held in a field may recur several times. Grammatical tags recur frequently, as do some orthographic words, such as *the*. These different forms can be held in ordered lists, some of which have familiar names. A list of tags, for instance, is a *tagset*, and a list of orthographic forms is a *lexicon*. Others, such as a list of pronouncing dictionary forms, or a list of words annotated for prosody, are more specific to this application. In the database these lists are stored as separate tables, and each item is given a unique identifier. The tag or orthographic form is then replaced in the original table by its identifier.

The database thus consists of a set of linked tables. Some tables are unreadable, and consist mainly or only of identifiers. An illustration is provided in Fig. 17.7.

phon_id	location	dpron_id	cpron_id
525400	M06121020	4371	6778
525410	M06121030	1251	2109
525420	M06121040	4369	6787
525430	M06121050	2041	3437
525440	M06121060	5459	1866
525450	M06121070	7204	8602
525460	M06121080	5643	6964

Figure 17.7

This figure gives a sample of the table *Phnwords*, which holds information on the phonetic form of words.

Take as an example the record with the phon_id 525420, which is the conjuction *that*. Its *location* M06121040 refers to its position in the original orthographic transcript: it comes from text 6 of section M of the corpus, where it was the second word on line 121. The corresponding dictionary form is no 4369, and the contextual form 6787. The dictionary forms are held in a separate table called *Dpronlex*, and the contextual forms in *Cpronlex*. The relevant portions of these tables are reproduced below in Fig. 17.8.

dpron_id	dpron
4363	Ask
4364	Asks
4365	Askt
4366	At
4367	AtS
4368	D&n
4369	D&t
4370	D&ts
4371	D@

cpron_id	cpron
6781	D@m'selvz
6782	D@n
6783	D@n~N
6784	D@n~m
6785	D@t
6786	D@t~k
6787	D@t~p
6788	DI
6789	DI[j]

Figure 17.8

Dpronlex has two fields, *dpron_id* and *dpron*, and 4369 corresponds to the form /D&t/ which in the computer-readable notation used corresponds to the ipa /ðæt/. The corresponding record in *Cpronlex* is 6787 which has the form /D@t~p/. The symbol "@" is used in the notation for shwa, which is the expected contextual form for this word. The final '~p' indicates that the word occurs in a position where it can be expected to assimilate to a following labial consonant. (The following word is *millions*.) Whenever we need to make use of the information in the table, for example when presenting it on the screen or sending it to another file, we can always replace the identity numbers with the corresponding phonetic forms.

This has important consequences for the way the database is used. The person who designs the database has to have a very clear understanding of the relationships among pieces of data. But if the user also carries out the same kind of task, the relationships between tables can be stored and reestablished every time the database is used. This means that the user might never have to know about the identity numbers, or how the data is stored in the different tables.

Parallel to *Phnwords* is another file *Prswords* which contains the prosodic information. Two important fields are *orthog* which holds the identifier of the orthographic form which was used for the prosodic transcription, and *prosody*, which holds the identifier of the prosodic transcription itself. These are looked up in tables in the same way, and the identifiers can be replaced by the corresponding form either on screen or in a new table. Putting together the information in *Phnwords* and *Prswords*, we can form the table shown in Fig. 17.9.

Now this table looks remarkably like the kind of flatfile we started with, but the resemblance is only superficial. The data is still stored on disk in the separate tables, and the related pieces of data are only brought together on the screen for the human observer. The point is that the links among the different kinds of data allow the data to be manipulated in a variety of ways.

Converting a corpus into a database

phon_id	orthog	dpron	cpron	prosody
525400	the	Di	D@	the
525410	gratitude	'gr&tItjud	'gr&tItjud	,gratitude
525420	that	D&t	D@t~p	that
525430	millions	'mIll@nz	'mIll@nz	~millions
525440	feel	fil	'fil	*feel
525450	towards	t@'wOdz	t@'wOdz	to'wards
525460	him	hIm	Im	him

Figure 17.9

Among the things we can do with the data is to recover the original flatfile. But we can also generate other interesting flatfiles. Different subsets of the data are used for different applications, such as the study of syntax, phonetic segments, or prosody. For example, by retrieving orthographic forms, tags, and dictionary pronunciations, and ordering the list according to the orthographic forms, we can generate a pronouncing dictionary. That is, the relational structure can do anything the flatfile can do, and a lot more besides.

6   Illustration: interpreting complex symbols

The prosodic transcription holds much useful information, but it is not immediately obvious how to make use of it. Using the corpus files, the researcher has to interpret every individual case, which makes for slow progress. Using a flatfile, it would be possible to separate the information out into several calculated fields, but at an enormous cost if the results had to be stored. The relational database requires some unstored calculated fields and a small table.

In the prosodic transcription, the direction of pitch movement is marked on the accented syllables by so-called *tonetic stress marks* (or 'tsms'). These marks represent the judgement of the transcriber according to a set of criteria. In order to make use of the tsm information, for example to explain their distribution in the text, or to relate them to measurable properties of the waveform, it is necessary to relate the symbols explicitly to the criteria for their use.

The first step is to isolate the tsm from the word in which it is included. The position of the tsm – if any – corresponds to the position of the primary stress mark in the *dpron* field. A slight problem here is that the dictionary from which the *dpron* was obtained does not mark primary stress on monosyllables: for this reason a new calculated field is required which copies words with a stress mark and preposes a stress mark to those without. In this way *feel* /fil/ is re-written /'fil/.

At this point we can set up a new *tsm* field, the value of which is extracted from the *prosody* field, or which is assigned the value 0 if there is no tsm. For the new table, see Fig. 17.10.

phon_id	dpron	prosody	tsm
525400	'DI	the	0
525410	'gr&tItjud	,gratitude	,
525420	'D&t	that	0
525430	'mIll@nz	~millions	~
525440	'fil	*feel	*
525450	t@'wOdz	to'wards	'
525460	'hIm	him	0

Figure 17.10

Extracting the tsm is a reasonably straightforward process in the case of words which only have one primary stress. However, there is a complication in the case of long words which have a 'secondary' stress close to the beginning (marked ',') followed by the 'primary' stress later in the word (see Fig. 17.11).

phon_id	orthog	dpron	prosody
140	unification	,junIfI'keISn	unifi\cation

Figure 17.11

In order to deal consistently with the *tsm* field, we first have to split these long words into two parts. These parts are close in size to the units conventionally described as 'feet'. We now need to create a new table (see Fig. 17.12), in which the record is a foot, and feet are given unique identifiers in a new field *foot_id*.

foot_id	phon_id	orthog	dpron2	prosody2	tsm
14	140	unification	,junIfI	unifi	0
15	140	unification	'keISn	\cation	\

Figure 17.12

Up to now the operations could have been carried out in a flatfile in the same way as in a relational database. In a flatfile, when a record is split, all the fields have to be copied, which not only uses up storage space, but could also be misleading. It looks from the above table as though there are now two occurrences of the word *unification*. There would indeed be two in a flatfile, but not in a relational database. There are two feet but both are associated with the same record (phon_id 140) in the *phnwords* table.

Having isolated the tsm for each foot, we can begin to manipulate this information. First, as a paper-and-pencil exercise, we need to associate the tsm symbols with their conventional descriptions (see Fig. 17.13).

tsm	description
0	unstressed
*	stressed but not accented
_	low level
~	high level
,	low rise
/	high rise
\,	low fall–rise
'/	high fall–rise
'	low fall
\	high fall

Figure 17.13

These descriptions can be reformulated in terms of six binary features:

- All tsms except '0' are stressed.
- All remaining tsms except '*' are accented.
- All accented tsms can be classed as high or not high.
- All accented tsms except '_~' have moving or kinetic tones.
- All remaining tsms except ', /' have a peak of pitch before the end.
- All remaining tsms except ' '/' have a final drop in pitch.

These features can be used to code fields with the Boolean values True or False, and entered in a table (Fig. 17.14), which is stored as an additional database file.

tsm	stress	pitch	kinetic	peak	fall	high
0	F	F	F	F	F	F
*	T	F	F	F	F	F
_	T	T	F	F	F	F
~	T	T	F	F	F	T
,	T	T	T	F	F	F
/	T	T	T	F	F	T
\,	T	T	T	T	F	F
'/	T	T	T	T	F	T
'	T	T	T	T	T	F
\	T	T	T	T	T	T

Figure 17.14

The symbols in the *tsm* field of this table are exactly the same as the symbols in the *tsm* field of the *feet* table. If the tables are linked through the *tsm* field, the Boolean values for any *tsm* in the *feet* table can be displayed automatically, as shown in Fig. 17.15.

foot_id	dpron	tsm	stress	accent	kinetic	peak	fall
54313	Di	0	F	F	F	F	F
54314	'gr&tltjud	,	T	T	T	F	F
54315	D&t	0	F	F	F	F	F
54316	'mlll@nz	~	T	T	F	F	F
54317	'fil	*	T	F	F	F	F
54318	t@'wOdz	'	T	T	T	T	T
54319	hlm	0	F	F	F	F	F

Figure 17.15

The prosodic information is now presented much more effectively than in the *tsms*. Other researchers will not necessarily want to know about the distribution of the set of symbols that the transcribers happened to use. The transcribers may even change their minds about the best way to transcribe a text. What everybody does want to know about is the distribution of stress, or of rises and falls in pitch.

Since this prosodic information is explicitly linked to grammatical tags, it is possible to find accented prepositions, or unaccented nouns. Since the punctuation of the orthographic text is also linked, we can find words which rise in pitch before a comma, or fall before a full stop.

7 The encoding of expert knowledge

The progression from book format to flatfile to relational database represents at each stage an apparent quantum increase in complexity which is rewarded by an increase in effective data manipulation. The increase in complexity is not real, however, because the separate but linked tables correspond more closely to expert knowledge. It has already been mentioned, for example, that tagsets and lexicons are concepts familiar to linguists.

The symbols used in the prosodic transcription belong to a set which is described in a separate manual (Taylor and Knowles 1988). Just as the database formally links information in separate corpus files, so it relates symbols formally to their descriptions. In the same way, phoneticians making phonemic transcriptions use symbols taken from an inventory which is stored in some other place (perhaps on a piece of paper). These symbols also have definitions (e.g. /k/ is a 'voiceless velar stop'), and this information is stored in textbooks and in the transcribers' heads. Using a relational database, phonemic information can be linked explicitly. The database actually enables experts to organize data according to the way they naturally categorize it.

Linguists have hitherto had to contend with dual systems of data handling. The first concerns the natural organization of data, and the second is the presentation of data in book format. Book format has been a dominant but totally irrelevant consideration in phonological theories from the phoneme to contemporary post-Sound Pattern of English (SPE) phonologies. The abandonment of book format may at first look superficially like a complication, but it actually brings release from an irrelevant encumbrance.

But the use of a relational database also has other important consequences for linguistic theory. It is traditionally assumed that the problems of linguistics are problems *sui generis*, that they are different in kind from the problems tackled by historians, psychologists or market researchers. But the very fact that a general-purpose database system can be used to handle linguistic data demonstrates that linguistics shares many problems with other disciplines. Relational logic is of course no more part of linguistics than statistics is part of psychology or mathematics part of engineering. However, if we can separate out the general problems of data organization, we will be left with a much clearer idea of the special concerns of linguistic theory proper.

8 Conclusion

This chapter has been concerned in the first instance with the practical problems of converting the original SEC files into a database using more modern techniques for data storage and retrieval. The issues involved in making this conversion go far beyond practical issues, and have major consequences for linguistic theory.

The intellectual discipline which the relational database enforces brings with it two major benefits. First, the problem of organizing data is quite clearly separated from the problem of presenting data on the printed page. It is time for linguists to abandon the conventional book format. Second, data organization is distinguished from linguistic theory proper. The general problems of organization are shared with many other disciplines. The theory is what is implemented in the design of fields, records, and tables, and the links established between them.

18 The International Corpus of English: mark-up for spoken language

GERALD NELSON

The International Corpus of English (ICE) is a collaborative project involving research teams in over 16 countries throughout the world (see Greenbaum 1992). Each team is compiling a corpus of one million words of their own national or regional variety of English, of which 600,000 words are taken from spoken sources. One of the primary aims of the project is to produce research material for comparative studies between varieties of English throughout the world, and to facilitate this, each corpus will be computerized, tagged and parsed using common conventions. The project, which began in 1990, is being coordinated by the Survey of English Usage, University College London.

1 Transcription extract

```
1   <$A> <#>I'll leave those wallflowers in <}><->as<.>w</.></->
2   <=>to</=></}> the last moment
3   <$B> <#>What <#>So all the flowers have died on them
4   <$A> <#>Well these other ones are not coming along very well
5   <{><[>so</[>
6   <$B> <#><[>The</[></{> ones on the right-hand side you can just cut
7   the tops off and leave them <#>They'll come up next year then
8   <$A> <#>I'm peeved about <}><->that</-><=>giving her
9   that</=></}> window <#>I was a fool <#>I <}><->was</->
10  <=>wasn't</=></}> growing seeds then of course
11  <$C><#>What window
12  <$B> <#>Piece <{><[>of glass</[>
13  <$A> <#><[>Her</[></{> next door when she was down or
14  something<,,> <#>A glazed uhm sash window <#>I could have used it to
15  bring these blasted seeds on<,,> <#>Could have cleared that square yard
16  <}><->in</-> <=>down</=></}> that right-hand border in the sun
17  put the seed boxes on the ground and the uh window glass over it<,,>
```

220

18 <$B> <#>No <#>You can't blame her for that really <{><[>can
19 you</[>
20 <$C> <#><[>If you </[></{> gave it to her <{><[>Dad</[>
21 <O>laughs</O>
22 <$B> <#><[>No</[></{>
23 <$A> <#>Well these damn plants have shot up in price so much over the last
24 year or <{><[>two</[>
25 <$B> <#><[>Yes</[></{>
26 <$B> <#>Those few begonias were a pound or<,>
27 <$A> <#>Yes <{><[><unclear> word </unclear></[>
28 <$B> <#><[>Absolute</[></{> daylight robbery really aren't they<,,>
29 <#>It is the only way to grow them yourself really I mean and plant them
30 out<,,> <#>What you want is a little greenhouse really<,> <{><[>don't
31 you</[>
32 <$A> <#><[>No <#>}><–>That</–></[></{>
33 <=>that's</=></}> <}><–>frame</–> <=>a little cold
34 frame</=></}>
35 <$B> <#> Has he got one
36 <$A> <#>No <#>I don't think so
37 <$B> <#>What <#>Not in his shed even
38 <$A> <#>No no <#>I brought that from Bow because I got it from the
39 place next door when they threw all their window frames out
40 <$B> <#>Oh<,>
41 <$A> <#>I got two <#>But <}><–>I I can't</–><=>I
42 think</=></}> I left the other one up at Bow <#><{><[>Didn't
43 <?>want it</?></[>
44 <$B> <#><[>What's</[></{> happened to the door we had out there
45 <#>Can't you<,> <{1><[1> saw the lower bit off and use
46 <{2><[2>that</[2>
47 <$A> <#><[1>Still out there</[1></{1>
48 <$A> <#><[2>No</[2></{2> <#>It's all frosted glass <#>It's
49 <{><[>almost</[> opaque
50 <$B> <#><[>Oh</[></{>
51 <$B> <#>Oh I
52 <$A> <#>Almost opaque<,,>

Key

<$>	Speaker identification
<#>	Text unit marker
<}>	Normalized sequence
<–>	Normative deletion
<=>	Original normalization
<{>	Overlapping string set

<[>	Overlapping string
<?>	Uncertain transcription
<O>	Untranscribed text
<unclear>	Unclear words or syllables
<,>	Short pause
<,,>	Long pause

2 Discussion

This extract is taken from the British component of ICE. It is a family conversation; speaker A is speaker B's husband, and speaker C is their daughter. The mark-up symbols are SGML-conformant and are of two types. Features of the text which have scope over one or more words are marked with an opening symbol <*symbol*> where they begin and with a closing symbol </*symbol*> where they end. Features which have no scope over any words and have position only, such as the pause marker, are represented by a single symbol where they occur.

The transcription is orthographic, and standard orthographic conventions for spelling, word-spacing, hyphenation and capitalization are observed. Enclitic forms such as *I'm*, *we're* and *you'll* are permitted and can be dealt with by the automatic tagger. No prosodic or phonetic features are marked, except short and long pauses. By convention, a short pause is equal in duration to a single syllable, uttered at the speaker's tempo, while a long pause is the equivalent of two or more syllables uttered at the same tempo. Voiced pauses are transcribed as *uh* and *uhm*. The basic unit of transcription is the text unit, marked with <#>. This is the approximate equivalent of the orthographic sentence, though in many instances it is syntactically incomplete, as in lines 26 and 51.

A large part of the mark-up in the extract shown has been applied to facilitate parsing. Common features of informal speech, such as repetitions, hesitations, incomplete words and self-corrections have been normalized, but in such a way that all features of the original utterance have been retained in the transcription. In lines 1 and 2, *as* and the incomplete word *w* have been normatively deleted using <–> and </–>. Deleted words are grammatically tagged but they do not form part of the parser input, so the input from lines 1 and 2 is *I'll leave those wallflowers in to the last moment*. Lines 32 to 34 illustrate a more complex example of normalization. Here the speaker repeats the word *that* and then corrects or re-formulates *frame* as *a little cold frame*. The self-correction is marked by normatively deleting *frame* and by marking *a little cold frame* as an original normalization. This indicates that the words were uttered by the speaker, but as part of a self-correction. Using this method, the self-correction phenomenon is clearly recorded, while at the same time allowing the utterance to be parsed as *That's a little cold frame*.

Overlapping speech is marked by enclosing each overlapping string in <[> and </[> and by enclosing both strings in <{> and </{>. Lines 5 and 6 show a simple example of this. Here, speaker A's *so* overlaps with speaker B's *the*. Speaker turns are not made discontinuous by overlapping interruptions. Instead, the position of the interruption is indicated and the complete turn is retained as a unit for parsing. One of the most common types of overlapping is shown in lines 45 to 47. This is overlapping with a pause. In line 45, speaker B pauses after *can't you*, allowing speaker A to say *still out there*, which is presumably a reply to B's question in line 44, *what's happened to the door we had out there*. After the interruption, speaker B continues her utterance and the whole sequence is transcribed as a single text unit. Note that the symbol indicating the overlap in line 45 has no corresponding closing symbol, since the interruption has no scope over any words. Lines 45 to 48 also illustrate multiple overlapping. The overlapping with speaker B's pause in line 45 is the first of two interruptions by speaker A. In line 48, A replies to B's question *can't you saw the lower bit off and use that* before she has fully finished, so A's *no* overlaps with B's *that*. Multiple overlaps in a single speaker turn are numbered in sequence and are transcribed after the turn. The numbering indicates clearly that *still out there* overlaps with the short pause in line 45, while *no* overlaps with *that* in line 46.

Non-verbal utterances are noted in the transcription and marked as untranscribed text only if they are contextually relevant. An example of this may be seen in line 21, where speaker C's laughter may be considered relevant to the discourse. Non-relevant background noises and anthropophonics are ignored. Line 27 shows an example of the mark-up for words or syllables which are unclear in the recording. Here the word is unclear because of its overlapping with *absolute* in line 28.

19 The BNC spoken corpus

STEVE CROWDY

1 Introduction

Lexicographers and linguists have long hoped for corpus evidence about spoken language, but the practical difficulties of transcribing sufficiently large quantities of text have until recently prevented the construction of a spoken corpus of over one million words. Now, as part of the British National Corpus (BNC) project,[1] Longman have produced an orthographically transcribed corpus of 10 million words covering a wide range of speech variation. A large proportion of the spoken corpus – approximately five million words – comprises spontaneous conversational English. The importance of conversational dialogue to linguistic study is unquestionable: it is the dominant component of general language both in terms of language reception and language production. Gathering this amount of conversational English has been made possible by employing a unique method of data collection, which is briefly described below (for more information see Crowdy 1993). In addition, this chapter considers (a) the methods used to process the 1200 hours of recordings and (b) the transcription scheme employed.

2 BNC spoken corpus design, sampling, and representativeness

The issues of corpus sampling and representativeness have been discussed at great length by many corpus linguists. Recently Biber (1993) stated that:

Whether or not a sample is 'representative' depends first of all on the extent to which it is selected from the range of text types in a population; an assessment of the representativeness thus depends on a prior full definition of the 'population' that the sample is intended to represent, and the techniques used to select the sample from that population.

With a corpus of spoken language there are no obvious objective measures that can be used to define the target population or construct a sampling frame. A comprehensive list of text types can be drawn up but there is no accurate way of estimating the relative proportions of each text type other than by a priori linguistically motivated analysis. An alternative approach, one well known to sociological researchers, is demographic sampling, and this is broadly the approach we have adopted. The sampling frame has been defined in terms of the language production of the population of British English speakers in the United Kingdom. Representativeness is achieved by sampling a spread of language producers in terms of age, gender, social group, and region, and recording their language output over a set period of time. We recognize, however, that many types of spoken text are produced only rarely by comparison with the total output of all 'speech producers': for example, broadcast interviews, lectures, legal proceedings, and other texts produced in situations where − broadly speaking − there are few producers and many receivers. A corpus constituted solely on the *demographic* model would thus omit important spoken text types. Consequently, we have complemented the demographic component of the corpus with a separate text typology intended to cover the full range of linguistic variation found in spoken language, termed the *context-governed* corpus.

The *demographic* approach to spoken corpus design and sampling used demographic parameters to sample the population of British English speakers in the United Kingdom. Using established random location sampling procedures, individual members of the population were selected by personal interview from across the country (with the assistance of a leading market research company − the British Market Research Bureau) taking into account age, gender, and social group. Selected individuals then recorded their own speech − and the speech of people they conversed with − using a portable tape recorder over a period of seven days. In this way a unique record of the language people use in everyday conversation was constructed.

For the *context-governed* approach, as in many other spoken corpora, the range of text types was divided into a priori linguistically motivated categories. At the top layer of the typology is a division into four equally sized contextually based categories: *educational, business, public/institutional,* and *leisure,* subdivided into monologue (40 per cent) and dialogue (60 per cent). Within each subcategory a range of text types is defined. These include lectures, classroom interaction, business meetings, interviews, sales demonstrations, political speeches, council meetings, legal proceedings, news broadcasts, and so on. The sampling methodology varied for each text type but the overall aim was to achieve a balanced selection within each text type, taking into account the following features: region, level, gender of speakers, and topic. All recordings were unscripted.

3 Processing of recordings

The processing stages of recordings from initial audio capture to the incorporation of transcriptions into the corpus are described below (see Fig. 19.1).

226   *Samples and systems of transcription*

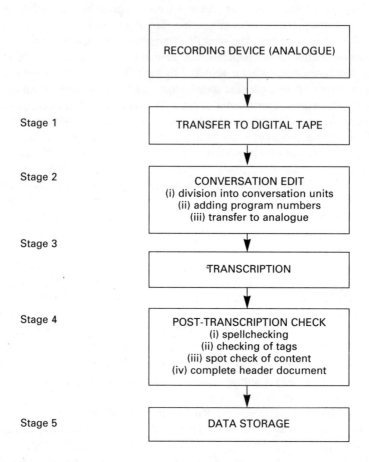

Figure 19.1 Processing of audio recording

Stage 1: Transfer to digital tape

Editing and retrieval of recordings in digital form is easier and quicker than in analogue. Using digital technology it is possible to edit with greater precision and speed and to put identification markers on the tape at the start of each text unit. Specific text units can then be retrieved simply by entering the appropriate identification number.

Stage 2: Conversation edit

Natural, spontaneous conversation is characterized by intermittent periods of dialogue that can vary in length from a few seconds to a few hours. During the course of a typical day many conversational exchanges are no more than a few words. The break point between one conversation and the next has to be a fairly subjective decision. In addition, many conversations do not have well-defined openings or closings. Conversations can be interrupted (by another conversation, or by an action of some kind) then resumed a few minutes later, or may never be finished. Participants in a conversation may depart, and others join. Participants may move from one setting to another, still continuing with the same conversation. Changes of topic can fluctuate considerably within the same conversation, or can mark the beginning of a new conversation. For the demographic corpus all recordings were divided into *conversational units* irrespective of whether the 'conversation' was several words or 10,000 words.

Each conversational unit exists as a separate document, complete with a header giving details of context and participants (see Crowdy 1993). The sequence of conversation units is indicated in the header. For practical reasons very short isolated utterances have been included within longer conversation units. A contiguous sequence of very short utterances has, on occasion, been grouped according to a common set of features. For example, a dialogue that consisted of two squash players exchanging the occasional utterance between rallies would be treated as a single unit of conversation. Within this unit each sub-unit of conversation is identified. Longer recordings that include multiple conversations will be split into units depending on the interaction of the following four factors: an elapsed period of silence, a change of participants, a change of setting, and a change of topic. The first, a period of time when no speaking is taking place, is the most frequent and reliable indicator that a change of conversation has occurred. Usually this is accompanied by a change in one of the other factors. If it is not there may be a resumption of the same conversation, although this likelihood diminishes the longer the silence continues. A change in conversation can take place without a significant pause in the flow of dialogue, such as if there is a change of participants coupled with a change of topic.

Most text units in the context-governed corpus are longer, with well defined openings and closings, making editing considerably easier.

Stage 3: Transcription

Transcription was carried out by a team of audio keyboarders using WordPerfect word-processing software. Each transcriber was trained over a period of several weeks during which time transcripts were carefully monitored. For particularly strong regional accents we recruited transcribers who were familiar with the accents. An average transcription rate of 750 words per hour was achieved, although this fluctuated considerably depending on the clarity of the recordings and speech and the complexity of the interchanges. In general, context-governed recordings were much easier to transcribe.

Stage 4: Post-transcription check

All transcripts were spell-checked and validated for tagging and structural errors. Detailed checks against the audio recordings were carried out on every fifth transcript to ensure consistency.

At this point transcriptions were incorporated into a corpus computer system for use by Longman lexicographers. However, this was only the first stage in the overall BNC processing 'sausage machine'. Details of the work of the other BNC partners are given in Chapters 5 and 13 above, but are summarized below.

From Longman the transcriptions were sent to Oxford University Computing Services, who were responsible for ensuring that all material was encoded in accordance with Text Encoding Initiative (TEI) guidelines for spoken corpus transcription (see Burnard, Chapter 5). This involved validation and translation of 'transcriber-friendly' codes (as described below in section 4) into common format SGML tags and features, defined in an agreed BNC Corpus Document Interchange Format, which will be the format in which the corpus will be delivered to other users.

From Oxford University Computing Services the data was sent to Lancaster University, who were responsible for the automatic word-class tagging of the BNC (see Garside, Chapter 13). The tagset was based on the CLAWS tagset, modified to meet the particular needs of the BNC.

4 Transcription

The design of any transcription scheme should involve consideration of: *Who is the transcription for? How will it be used? What are the important features?* The first users of the BNC are from the BNC consortium, principally the dictionary publishers Longman Group, Oxford University Press, and Chambers Harrap, so lexicographic applications are naturally of immediate concern. However, the BNC is also intended for discourse researchers, grammarians, general linguists, language teachers/authors, social scientists, and others, and as far as possible caters for their needs also. The corpus will be used in many ways, but in the main will be accessed for particular features or patterns, or viewed in concordanced form. (It has already been used extensively by Longman in the creation of a major new dictionary – the *Longman Language Activator*.) The transcription scheme needs to be easily assimilated and consistently coded. It is possible to access the corpus by a number of different text features, including lexical item, 'sentence', speaker turn, or text unit.

The overall extent of the corpus clearly also impacts on the transcription design, as this is determined by non-linguistic factors such as time and budget. The target of 10 million words was much bigger than any existing representative spoken corpus, and was achieved by using a broad orthographic transcription scheme, with little prosodic information and no phonetic features marked. It is hoped that audio recordings will be made available (initially through the National

Sound Archive in London) to researchers wishing to analyse the text in more detail, and in this case the transcript can be used as a baseline.

5   Transcription features

The following features are being transcribed (examples are given in Fig. 19.2)[2].

1)   Header document   notes

<REG>	M	region (M= Midlands)
<REF>	048902	reference number
<TIT>		title (optional)
<DAT>	14-01-92	date of recording
<TIM>	10:45	time of recording
<DEV>	wlk	recording device
<DUR>	1.50	duration of recording
<CTY>	Leicestershire	county
<LOC>	Leicester	location
<SET>	in the kitchen	setting
<ACT>	discussing newspaper article	activity
<TYP>	conversation	type of discourse
<SUP>		⎧ topic/domain classification
<SUB>		⎨ system (superfield, subject field,
<IND>		⎩ individual topic)
<SPN>	3	spontaneity
<AUD>	2	audience
<IDT1>	1	details for person 1:
<NAM1>	Sid	first name
<GEN1>	m	gender
<AGE1>	76	age
<LAN1>	BrE	language variety
<DIA1>	M	Midlands
<OCC1>	retired	occupation
<EDU1>	14	age left education
<SOC1>	D	social class
<REL1>	brother2	relationship to others
<IDT2>	2	details of person 2
<NAM2>	Fred	
<GEN2>	m	
<AGE2>	73	
<LAN2>	BrE	
<DIA2>	M	
<OCC2>	retired	
<EDU2>	14	
<SOC2>	?	
<REL2>	brother1	

2)   Transcription

<1>   The best paid jobs these days, say what you like,   notes:
      or what you don't like, is either in local government   (items in transcription
      or something like that. They're overpaid vastly,   have been italicized
      local government   for identification, and
                                                                 not as part of the
                                                                 transcription scheme)

<2>   Hm. Erm well I don't really know how much they get.   vocalized pauses

Samples and systems of transcription

```
<1>  Pardon?
<2>  <shouting>I don't really know how much money      paralinguistic tagging
     they get</>
<1>  Well you've only got to look at adverts in the ruddy
     paper for...                                       ... = short pause
<2>  I mean <unclear> I no, I'm, I'm thinking more on the   tag for unclear word or
                                                           passage
     ordinary clerical and that executive stuff, [not the
     <unclear> jobs].                                   overlapping text brackets
<1>  [Oh well, I was].
<2>  Yeah, yeah.
<1>  <unclear>.
<2>  I mean I don't think they're partic= particularly well   truncated word
     paid, but they they're <nv>cough</nv> well paid for     non-verbal sound
     what they flipping well do cos they don't, they, they,   repetition
     they don't do it, but I mean eh, that's the fault of
     the bosses, they should cut down the staff. You can't
     blame you can't blame people for hanging about doing
     nowt if they've got twice as many staff as they should
     have, and they're paying them, I mean, that, that's an
     administrative error, not a ... well it seems to be very
     rife in local [government that they're overstaffed]
<1>  [I, I think all these, all these people in] local
     government and things, and er, it's obvious when, you   vocalized pause
     see adverts for jobs, what a bloody salaries they're
     paying them, for a mediocre job.
<2>  Well I never look at the adverts do I? I'm not int= <nv>laugh</nv>.
<1>  No, I don't suppose you do now, but, but I never would
     work for local authorities, because at one time they
     were very poorly paid. ***(10) But it's all changed    pause of approx
     now, they're the best paid people in the ruddy country.  10 seconds
```

Figure 19.2 Sample transcription from British National Corpus

Speaker turns

The basic structural unit of spoken text is the speaker turn. Speaker turns are indicated by numerical references within angle bracket delimiters (e.g. <1>, <2>). Speakers are numbered sequentially as they enter the conversation; this number is linked to participant details given in a header document (see Fig. 19.2) attached to each unit of conversation. Speakers are uniquely coded to enable their speech to be tracked from one conversation to the next. If the transcriber cannot identify a particular speaker a question mark within angle brackets is used in place of a number.

Overlapping speech

Overlapping speech is very common in natural, informal conversation and any marking system has to be easy to employ (so that the transcription rate is not severely affected) and easy to interpret. The following system has a minimal effect on the speed of transcription, and although the precise positioning of markers may not always be accurate enough for detailed syntactic or conversational analysis it clearly shows that an interruption has taken place and who has made that interruption. In addition it is visually unobtrusive enough not to disrupt the analysis of those not specifically interested in overlap.

When an overlap occurs between two speakers the text that overlaps is shown within two sets of square brackets. If the text of a third speaker overlaps this is shown within curly brackets. For example:

Two speakers:

<1>   The clarinetist was a forlorn [looking]
<2>   [black-haired]
<1>   fellow

Three speakers:

<1>   So she was virtually a [a house prisoner]
<2>   [house {bound}]
<3>   {prisoner}

Note: speakers <1> and <2> simultaneously say 'a house prisoner' and 'house bound' respectively, whereas speaker <3> says 'prisoner' simultaneously with speaker <2> saying 'bound'.

Use of punctuation, and 'sentence' boundaries

The identification of intonational units requires a great deal of experience and is very time consuming. Often the division into intonational units is a separate preliminary phase prior to further mark-up. As stated previously, the intention for the BNC was to transcribe orthographically, not prosodically. We have used written text conventions to identify 'sentence-like' units which, although not strictly intonational, approximate to the behaviour of intonational units in terms of pausing and syntax. So, for example, if a spoken phrase ends with a falling contour and pause, the transcriber will add a full stop; if there is a slight terminal rise followed by a shorter pause, the transcriber will add a comma. The transcribers may not be overtly aware of any rhythmical or prosodic contour fluctuations, but intuitively feel that punctuation is required, as they would in written text. Transcribers are instructed to add punctuation only if it is syntactically appropriate, even if a pause has not occurred. Punctuation has not been added if it is syntactically inappropriate.

- A full stop or comma marks a syntactically appropriate termination or pause in an utterance, approximating to use in written text.
- Question marks and exclamation marks indicate questioning and exclamatory utterances.
- An equals sign (=) indicates an incomplete word, e.g. *diff=* (for *different*).

232   *Samples and systems of transcription*

- Three dots (...) indicate a pause (see following section).
- Apostrophes are used as in written text, for example in contractions and to indicate possessives.
- Speech marks (') are not used.

Pauses

As mentioned above, full stops and commas are used only where it would be syntactically appropriate to indicate pauses in written text. A longer pause – up to five seconds – is indicated by three dots (...). A pause of longer than five seconds is indicated again using three dots but followed by the duration in round brackets (measured to the nearest five seconds). A much longer pause, of say two or more minutes, would be treated as a break point for that conversation. Initially a more complex system of pause indicators was considered, but this was rejected because it could not be accurately applied without slowing down the transcription rate considerably.

Vocalized pauses

Vocalized pauses are represented orthographically, in accordance with an updatable control list of permissible forms. Examples are given in Fig. 19.2.

Accent, dialect, and representation of non-standard forms

Many non-standard forms are represented orthographically, such as *dunno, gonna,* and *cos*. As a rule, non-standard forms that appear as head-words in general dictionaries can be used in transcriptions. Distinct dialectal forms are also used, such as *lorra, nowt, owt, gradely, och,* and *ken*. Variations in pronunciation are not shown. Control lists of acceptable and normalized forms have been maintained.

Paralinguistic features

Where a particular stretch of text is characterized by an obvious paralinguistic feature, the start and end points of that text is tagged. For example:

<1>   <shouting>Mum, can I have a drink?</>
<2>   <whispering>Shh, you'll wake the baby.</>

Other tagged paralinguistic features include *<laughing>*, *<yawning>*, *<singing>*, and *<mimicking>*.

Non-verbal sounds

Non-verbal vocal sounds are represented using a generic <nv> tag to encode descriptions such as *cough, sneeze, laugh, yawn, whistling*. If these sounds continue for more than five seconds the duration may be added in round brackets after the description: <nv>laugh</nv>(10).

Contextual comments

Contextual comments can be added giving any relevant supplementary information, such as details of background noise or non-linguistic activities that might affect what is being spoken. Comments appear within round brackets, added by the transcriber as they are noticed, and include: *(loud traffic noise), (TV on), (playing croquet), (eating biscuits)* and *(drumming fingers on table)*.

Unclear or inaudible text

Because of the large quantity of spoken material that needs to be transcribed, transcribers are instructed not to spend too much time attempting to understand words that are unclear (for whatever reason – poor recording, too much background noise, unusual accent, poor enunciation, etc.). For single words or short extracts of less than five seconds, if the text is unclear the transcribers add the code <unclear>. Longer inaudible extracts are timed to the nearest five seconds, for example: <unclear>(15). If a transcriber is unable to understand somebody because he or she has an unfamiliar accent or dialect the passage is marked for the attention of the transcription checker. In some cases it may be necessary to recruit transcribers who are familiar with a particular accent.

Unfamiliar words

Words that are unfamiliar to the transcriber or that the transcriber is not sure how to spell are marked with the tag <??>. For example, <??>Lemster</> (=Leominster) and <??>skuzzy</> (=SCSI). This alerts the transcription checker who will then add the correct spelling, if known.

Spelt-out words

Words that the speaker spells out letter by letter are transcribed in capitals with spaces between each letter. For example:

> I live in Hinxton. That's spelt H I N X T O N.

Acronyms and abbreviations

Acronyms and abbreviations will be transcribed as a sequence of upper-case letters separated by spaces (P H D, M P H, V A T). Where acronyms and abbreviations are pronounced as words they will be represented as sequences of upper-case letters without spaces (VAT – pronounced *vat*, RIBA – pronounced *riba*).

Telephone conversations

Telephone conversations do not form part of the demographic corpus and have been gathered as part of the context-governed corpus approach. However, it is important to mark where a telephone conversation is taking place in the text, and for this the code <*tel*> is followed, where necessary, by an indication of the length of the conversation (unless the telephone call marks the end of conversation).

Codes used to preserve anonymity

During a conversation any reference that would allow an individual to be identified is omitted from the transcription. Full names of participants are not given, and any other full-name references are replaced with <*name*> tag. Personal addresses that include house or street names are replaced with an address tag <*address*>. Similarly, telephone numbers are replaced with a <*tel_num*> tag. The names of publicly known figures and addresses are not changed.

Text read out

Occasionally during a conversation one participant might read out a passage from a newspaper or magazine, or read out a notice or road sign. The tag <*read*> is used to indicate the beginning of passages that are predominantly read, terminated with an end tag </>.

Note

1. The British National Corpus (BNC) is a major collaborative venture, containing 100 million words of contemporary written (90 million words) and spoken (10 million words) British English. The participants in the project are Oxford University Press, Longman Group UK Ltd, Chambers Harrap, the British Library and the universities of Oxford (Oxford University Computing Services) and Lancaster (Unit for Computer Research on the English Language). For details of availability for research please contact Oxford University Computing Services, 13 Banbury Road, Oxford OXN 6NN.
2. [*Editors' note*] The following transcription features illustrate the 'transcriber-friendly' mark-up devised by Longman. Compare Garside, Chapter 13, for examples of the full TEI version of the mark-up, used in the distributable version of the British National Corpus.

20 The Bergen Corpus of London Teenager Language (COLT)

VIBECKE HASLERUD and ANNA-BRITA STENSTRÖM

1 Introducing COLT

The Bergen Corpus of London Teenager Language (COLT) was launched in March 1993 with support from the Norwegian Research Council for the Humanities. It consists of about half a million words of spontaneous conversations between 13- to 17-year-old boys and girls from London with varying social backgrounds, ranging from lower working class to upper class. The method used for recording the data was patterned on the Longman model used for collecting the British National Corpus (BNC) (described in Crowdy, Chapter 19). The entire corpus was transcribed by the Longman Group and was ready for checking by the Bergen team in March 1994. The corrected version was then included as part of the BNC (for further processing of the BNC see, e.g. Quirk 1992: 460–1). At the Bergen end, the transcription will be refined to suit our purposes, and COLT will ultimately be available on CD-ROM, with text, sound and search program.

The transcription of COLT involves the following levels:

1. the Longman level (orthographic; sentence orientated)
2. the Bergen level (prosodic; tone-unit orientated)
3. the TEI level (tagged to conform with international mark-up standards)

In what follows we shall compare the Longman and the Bergen transcription schemes applied to the same piece of talk, an extract from a conversation between two 17-year-old public school girls.

Tagging at the TEI (Text Encoding Initiative) level will not be discussed in this chapter (for a description of TEI, see Burnard, Chapter 5).

2 Transcription

2.1 Aims

The primary concern of the Longman Group when transcribing the BNC has been lexicographic applications which, first of all, requires accessibility by lexical item. The corpus has not been made accessible by lexical item alone, however, but also by 'sentence', speaker turn and text unit to make it available for other types of research (cf. Crowdy this volume Chapter 19).

The primary concern of the Bergen team is to make COLT available for linguistic research in general and discourse and sociolinguistic research in particular. Therefore, the Bergen transcription differs from the Longman transcription both in terms of focus and degree of delicacy.

2.2 The Longman scheme

The Longman scheme, characterized as 'enhanced orthographic transcription', aims at identifying 'sentence-like units' which, according to Crowdy (Chapter 19), 'although not strictly intonational approximate to the behaviour of intonational units in terms of pausing and syntax' (see Fig. 20.1).

		Line
<1>	He's as changeable as the weather.	1
<2>	Who me?	2
<1>	No <name>	3
<2>	Well I'll think about it then.	4
<1>	He's the kind of person you fancy and you think no, I	5
	don't, no.	6
<2>	<unclear> it's just such a dilemma. I do actually quite	7
	fancy <name>. I don't want to but I do. What are you	8
	doing? Oh you're just so good.	9
<1>	<unclear> my left hand and a fist	10
<2>	You doing step aerobics tomorrow?	11
<1>	No way!	12
<2>	I was going to and then erm me and <name> have got to do	13
	our French oral.	14
<1>	<unclear>	15
<2>	Yeah me too. Actually I don't think I can afford it if	16
	I'm [going to the pub]	17
<1>	[No I'm not]	18
<2>	No if I'm going to the pub on Saturday, then I'm going	19
	to the Galleria on [Sunday]	20
<1>	[Sunday] How are you getting to the Galleria?	21
<2>	I don't know yet.	22
<1>	Cost you loads by taxi.	23
<2>	I know. I've got twelve quid for the week=, I've got	24
	twelve quid for the weekend.	25
<1>	<unclear>	26
<2>	Well <name> might be able to give me a lift. Me and	27
	<name> a lift. Yeah. I don't know how the fuck we're	28
	gonna get back.	29
<1>	Well it depends.	30
<2>	I can always phone up my mum and go can you pick me up	31
	from the Galleria and take me back to <name> please.	32
<1>	She'll go no.	33
<2>	You reckon. Dunno, might ask me Dad cos he'll probably	34
	take us back to the pub <nv>laugh</nv>.	35

Figure 20.1 Longman transcription

2.2.1 Sentences

'Sentences' are marked off by a capital letter at the beginning and a punctuation mark (. , ? !) at the end according to writing conventions – and the transcriber's intuition. In addition, the punctuation marks have a functional role; they are used to mark continuing, terminating, questioning and exclamatory intonation.

2.2.2 Pauses

Punctuation marks have also been used for silent pauses occurring at a syntactic boundary, a comma for brief pauses after a slight rise (e.g. lines 5 and 6 in Fig. 20.1) and a full stop for somewhat longer pauses after a falling contour (e.g. lines 1,4,6). The spelling *erm* (line 13) is used for a filled pause. (Other spellings of 'vocalized pauses' are listed in Crowdy, Chapter 19, Figure 19.2.)

2.2.3 Non-standard forms

The scheme allows certain non-standard forms reflecting spoken language, such as contractions (*He's* line 1, *I'll* line 4) and spelling variants reflecting pronunciation (*gonna* line 29, *Dunno* and *cos* line 34).

2.2.4 Overlaps

Square brackets ([]) indicate single speech overlaps; *[No I'm not]* in line 18, for instance, is uttered at the same time as *[going to the pub]* in line 17. The brackets are not vertically aligned.

2.2.5 Unintelligible speech

Angle brackets (<>) are used for unintelligible speech (lines 7, 15, 26), omission of proper names (lines 3, 8, 27, 32) and non-verbal sounds (line 35).

2.2.6 Incomplete words and sentences

The equal sign is used for incomplete words (*week=* line 24), but there is no indication of incomplete sentences.

2.2.7 Non-verbal sounds

All non-verbal sounds, except filled pauses, are indicated in the same way. The only example of a non-verbal sound in the text is *<nv>laugh</nv>* (line 35).

2.2.8 Anonymity

All names and addresses have been deleted to assure full anonymity. This is illustrated in lines 3, 8, 27, and 32 (*<name>*).

Additional conventions, not illustrated in this extract, are listed in Fig. 20.3 below.

2.2.9 Comments

This written-like transcript of spoken text has certain advantages. To begin with, it is simple and straightforward and easy to read (cf. Edwards 1993b: 6); second, it gives a fair picture of the syntactic structure of the speaker turns in terms of 'sentence-like' units; third, it also gives some indication of intonation and utterance function.

However, the use (and non-use) of punctuation marks may lead to confusion because commas and full stops play a dual role. In addition to functioning as syntactic markers, they also represent short and medium pauses. These two roles sometimes conflict with each other. For example, one does not always pause between sentences, but the transcribers are instructed to add a full stop if there is a falling intonation contour. How, then, will the analyst recognize whether the full stop serves only to mark end of sentence or end of sentence plus a medium-length pause? And what about a brief pause after a falling contour and a long pause after a rise? Would they still be indicated by comma and full stop, respectively? Moreover, pauses within sentences are frequent, but these will not be marked in the transcript, since 'Transcribers are instructed to add punctuation only if it is syntactically appropriate' (Crowdy, Chapter 19). It seems that even if punctuation increases the readability, it will not invariably correspond to the recorded speech studied; it may interfere with our perception of the sound material.

2.3 The Bergen scheme

With the Longman level of transcription as a starting-point, we are aiming at a transcription that is closer to the spoken language, in other words a transcription scheme that captures what we think are the main features of spontaneous conversation. The Bergen transcription scheme focuses on the tone unit, notably a simplified version of the tone unit proposed by Crystal (1969, 1975), and used in a more elaborate form in the London–Lund Corpus (LLC) (see Svartvik and Quirk 1980). In its simplest form, the tone unit consists of a *tonic syllable* expounded by a *nuclear tone* and optionally preceded and/or followed by other syllables (cf. Crystal 1975: 11).

2.3.1 Tone units

Tone units are divided by tone unit boundaries (#). Capital letters are used for the syllable in the tone unit carrying the nuclear tone, which is often the last word in the tone unit (*he's as changeable as the W_EATHer#* line 1). A falling (\), rising (/), level (_), falling-rising (V) or rising-falling (∧) tone marker precedes the first vowel sound in the nuclear syllable.

		Line
<1>	he's as changeable as the W_EATHer#.	1
<2>	who M\E# .	2
<1>	no . C\OLin# .	3
<2>	well I'll TH\INK about it then# . .	4
<1>	yeah he's the kind of person you F\ANcy and you think# N\O#	5
	oh I D\ON't# . N\O . .	6
<2>	<10 sylls> it's just S\UCH# a diL\EMma# I D\ O actually quite	7
	fancy Kirian# . . I don't W\ANT to# but I D/O# . . what are	8
	you D_Oing# . oh you're just so . G_OOD#	9
<1>	with my left hand . in a F\IST#	10
<2>	@@ . . mh . .	11
<1>	[<10 sylls>]	12
<2>	[you doing] step aeR\Obics tomorrow#	13
<1>	no W\AY#	14
<2>	I ca= * I was G\Oing to and then erm# . . me and R\OBin have	15
	got to do . our French /ORal# . .	16
<1>	<unclear> (5)	17
<2>	yeah me T\OO# . . [actually I don't think I can] afF\ORD it#	18
	if I'm [going to the P\UB]#	19
<1>	[no I'm N\OT#]	20
<2>	no if I'm going to the pub on S\/Aturday# . . and I'm	21
	going to the Galleria on [S\UNday]#	22
<1>	[S\UNday]# how are you getting to	23
	the GalleR\Ia#	24
<2>	I don't know Y/ET#	25
<1>	cost you L\OADS# by T\AXi#	26
<2>	oh I KN_OW# . . I've got TW\ELVE [quid# for the week= +I've	27
	got TW\ELVE] quid for the# week/END# . . .	28
<1>	[<5 sylls>] you'll N\EVer	29
	be able to <6 sylls> Galleria#	30
<2>	N/O# . . well ChaN\EL might be able to give me a L\IFT#.	31
	[me and] Robin a L\IFT#	32
<1>	[TH\ERE]#	33
<2>	Y/EAH# . . but I don't know how the F\UCK# we're gonna get	34
	B\ACK# . .	35
<1>	well it depends on [if you] ==	36
<2>	[I can _ALways] phone up my mum and go#	37
	can you pick me up from the <laughing> GalleR\Ia# and take	38
	me back </> to H\Onevalley please#	39
<1>	she'll go . . N\O#	40
<2>	you R\/ECKon# . . dunN\O# might ask me D\AD# . cos he'll	41
	probably take us back to the @ P\UB#	42

Figure 20.2 Bergen transcription

2.3.2 Pauses

Brief pauses are indicated by a full stop (.) instead of a comma, with a space on either side to distinguish it from a punctuation mark. We use two full stops instead of one for the medium pause, while longer pauses are indicated by three full stops, as in the Longman transcripts. Notice that pauses do not necessarily co-occur with tone unit boundaries; many tone unit boundaries do not have a pause, and some pauses come within tone units (e.g. lines 3, 9).

2.3.3 Non-standard forms

The spelling of non-standard forms follows the Longman pattern. We accept *you're* (line 9) and *gonna* (line 34), and so on. Due to the nature of COLT, we may have to be more liberal, however. Teenager language may very well prove to contain more non-standard forms than adult language, and the idea is of course to highlight the differences.

2.3.4 Overlaps

We use the same conventions as the Longman Group for overlapping speech but prefer to align the left brackets in order to make the overlapping 'unit' stand out (e.g. lines 22 and 23, 32 and 33).

2.3.5 Unintelligible speech

Instead of <unclear> for unintelligible speech we prefer to indicate the number of unclear syllables, for instance <10 sylls> (line 12). If, however, the unintelligible speech lasts for more 5 seconds, we indicate it in the same way as Longman, by <unclear>(5) (line 17).

2.3.6 Incomplete words and tone units

Incomplete words are marked by an equal sign as in the Longman transcripts (*week=* line 27). In addition, we have decided to mark incomplete tone units by double equal signs (==), as in line 36 (*well it depends on if you==*).

2.3.7 Non-verbal sounds

Laughter is an extremely important feature of conversation and worth much more consideration than it is usually given. It is, for instance, used both as an interactive and as a strategic device. Therefore, we have decided to use the @ symbol, introduced by Du Bois (1991: 87) and Du Bois et al. (1993: 67), to indicate laughter 'syllables' instead of using the convention <nv>xxx</nv> for non-verbal sounds in general. When the speaker laughs while talking, on the other hand, we use the Longman convention (*<laughing> GalleR\Ia# and take me back </>* lines 38–39).

2.3.8 Restarts and repetitions

We have introduced the use of the asterisk (*) to mark a restart (*I ca= *I was G\Oing to and* line 15) and the plus sign (+) for repetitions (*I've got TW\ELVE quid# for the week= +I've got TW\ELVE quid for the# week/END#* lines 27–28).

2.3.9 Anonymity

For the Bergen level of transcription, which does not involve accompanying sound, we have substituted original names and addresses by faked names and addresses consisting of the same number of syllables as the originals to preserve the speech rhythm. As regards the TEI level, which involves a CD-ROM version with sound, we hope to be able to produce the faked names and addresses by synthetic means.

2.3.10 Comments

The Bergen transcription, illustrated in this chapter, involved checking, refining and sometimes adding to the Longman transcription, which explains the difference in length between the two versions. We have, however, taken maximal advantage of the Longman transcription scheme and, despite our intention to produce a prosodic rather than orthographic transcription, we have not departed from it more than is absolutely necessary (see Fig. 20.3). The fact that we have restricted the features of the tone unit to the minimum makes the transcription easy to read without leaving out basic information. The idea is that whoever needs more prosodic and paralinguistic information does his/her own additional analysis. As we see it, the principles of the Bergen scheme correspond reasonably well to the properties that Edwards (1992b: 130) regards as desirable for a transcription system: 'minimally theory-committal, easily readable, computationally tractable, minimally time-consuming to learn and to use, and expandable for more specific research needs'.

Longman	Bergen	
. , ? !		sentence-like boundaries
CAPS		sentence beginnings
	#	tone unit boundaries
	CAPS	nuclear syllable
	\	falling tone
	/	rising tone
	_	level tone
	*	restart
	+	repetition
	==	incomplete tone unit
=	=	incomplete word
,	.	brief pause
.	. .	medium pause
. . .	. . .	long pause
. . . (5 secs)	. . . (5 secs)	pause 5 secs or longer

242 *Samples and systems of transcription*

<nv>laugh</nv>	@@@@@	laughter syllables
<name>	substitute	name
<address>	substitute	address
<unclear>	<3 sylls>	unintelligible speech
<unclear> (5)	<unclear> (5)	–"– 5 secs or longer
[ ]	[ ]	single overlap
{ }	{ }	" "
[{ }]	[{ }]	double overlap
<singing> text</>	<singing>text</>	paralinguistic features
<nv>yawn</nv>	<nv>yawn</nv>	nonverbal sound
(hairdryer on)	(hairdryer on)	contextual comment
<??>text</>	<??>text</>	uncertain transcription

Figure 20.3 Coding conventions

Bibliographical references

Aijmer K, Altenberg (eds) B 1991 *English corpus linguistics: studies in honour of Jan Svartvik*. Longman, London

Alderson P, Knowles G forthcoming *Working with the Spoken English Corpus*. Longman, London

Altenberg B 1991 A bibliography of publications relating to English computer corpora. In Johansson S, Stenström A-B (eds) *English computer corpora: selected papers and research guide*. Mouton de Gruyter, Berlin/New York pp 355–95

Altenberg B 1993 Recurrent verb-complement constructions in the London–Lund corpus. In Aarts J, Haan P de, Oostdijk N (eds) *English language corpora: design, analysis and exploitation. Papers from the Thirteenth International Conference on English Language Research on Computerized Corpora, Nijmegen*. Rodopi, Amsterdam/Atlanta pp 227–46

Anderson A H, Badger M, Bard E G, Boyle E, Doherty G, Garrod S, Isard S, Kowtko J, McAllister J, Miller J, Sotillo C, Thompson H S, Weinert R 1991 The HCRC Map Task Corpus, *Language and Speech*, **34**(4) 351–66

Argyle M, Alkema F, Gilmour R 1971 The communication of friendly and hostile attitudes by verbal and non-verbal signals. *European Journal of Social Psychology* **1**: 385–402

Argyle M, Salter V, Nicholson H, Williams M, Burgess P 1970 The communication of inferior and superior attitudes by verbal and non-verbal signals. *British Journal of Social and Clinical Psychology* **9**: 222–31

Arnfield S, Atwell E A 1993 A syntax-based grammar of stress sequences *Proceedings of the IE Conference on Grammatical Inference*. Essex University

Atkinson J M, Heritage J (eds) 1984 *Structures of social action: studies in conversation analysis*. Cambridge University Press, Cambridge

Atwell E, Elliott S 1987 Dealing with ill-formed English text. In Garside R, Leech G N, Sampson G (eds) *The computational analysis of English: a corpus-based approach*. Longman, London pp 120–38

Austin J L 1962 *How to do things with words*. Clarendon, Oxford

Auteserre G, Pérennou, G P, Rossi M 1991 Methodology for the transcription and labeling of a speech corpus. *Journal of the International Phonetic Association* **19**: 2–15

Baker M, Francis G, Tognini-Bonelli E (eds) 1994 *Text and Technology*. Benjamins, Amsterdam

Bakhtin M M [1936] 1986 *Speech genre and other late essays*. University of Texas, Austin
Bates E, Friederici A, Wulfeck B 1987 Grammatical morphology in aphasia. Evidence from three languages. *Cortex* **23**: 545–74
Batstone R 1994 *Grammar*. Oxford University Press, Oxford
BBC 1992 *BBC English dictionary: a dictionary for the world* Collins COBUILD, London
Berman R A, Slobin D 1986 *Coding manual: temporality in discourse*. University of California, Institute of Cognitive Studies, Berkeley
Biber D 1988 *Variation across speech and writing*. Cambridge University Press, Cambridge
Biber D 1992 Using computer-based text corpora to analyze the referential strategies of spoken and written texts. In Svartvik J (ed) *Directions in corpus linguistics. Proceedings of Nobel Symposium 82, Stockholm, 4–8 August 1991*. Mouton de Gruyter, Berlin/New York pp 213–52
Biber D 1993 Representativeness in corpus design. *Literary and Linguistic Computing* **8**(4): 243–57
Biber D, Finegan E 1991 On the exploitation of computerized corpora in variation studies. In Aijmer K, Altenberg B (eds) *English corpus linguistics: studies in honour of Jan Svartvik*. Longman, London pp 204–20
Birdwhistell R 1973 *Kinesics and context*. Penguin, Harmondsworth
Bishop D V M 1984 Automated LARSP: computer-assisted grammatical analysis. *British Journal of Disorders of Communication* **19**: 78–87
Bliss L 1988 The development of modals. *Journal of Applied Developmental Psychology* **9**: 253–61
Bloom L 1973 *One word at a time: the use of single word utterances before syntax*. Mouton, The Hague
Bloom L 1993 Transcription and coding for child language research: the parts are more than the whole. In Edwards J A, Lampert M D (eds) *Talking data: transcription and coding in discourse research*. Lawrence Erlbaum, Hillsdale, NJ pp 149–66
Boase S 1990 *London–Lund Corpus: example text and transcription guide*. Survey of English Usage, University College London
Bolinger D L 1961 *Generality, gradience, and the all-or-none*. Mouton, The Hague
Boyle E A 1990 *User's guide to the HCRC Dialogue Database. Technical Report HCRC/TR-11*. Human Communication Research Centre, University of Edinburgh, Edinburgh
Brierley L, Cassar I, Loader P, Norman K, Shantry I, Wolfe S, Wood D 1992 *Thinking voices: the work of the National Oracy Project*. Hodder Stoughton, London
Brodda B 1988 Tracing turns in the London–Lund Corpus. *Literary and Linguistic Computing* **3**: 94–104
Brown R 1973 *A first language: the early stages*. Allen and Unwin, London
Bruce G 1992 Comments on the paper by Jane Edwards. In Svartvik J (ed) *New directions in corpus linguistics*. Mouton de Gruyter, Berlin pp 145–47
Burnard L 1991a What is TEI? In Greenstein D (ed) *Modelling historical data*. Scripta Mercaturae Verlag, St Katharinen pp 130–45
Burnard L 1991b Speaking with one voice. In Greenstein D (ed) *Modelling historical data*. Scripta Mercaturae Verlag, St Katharinen
Burnard L 1992 The TEI: a progress report. In Leitner G (ed) *New dimensions in corpus linguistics*. Mouton de Gruyter, Berlin/New York pp 97–107
Burnard L 1993b The TEI: a further report. In Souter C, Atwell E (eds) *Corpus-based computational linguistics*. Rodopi, Amsterdam pp 37–45

Burnard L 1993c The TEI: Towards an extensible standard for the encoding of texts. In Sperberg-McQueen C M, Burnard L (eds) *Guidelines for electronic text encoding and interchange*. Text Encoding Initiative, Chicago/Oxford pp 1–9

Calzolari N, McNaught J (eds) 1994 *Interim report of EAGLES (Expert Advisory Groups on Language Engineering Standards)*. ILC, University of Pisa; CCL, University of Manchester Institute of Science and Technology; available on File Transfer Protocol (FTP)

Caplan D 1987 *Neurolinguistics and linguistic aphasiology*. Cambridge University Press, Cambridge

Carroll L [1893] 1982 Sylvie and Bruno concluded. In *The Penguin complete Lewis Carroll*. Penguin, Harmondsworth

Chafe W L (ed) 1980 *The pear stories: cognitive, cultural and linguistic aspects of narrative production*. Ablex, Norwood, NJ.

Chafe W L 1987 Cognitive constraints on information flow. In Tomlin R W (ed) *Coherence and grounding in discourse*. John Benjamins, Amsterdam pp 21–55

Chafe W L 1988 Punctuation and the prosody of written language. *Written Communication* **5**: 396–426

Chafe W L 1993 Prosodic and functional units of language. In Edwards J A, Lampert M D (eds) *Talking data: transcription and coding in discourse research*. Lawrence Erlbaum, Hillsdale, NJ pp 33–43

Chafe W L 1994 *Discourse, consciousness, and time: the flow and displacement of conscious experience in speaking and writing*. University of Chicago Press, Chicago

Cheepen C 1988 *The predictability of informal conversation*. Pinter, London

Cheepen C, Monaghan J 1990 *Spoken English: a practical guide*. Pinter, London

Chomsky N 1965 *Aspects of the theory of syntax*. MIT Press, Cambridge, MA.

Chomsky N, Halle M 1968 *The sound pattern of English*. Harper and Row, New York/London

Church K W, Mercer, R L 1993 Introduction to the Special Issue on Computational Linguistics Using Large Corpora. *Computational Linguistics* **19**(1): 1–24

Conti-Ramsden G, Dykins J 1989 Mother–child interaction with language-impaired children and their siblings. Unpublished manuscript, University of Manchester

Cook G 1990 Transcribing infinity: problems of context presentation. *Journal of Pragmatics* **14**(1): 1–24

Cook G 1992 *The discourse of advertising*. Routledge, London

Cook G 1994a Repetitions and knowing by heart: an aspect of intimate discourse and its implications. *English Language Teaching Journal* **48**(2): 133–42

Cook G 1994b *Discourse and literature: the interplay of form and mind*. Oxford University Press, Oxford

Coulthard M, Mongomery M (eds) 1981 *Studies in discourse analysis*. Routledge and Kegan Paul, London

Couper-Kuhlen E 1986 *An introduction to English prosody*. Edward Arnold, London

Crowdy S 1993 Spoken corpus design and transcription. *Literary and Linguistic Computing* **8**(4): 259–65

Crowdy S 1994 Spoken corpus transcription. *Literary and Linguistic Computing* **10**: 25–8

Cruttenden A 1986 *Intonation* Cambridge. University Press, Cambridge

Crystal D 1969 *Prosodic systems and intonation in English*. Cambridge University Press, Cambridge

Crystal D 1974 Review of Brown, R. 1973. *Journal of Child Language* **1**: 289–307

Crystal D 1975 *The English tone of voice: essays on intonation, prosody and paralanguage*. Edward Arnold, London

Crystal D 1979 Neglected grammatical factors in conversational English. In Greenbaum S, Leech G, Svartvik J (eds) *Studies in English linguistics: for Randolph Quirk*. Longman, London pp 153–66

Crystal D 1982 *Profiling linguistic disability*. Edward Arnold, London

Crystal D 1991 *A dictionary of linguistics and phonetics*, 3rd edn. Blackwell, Oxford

Crystal D, Fletcher P, Garman M 1989 *The grammatical analysis of language disability*, 2nd edn. Edward Arnold, London

Crystal D, Varley R 1993 *Introduction to language pathology*, 3rd edn. Whurr, London

Darwin C 1877 A biographical sketch of an infant. *Mind* **2**: 285–94

Davis W S 1983 *Systems analysis and design*. Addison Wesley, Reading, Mass.

Derrida J [1967] 1976 *Of grammatology*. Johns Hopkins University Press, Baltimore

Derrida J [1978] [1967] 1988 Structure, sign and play in the discourse of the human sciences. In Lodge D (ed) *Modern criticism and theory: a reader*. Longman, London pp 107–24

Du Bois J W 1991 Transcription design principles for spoken discourse research. *Pragmatics: Quarterly Publication of the International Pragmatics Association* **1**(1): 71–106

Du Bois J W, Schuetze-Coburn S, Paolino D, Cumming S 1990 *Discourse transcription*. University of California, Santa Barbara

Du Bois J W, Schuetze-Coburn S 1993 Representing hierarchy: constituent structure for discourse databases. In Edwards J A, Lampert M D (eds) *Talking data: transcription and coding in discourse research*. Lawrence Erlbaum, Hillsdale, NJ pp 221–60

Du Bois J W, Schuetze-Coburn S, Cumming S, Paolino D 1993 Outline of discourse transcription. In Edwards J A, Lampert M D (eds) *Talking data: transcription and coding in discourse research*. Lawrence Erlbaum, Hillsdale, NJ pp 45–89

Duckworth M, Allen G, Hardcastle W, Ball M 1990 Extensions to the International Phonetic Alphabet for the transcription of atypical speech. *Clinical linguistics and phonetics* **4**: 273–80

Edwards J A 1989 *Transcription and the new functionalism: a counterproposal to the CHILDES CHAT conventions. Cognitive Science Program Technical Report, No. 58*. University of California, Berkeley (ERIC Document Reproduction No. ED 341 236)

Edwards J A 1991 Transcription in discourse. In Bright W (ed) *Oxford international encyclopedia of linguistics*. Oxford University Press, Oxford pp 367–71

Edwards J A 1992a Computer methods in child language research: four principles for the use of archive data. *Journal of Child Language* **19**: 435–58

Edwards J A 1992b Design principles in the transcription of spoken discourse. In Svartvik J (ed) *Directions in corpus linguistics. Proceedings of the Nobel Symposium 82, Stockholm, August 4–8, 1991*. Mouton, New York pp 129–44

Edwards J A 1993a Perfecting research techniques in an imperfect world: response to MacWhinney and Snow. *Journal of Child Language* **20**: 209–16

Edwards J A 1993b Principles and contrasting systems of discourse transcription. In Edwards J A, Lampert M D (eds) *Talking data: transcription and coding in discourse research*. Lawrence Erlbaum, Hillsdale, NJ pp 3–31

Edwards J A, Lampert M D (eds) 1993 *Talking data: transcription and coding in discourse research*. Lawrence Erlbaum, Hillsdale, NJ

Edwards S, Garman M, Knott R 1992 Project report: the linguistic characterization of aphasic speech. *Clinical Linguistics and Phonetics* **6**: 161–4

Edwards S, Garman M, Knott R 1993 Short report: the grammatical characterization of aphasic language. *Aphasiology* **7**: 217–20

Ehlich K 1993 HIAT: a transcription system for discourse data. In Edwards J A, Lampert M D (eds) *Talking data: transcription and coding in discourse research*. Lawrence Erlbaum, Hillsdale, NJ pp 123–48

Feldman H, Keefe K, Holland A 1989 Language abilities after left hemisphere brain injury: a case study of twins. *Topics in Special Education* **9**: 32–47

Fillmore C J 1992 'Corpus linguistics' or 'Computer-aided armchair linguistics'. In Svartvik J (ed) *Directions in corpus linguistics. Proceedings of Nobel Symposium 82, Stockholm, 4–8 August 1991*. Mouton de Gruyter, Berlin/New York pp 35–60

Fillmore L W, Peters A, Östman J-O, Larsen T, O'Connor M C, Parker L 1982 *Coding manual for the Individual Differences in Language Learning Project*. University of California, School of Education, Berkeley

Fishman J A 1965 Who speaks what language to whom and when? *Linguistique* **2**: 57–88

Fletcher P, Garman M, Johnson M, Schelletter C, Stodel L 1986 Characterising language impairment in terms of normal language development: advantages and limitations. In *Proceedings of the seventh annual Wisconsin symposium on research in child language disorders*. University of Wisconsin-Madison, Madison pp 74–84

Fletcher P, Ingham R 1995 Grammatical impairment. In Fletcher P, MacWhinney B (eds) *The Handbook of child language*. Blackwell, Oxford pp 602–22

Francis W N, Kucera H 1979 *Manual of information to accompany a standard sample of present-day edited American English, for use with digital computers*. First published 1964, revised and augmented 1979. Department of Linguistics, Brown University, Providence, R.I.

French J P 1992a Notes and conventions for soundprint transcribers. Unpublished paper: J P French Associates

French J P 1992b Transcription proposals: multi-level system. NERC-WP4-50. Working paper for NERC

Freund E 1987 *The return of the reader*. Methuen, London

Fries C C 1940 *American English grammar*. Appleton-Century Crofts, New York

Gardner-Chloros P 1991 *Language selection and switching in Strasbourg*. Clarendon, Oxford

Garman M 1989 The role of linguistics in speech therapy: assessment and interpretation. In Grunwell P, James A (eds) *The functional evaluation of language disorders*. Croom Helm, London pp 29–57

Garside R, Leech G and Sampson G (eds) 1987 *The computational analysis of English: a corpus-based approach*. Longman, London

Gee J P, Grosjean F 1983 Performance structures: a psycholinguistic and linguistic appraisal. *Cognitive Psychology* **15**: 411–58

Ghali N, Arnfield S, Roach P 1992 Statistical relationships between acoustic and auditory records of intonation. *Proceedings of the Institute of Acoustics* **14**(6): 207–15

Goffman E 1967 *Interaction ritual* Anchor Books, New York

Greenbaum S 1992 A new corpus of English: ICE. In Svartvik J (ed) Directions in corpus linguistics. *Proceedings of Nobel Symposium 82, Stockholm, 4–8 August 1991*. Mouton de Gruyter, Berlin/New York pp 171–9

Bibliographical references

Grodzinsky Y 1990 *Theoretical perspectives on language deficits*. MIT. Press, Cambridge, Mass.

Gumperz J J, Berenz N 1993 Transcribing conversational exchanges. In Edwards J A, Lampert M D (eds) *Talking data: transcription and coding in discourse research*. Lawrence Erlbaum, Hillsdale, NJ pp 91–121

Guo J 1992 Table five chu can ng gai! Conversation analysis of English-Mandarin-Cantonese code-switching in a local Chinese restaurant. Unpublished MA Thesis. Department of Linguistics, Lancaster University.

Halliday M A K 1967 *Intonation and Grammar in British English*. Mouton, The Hague

Halliday M A K 1975 Language as social semiotic: towards a general sociolinguistic theory. In Makkai A, Makkai V B (eds) *The first LACUS forum*. Hornbeam Press, Columbia S.C. pp 17–46

Halliday M A K 1985 *An introduction to functional grammar*. Arnold, London

Halliday M A K 1991 Corpus studies and probabilistic grammar. In Aijmer K, Altenberg B (eds) *English corpus linguistics: studies in honour of Jan Svartvik*. Longman, London pp 30–43

Halliday M A K, McIntosh A, Strevens P 1964 *The linguistic sciences and language teaching*. Longman, London

Hargrove P M, Holmberg C, Ziegler M 1986 Changes in spontaneous speech associated with therapy hiatus: a retrospective study. *Child Language Teaching and Therapy* 2: 266–80

Harris Z S 1946 From morpheme to utterance. *Language* 22: 161–83

Harris Z S 1951 *Methods in structural linguistics*. Chicago University Press, Chicago

Heath C 1984 Talk and recipiency. In Atkinson J M, Heritage J (eds) *Structures of social action: studies in conversation analysis*. Cambridge University Press, Cambridge pp 247–65

Hoey M 1982 *On the surface of discourse*. George Allen and Unwin, London

Holland A, Miller J, Reinmuth O, Bartlett C, Fromm D, Pashek G, Stein D, Swindell C 1988 Rapid recovery from aphasia: a detailed language analysis. *Brain and Language* 24: 156–73

Holub R C 1984 *Reception theory*. Methuen, New York and London

Hooshyar N 1985 Language interaction between mothers and their nonhandicapped children, mothers and their Down children, and mothers and their language. *International Journal of Rehabilitation Research* 4: 475–7

Hunt K 1965 *Grammatical structures written at three grade levels*. National Council of Teachers of English, Champaign, Illinois

Jefferson G 1984 Transcription notation. In Atkinson J M, Heritage J (eds) *Structures of social action: studies in conversational analysis*. Cambridge University Press, Cambridge pp ix–xvi

Jefferson G 1985 An exercise in the transcription and analysis of laughter. In van Dijk T (ed) *A handbook of discourse analysis*. Academic Press, London pp 25–35

Jelinek F 1976 Continuous speech recognition by statistical methods. *Proceedings of the IEEE* **64**(4): 532–55

Johansson S 1991 *Some thoughts on the encoding of spoken texts in machine-readable form*. University of Oslo, Department of English, Oslo

Johansson S 1994 Encoding a corpus in machine-readable form. In Atkins, T S (ed) *Computational approaches to the lexicon: an overview*. Oxford University Press, Oxford pp 83–102

Johansson S, Burnard L, Edwards J A, Rosta A 1991 *Text Encoding Initiative, Spoken Text Working Group, final report*. Department of English, University of Oslo

Johnson M 1986 A computer-based approach to the analysis of child language data. Unpublished PhD thesis. University of Reading.

Jones K 1992 Creating new identities and new language functions: the implications of the language values and practices of adult Welsh learners for reversing language shift in Wales. Unpublished MA thesis. Department of Linguistics, Lancaster University.

Kennedy G 1992 Preferred ways of putting things with implications for language teaching. In Svartvik J (ed) *Directions in corpus linguistics. Proceedings of Nobel Symposium 82, 4–8 August 1991*. Mouton de Gruyter, Berlin/New York pp 335–73

Knowles G 1991 Prosodic labelling: the problem of tone group boundaries. In Johansson S, Stenström A-B (eds) *English computer corpora: selected papers and research guide*. Mouton de Gruyter, Berlin/New York pp 149–63

Knowles, G. 1994 Review of Jane A. Edwards and Martin D. Lampert (eds) 1993 Talking data: transcription and coding in discourse research. *ICAME Journal* **18**:107–12

Knowles G, Alderson P (eds) 1994 *Working with speech: perspectives on research into the Lancaster/IBM Spoken English Corpus*. Longman, London

Knowles G, Taylor L 1988 *Manual of information to accompany the Spoken English Corpus*. UCREL, University of Lancaster, Lancaster

Kytö M 1990 Introduction to the use of the Helsinki Corpus: diachronic and dialectal. In Ljung M (ed) *Proceedings from the Stockholm conference on the use of computers in language research and teaching, September 7–9, 1989*. English Department, University of Stockholm, Stockholm pp 41–56

Lampert M D, Ervin-Tripp S M 1993 Structured coding for the study of language and social interaction. In Edwards J A, Lampert M D (eds) *Talking data: transcription and coding in discourse research*. Lawrence Erlbaum, Hillsdale, NJ pp 169–206

Langendoen D T, Simons G F 1993 A rationale for the TEI recommendations for feature–structure make-up. In *Computers and humanities*.

Lecercle J-J 1990 *The violence of language*. Routledge, London

Leech G N 1992a Corpora and theories of linguistic performance. In Svartvik J (ed) *Directions in corpus linguistics. Proceedings of Nobel Symposium 82, Stockholm, 4–8 August 1991*. Mouton de Gruyter, Berlin/New York pp 105–22

Leech G N 1992b Corpus processing. In Bright W (ed) *International encyclopaedia of linguistics, Vol. 1*. Oxford University Press, Oxford pp 313–14

Leech G N, Fligelstone S 1992 Computers in corpus analysis. In Butler C S (ed) *Computers in written texts*. Blackwell, Oxford pp 115–40

Leung H C and Zue V W 1984 A procedure for automatic alignment of phonetic transcriptions with continuous speech *Proceedings of ICASSP 84* pp 271–274

Lieberman P 1965 On the acoustic basis of the perception of intonation by linguists. *Word* **21**: 40–54

Loman B, Jörgensen N 1971 *Manual för analys och beskrivning av makrosyntagmer*. Studentlitteratur, Lund

Long S H 1987 'Computerized profiling' of clinical language samples. *Clinical Linguistics and Phonetics* **1**: 97–105

Lyons J 1968 *Introduction to theoretical linguistics*. Cambridge University Press, Cambridge

Lyons J 1977 *Semantics*. Cambridge University Press, Cambridge

MacWhinney B 1988 *CHAT manual*. Department of Psychology, Carnegie-Mellon University, Pittsburgh, PA

MacWhinney B 1991 *The CHILDES project: tools for analyzing talk*. Lawrence Erlbaum, Hillsdale, NJ

MacWhinney B, Snow C 1990 The Child Language Data Exchange System. *ICAME Journal* **14**: 3–25

MacWhinney B, Snow C 1992 The wheat and the chaff: or four confusions regarding CHILDES. *Journal of Child Language* **19**: 459–71

Malinowski B 1923 The problem of meaning in primitive languages. In Ogden C K, Richards I A (eds) *The meaning of meaning*. Routledge and Kegan Paul, London pp 296–336

Martin-Jones M, Saxena M (in progress) Transcribing bilingual classroom discourse. Lancaster University/University College of Ripon and York St John

Martin-Jones M, Saxena M, Chana V, Barton D and Ivanič R 1992 *Bilingual Resources in Primary Classroom Interaction* Centre for Language in Social Life Working Paper Series No 53 Lancaster University, Lancaster

Martindale C 1991 *Cognitive psychology*. Brooks/Cole, Pacific Grove, CA

Melby A 1993 *Terminology Interchange Format (TIF): a tutorial*. Infoterm, Vienna

Melchers G 1972 *Studies in Yorkshire dialects. Based on recordings of 13 dialect speakers in the West Riding*. English Department, University of Stockholm, Stockholm

Menn L, Obler L K 1990 Theoretical motivations for the cross-language study of agrammatism. In Menn L, Obler L K (eds) *Agrammatic aphasia: a cross-language narrative sourcebook, Vol. 1*. Benjamins, Amsterdam

Miller J, Chapman R 1985 *SALT: systematic analysis of language transcripts*. Language Analysis Laboratory, Waisman Centre on Mental Retardation and Human Development, University of Madison-Wisconsin

Monaghan J 1982 On the phonological signalling of text structure. In Gutwinski W, Jolly G (eds) *The eighth LACUS forum*. Hornbeam Press, Columbia, S.C. pp 418–427

Monaghan J 1987 *Grammar in the construction of texts*. Pinter Publishers, London

Monaghan J 1992 Fundamental research underlying the design of an automated dictation system. In R Lawrence (ed) *Proceedings of the Institute of Acoustics: 1992 Autumn conference on Speech and Hearing*. The Institute of Acoustics, St Albans, Herts. pp. 645–51

Nakamura J 1993 Statistical methods and large corpora. In Baker M, Francis G and Tognini-Bonelli E (eds) *Text and technology*. Benjamins, Amsterdam pp 645–51

Nelson G 1991 Markup manual for spoken texts. *ICE Newsletter* **10** Survey of English Usage, University College London

Nespoulous J-L, Lecours A R 1990 *Pourquoi l'aphasique peut-il dire 'Je ne peux pas le dire' et pas 'Elle ne peut pas la chanter?'. De l'intérêt des dissociations verbales dans l'étude du 'parler aphasique'*. Université de Toulouse-le Mirail, Toulouse

New York Times Staff for the Whitehouse Transcripts 1974 *The White House transcripts. Submission of recorded presidential conversations to the Committee on the Judiciary of the House of Representatives by President Richard Nixon*. Bantam Books, New York

O'Connor J D, Arnold G 1973 *Intonation of colloquial English*, 2nd edn. Longman, London

O'Connor J D, Tooley O 1964 The perceptibility of certain word-boundaries. In Abercrombie D (ed) *In honour of Daniel Jones*. Longman, London pp 171–6

Ochs E 1979 Transcription as theory. In Ochs E, Schieffelin B B (eds) *Developmental pragmatics*. Academic Press, New York pp 43–72

Olson D R, Torrance N (eds) 1991 *Literacy and orality*. Cambridge University Press, Cambridge

Ong W J 1982 *Orality and literacy*. Routledge, London

Palmer H E 1939 *A grammar of spoken English on a strictly phonetic basis*. Heffer, Cambridge

Pawley A, Syder F H 1983 Two puzzles for linguistic theory: nativelike selection and nativelike fluency. In Richards J C, Schmidt R W (eds) *Language and communication*. Longman, London pp 191–226

Payne J 1993 Speaking the same language – listening to the speech community. NERC Working Paper 4

Payne J A 1993 *A report on the compatibility of J P French's spoken corpus transcription conventions with the TEI guidelines for transcription of spoken texts* COBUILD. University of Birmingham, Birmingham

Penn C, Behrmann M 1986 Towards a classification scheme for aphasic syntax. *British Journal of Disorders of Communication* **21**: 21–38

Perkins M R 1994 Productivity and stereotypy in language disorders. In Aulanko R, Korpijaakko-Huuhka A-M (eds) *Proceedings of the third congress of the International Clinical Phonetics and Linguistics Association, 9–11 August 1993, Helsinki, Publication of the Department of Phonetics, 38*. University of Helsinki, Helsinki pp 129–36

Perkins M R, Howard S J 1995 *Case studies in clinical linguistics*. Whurr, London

Pierrehumbert J B 1980 The phonology and phonetics of English intonation. Unpublished PhD thesis. MIT.

Pittenger R E, Hockett C F, Danehy J J 1960 *The first five minutes: a sample of microscopic interview analysis*. P. Martineau, Ithaca, NY

Poplack S 1980 Sometimes I'll start a sentence in Spanish y termino en Español: toward a typology of code-switching. *Linguistics* **18**: 581–618

Quirk R 1992 On corpus principles and design. In Svartvik J (ed) Directions in corpus linguistics. *Proceedings of Nobel Symposium 82 Stockholm, 4–8 August 1991*. Mouton de Gruyter, Berlin pp 458–69

Quirk R, Greenbaum S, Leech G, Svartvik J 1985 *A comprehensive grammar of the English language*. Longman, London

Rabiner L R 1990 A tutorial on hidden Markov models and selected applications in speech recognition. In A.Waibel, K-F.Lee (eds) *Readings in speech recognition*. Morgan Kaufman, Los Altos, CA. pp 267–96

Radford A 1988 *Transformational grammar: a first course*. Cambridge University Press, Cambridge

Rampton M B H 1990 The 'native speaker'; expertise, affiliation and inheritance. *English Language Teaching Journal* **44**(2): 97–101

Reichman R 1985 *Getting computers to talk like you and me: discourse context, focus and semantics*. MIT Press, Cambridge, MA.

Renouf A 1986 The elicitation of spoken English. In Tottie G, Bäcklund I (eds) *English in speech and writing: a symposium*. Almqvist and Wiksell, Stockholm pp 177–97

Roach P 1991 *English phonetics and phonology*, 2nd edn. Cambridge University Press, Cambridge

Roach P J 1994 Conversion between prosodic transcription systems: 'Standard British' and ToBI. *Speech Communication* **15**, 1–2, pp 91–9

Rondal J 1978 Maternal speech to normal and Down's Syndrome children matched for mean length of utterance. In Myers C E (ed) *Quality of life in severely and profoundly mentally retarded people: research foundations for improvement.* American Association on Mental Deficiency, Washington, D.C.

Rosta A 1990 The system of preparation and annotation of ICE texts. *ICE Newsletter* **9**: supplement. Survey of English Usage, University College London

Sanford A J, Garrod S C 1981 *Understanding written language.* Wiley, Chichester

Saussure F de [1916] 1974 *Course in general linguistics.* Fontana/Collins, Glasgow

Schank R C, Abelson R 1977 *Scripts, plans, goals and understanding.* Lawrence Erlbaum, Hillsdale, NJ

Schegloff E 1968 Sequencing in conversational openings. *American Anthropologist* **70**: 1075–95

Schegloff E, Sacks H [1973] 1974 Opening up closings. In Turner R (ed) *Ethnomethodology.* Penguin, Harmondsworth pp 233–64

Scholes R J, Willis B J 1991 Linguists, literacy and the intentionality of Marshall McLuhan's Western Man. In Olson D R, Torrance N (eds) *Literacy and orality.* Cambridge University Press, Cambridge pp 236–50

Schuetze-Coburn S, Shapley M, Weber E G 1991 Units of intonation in discourse: a comparison of acoustic auditory analyses. *Language and Speech* **34**: 207–34

Searle J R 1969 *Speech acts: an essay in the philosophy of language.* Cambridge University Press, Cambridge

Searle J R 1976 A classification of illocutionary acts. *Language in Society* **5**: 1–23

Sebba M 1993 *London Jamaican: language systems in interaction.* Longman, London

Shippey T A 1993 Principles of conversation in Beowulfian speech. In Sinclair J M, Hoey M, Fox G (eds) *Techniques of description: spoken and written discourse.* Routledge, London pp 109–27

Shriberg L D, Lof G L 1991 Reliability studies in broad and narrow phonetic transcription. *Clinical Linguistics and Phonetics* **5**(3): 225–79

Silverman K, Beckman M, Pitrelli J, Ostendorf M, Wightman C, Price P, Pierrehumbert J and Hirschberg J 1992 ToBI: A Standard for Labeling English Prosody, *Proceedings of the 1992 International Conference on Speech and Language Processing*, Banff.

Sinclair J, Coulthard M 1975 *Towards an analysis of discourse: the English used by teachers and pupils.* Oxford University Press, Oxford

Sinclair J M 1991 *Corpus, concordance, collocation.* Oxford University Press, Oxford

Sinclair J M, Hoey M, Fox G (eds) 1993 *Techniques of description: spoken and written discourse.* Routledge, London

Slobin D I 1993 Coding child language data for crosslinguistic analysis. In Edwards J A, Lampert M D (eds) *Talking data: transcription and coding in discourse research.* Lawrence Erlbaum, Hillsdale, NJ pp 207–19

Sokolov J L, MacWhinney B 1990 The Chip framework – automatic coding and analysis of parent–child conversational interaction. *Behavior Research Methods, Instruments and Computers* **22**(2): 151–61

Sperber D, Wilson D 1986 *Relevance: communication and cognition.* Blackwell, Oxford

Sperberg-McQueen C M 1991 Texts in the electronic age: textual study and text encoding, with examples from medieval text. *Literary and Linguistic Computing* **6**(1): 34–6

Sperberg-McQueen C M, Burnard L (eds) 1994 *Guidelines for electronic text encoding and interchange (TEI P3)*. Association for Computers and the Humanities/Association for Computational Linguistics/Association for Literary and Linguistic Computing, Chicago and Oxford

Svartvik J (ed) 1990 *The London–Lund corpus of spoken English: description and research*. Lund University Press, Lund

Svartvik J 1992 Corpus linguistics comes of age. In Svartvik J (ed) Directions in corpus linguistics. *Proceedings of Nobel Symposium 82, Stockholm, 4–8 August 1991*. Mouton de Gruyter, Berlin/New York pp 7–13

Svartvik J (ed) 1992 Directions in corpus linguistics. *Proceedings of Nobel Symposium 82, Stockholm, 4–8 August 1991*. Mouton de Gruyter, Berlin/New York

Svartvik J, Quirk R (eds) 1980 *A corpus of English conversation*. Lund University Press, Lund

Swales J 1990 *Genre analysis*. Cambridge University Press, Cambridge

Tait M, Shillcock R 1993 Research in progress: syntactic theory and the characterization of dysphasic speech. *Clinical Linguistics and Phonetics* **7**: 237–9

Tannen D 1992 *Women and men in conversation*. Virago, London

Taylor L J, Knowles G 1988 *Manual of information to accompany the SEC corpus*. Unit for Computer Research on the English Language, Lancaster University.

Terkel S 1975 *Working with people. People talk about what they do all day and how they feel about what they do*. Avon Books, New York

Trager G L, Smith H L 1951 *An outline of English structure*. American Council of Learned Societies, Washington

Vološinov V N [1929] 1973 *Marxism and the philosophy of language*. Harvard University Press, Cambridge, MA.

Warren M 1993 Naturalness in conversation. Unpublished PhD thesis. University of Birmingham.

Wells G 1985 *Language development in the pre-school years*. Cambridge University Press, Cambridge

Wells J C 1987 Computer-coded phonetic transcription. *Journal of the International Phonetics Association* **17**: 94–114

Wichmann A 1991 Beginnings, middles and ends: a study of initiality and finality in the Spoken English Corpus. Unpublished PhD thesis. University of Lancaster.

Widdowson H G 1990 *Aspects of language teaching*. Oxford University Press, Oxford

Willis J D, Willis J W 1990 *Collins Cobuild English course*. Harper Collins, London

Winograd T 1983 *Language as a cognitive process. Volume 1: syntax*. Addison Wesley, Reading, Mass.

Winter E O 1977 A clause relational approach to English texts. *Instructional Science* **6**(1): 1–92

Author Index

Abelson, R 49
Alderson, P 149, 184
Alkema, F 40
Allen, G 130
Altenberg, B 132, 186n
Argyle, M 40
Arnfield, S 8, 113, 114, 115, 150, 155
Arnold, G 150, 192, 209
Atkinson, J M 83, 88, 89, 92
Atwell, E 134n
Austin, J L 49

Baker, M 99
Bakhtin, M M 39
Ball, M 130
Bartlett, C 129
Barton, D 148
Bates, E 129
Batstone, R 45
Beckman, M 29, 156
Behrmann, M 129
Berenz, N 26
Berman, R A 26
Biber, D 85, 106, 128, 132, 224
Birdwhistell, R 38, 52n
Bishop, D V M 129
Bliss, L 129
Bloom, L 28
Boase, S 94
Bolinger, D L 56
Brierley, L 142
Brodda, B 93
Brown, R 34n, 117, 118, 129
Burgess, P 40
Burnard, L 7, 9, 16, 17, 21, 39, 81n, 82, 85, 87, 93, 94, 95, 97n, 98n, 101, 107, 108, 128, 161, 185, 203, 228, 235

Calzolari, N 103
Caplan, D 122

Carroll, L 45, 47
Cassar, I 142
Chafe, W L 8, 16, 17, 26, 27, 47, 55, 56, 57, 208
Chana, U 148
Chapman, R 116
Cheepen, C 63, 66, 67, 114, 137, 138, 139, 140, 141, 143n
Chomsky, N 42, 68n, 131, 219
Church, K W 6
Conti-Ramsden, G 129
Cook, G 16, 17, 36, 43, 100, 104
Coulthard, M 44, 87, 99, 142, 143
Crowdy, S 7, 52n, 87, 162, 185, 224, 227, 235, 236, 237, 238
Cruttenden, A 27, 31
Crystal, D 98n, 118, 120, 122, 123, 129, 130, 131, 156, 158, 188, 192, 193, 238
Cumming, S 31, 56, 58, 82, 83, 86, 89, 91, 93, 94, 98n, 240

Danehy, J J 20
Darwin, C 129
Davis, W S 63, 64
Du Bois, J W 23, 25, 27, 29, 30, 31, 56, 58, 82, 83, 86, 89, 91, 93, 94, 98n, 240
Duckworth, M 130
Dykins, J 129

Edwards, J A 1, 5, 8, 11n, 16, 21, 23, 26, 27, 31, 36, 55, 82, 97n, 98n, 101, 116, 117, 208, 238, 241
Edwards, S 122, 129
Ehlich, K 27
Elliott, S 134n
Ervin-Tripp, S M 22, 30, 31

Feldman, H 129
Fillmore, C J 131
Fillmore, L W 29

255

Author Index

Finegan, E 128, 132
Fishman, J A 144
Fletcher, P 7, 8, 113, 114, 118, 122, 123, 129
Fligelstone, S 6
Francis, W N 6
French, J P 99, 203, 204, 206
Freund, E 49
Friederici, A 129
Fries, C C 68n
Fromm, D 129

Gardner-Chloros,. P 147
Garman, M 7, 8, 113, 114, 122, 123, 129
Garrod, S C 49
Gee, J P 26
Ghali, N 155
Gilmour, R 40
Goffman, E 137
Greenbaum, S 120, 185, 220
Grodzinsky, Y 132
Grosjean, F 26
Gumperz, J J 26
Guo, J 147

Halle, M 219
Halliday, M A K 39, 43, 66, 132, 192
Hardcastle, W 130
Hargrove, P M 129
Harris, Z S 68n
Heath, C 24
Heritage, J 83, 88, 89, 92
Hockett, C F 20
Hoey, M 140
Holland, A 129
Holmberg, C 129
Holub, R C 49
Hooshyar, N 129
Howard, S J 131
Hunt, K 120

Ingham, R 118
Ivanič, R 148

Jefferson, G 24, 38, 46, 83, 140, 141
Johansson, S 7, 8, 9, 16, 17, 21, 23, 28, 39, 76, 97n, 98n, 101, 128, 161, 185
Johnson, M 116, 118, 122, 129
Jones, K 148
Jörgensen, N 86

Keefe, K 129
Kennedy, G 128
Knott, R 122, 129
Knowles, G 10, 149, 152, 183, 184, 208, 209, 218
Kucera, H 6
Kyto, M 84

Lampert, M D 11n, 22, 30, 31, 82, 208

Larsen, T 29
Lecours, A R 132
Leech, G N 6, 99, 120, 131
Leung, H C 150
Lieberman, P 156
Loader, P 142
Loman, B 86
Long, S H 129
Lyons, J 22, 42

MacWhinney, B 7, 83, 84, 91, 93, 98n, 116, 117, 129
Malinowski, B 139
Martin-Jones, M 145, 148
Martindale, C 50
McIntosh, A 43
McNaught, J 103
Melby, A 81n
Melchers, G 93, 98n
Menn, L 129
Miller, J 116, 129
Monaghan, J 17, 38, 63, 66, 67, 101, 102, 107, 140, 143n
Montgomery, M 87

Nakamura, J 106
Nelson, G 7, 185
Nespoulos, J-L 132
Nicholson, H 40
Norman, K 142

Obler, L K 129
Ochs, E 15, 19, 36, 51, 55
O'Connor, J D 150, 156, 192, 209
Olson, D R 42
Ong, W J 42
Ostendorf, M 29, 156
Östman, J-O 29

Paolino, D 31, 56, 58, 82, 83, 86, 89, 91, 93, 94, 98n, 240
Pashek, G 129
Pawley, A 132
Payne, J A 95–97, 101, 102, 107, 108, 184, 203
Penn, C 129
Perkins, M R 8, 34n, 113, 114, 131, 132
Peters, A 29
Pierrehumbert, J B 29, 156
Pitrelli, J 29, 156
Pittenger, R E 20
Poplack, S 147
Price, P 29, 156

Quirk, R 24, 83, 86, 90, 93, 94, 120, 137, 140, 141, 184, 187, 201, 235, 238

Rabiner, L R 152
Radford, A 125
Rampton, M B H 52n

Reichman, R 44
Reinmuth, O 129
Roach, P 8, 17, 113, 114, 115, 149, 150, 155, 158, 209
Rondal, J 129
Rosta, A 21, 83, 98n, 101

Sacks, H 138
Salter, V 40
Sanford, A J 49
Saussure, F de 39, 42
Saxena, M 145, 148
Schank, R C 49
Schegloff, E 138
Schelletter, C 122, 129
Scholes, R J 52n
Schuetze-Coburn, S 27, 29, 30, 31, 56, 58, 82, 83, 86, 89, 91, 93, 94, 98n, 240
Searle, J R 22, 49
Sebba, M 8, 113, 114, 115, 144, 147
Shantry, I 142
Shapley, M 27
Shillcock, R 132
Shippey, T A 36
Silverman, K 29, 156
Sinclair, J M 7, 15, 17, 18, 40, 44, 87, 99, 132, 133, 142, 143, 150, 184
Slobin, D I 26, 27
Smith, H L 156. 157
Snow, C 7, 116
Sperber, D 49
Sperberg-McQueen, C M 81n, 82, 85, 87, 93, 94, 95, 98n, 203
Stein, D 129
Stodel, L 122, 129

Strevens, P 43
Svartvik, J 24, 27, 83, 86, 90, 93, 94, 120, 132, 137, 140, 141, 184, 187, 201, 238
Swales, J 49, 50
Swindell, C 129
Syder, F H 132

Tait, M 132
Tannen, D 36, 37
Taylor, L 149, 218
Terkel, S 93
Torrance, N 42
Trager, G L 156, 157

Varley, R 131
Volosinov, V N 39, 42

Warren, M 103
Weber, E G 27
Widdowson, H G 49
Wightman, C 29, 156
Williams, M 40
Willis, B J 52n
Willis, J D 103
Willis, J W 103
Wilson, D 49
Winograd, T 52
Winter, E O 67, 140
Wolfe, S 142
Wood, D 142
Wulfeck, B 129

Ziegler, M 129
Zue, V W 29, 150, 155

Subject Index

ACL/DCI (Data Collection Initiative) 172
acoustic data 64, 100–2, 114, 130, 149–60, 172, 178, 209
adequacy 54–61, 101–2, 105–6
agrammatism 122, 132
ALEP 108
alignment 51, 78, 90, 95–6, 98n, 114, 150–5, 185, 210, 211, 214–15, 218
analytical units (see sentence, clause, utterance, word, turn, T-unit)
annotations (see coding)
anonymity 234, 237, 241
aphasic speech 116, 122–6, 129
automatic corpus processing model 131–2

BNC (British National Corpus) 7, 9, 87, 161–7, 185, 224–34, 235

CD-ROM 6, 15–16, 17, 61, 114, 150, 168–80, 184, 185, 186n, 209, 235, 241
checking, correcting, proofreading, normalisation 176–8, 188, 204, 226, 227, 228, 233
CHILDES 7, 11n, 91, 94, 116, 117, 129, 183
clause 120, 125, 171, 192
COBUILD 9, 40, 46, 95, 99, 102, 103, 107, 113, 184, 185, 203–7
coding (see also alignment)
   discourse components 135–43
   discourse markers 142
   editorial comment 75, 76, 94–5, 96, 233
   interlineal glosses 146
   paralinguistic 16, 28, 44–8, 52n, 88–9, 94, 187–8, 201, 232
   phonetic and phonemic 93–4, 98n, 114, 135, 152, 155, 213–14, 218
   prosodic 31, 57–61, 93–4, 96, 102, 149–60, 187–8, 191–8, 199, 200–1, 204, 208, 209, 210, 211, 213, 214, 215–18, 231, 235, 237, 238, 239, 240, 241
   semantic 76, 130
   structure 138
   stories 139–41, 143
   s-units 164
   syntactic 26, 29, 30, 65, 125–6, 150, 209, 231, 237, 238
   textual divisions 21, 66–7, 73–4, 75, 76, 86–7, 125–6, 162–4, 227, 228, 236
   t-units 120–1
   word class tagging 2, 29, 135, 150, 161–7, 209, 210, 213, 228
collocations 133, 143
COLT (Corpus of London Teenager Language) 9, 184, 185, 235–42
context-governed model 225
conversation 103, 113, 137–41, 142–3, 145, 162, 168, 176, 187, 203, 207, 220–3, 223, 226–7, 229–34, 235–42
corpora, text collections, and initiatives (see ACL/DCI, BNC, CHILDES, COBUILD, COLT, CSAE, HCRC Map Task Corpus, ICE, LOB, SALT, SEC, TEI, TIMIT)
CSAE 10, 55, 86, 183

DAT (Digital Audio Tape) 172–4, 226
demographic model 225
discourse markers 142
DTD (Document Type Description) 69, 72, 76, 77, 78, 80, 107, 163

EAGLES 7, 72, 99, 102

format 16, 17, 19, 23–30, 51, 87, 118–20, 122–6, 146, 162, 172, 189, 203, 208, 209, 210, 218–19

hardware 6, 115, 173–6, 179–80
HCRC (Human Communication Research

Subject Index 259

Centre) Map Task Corpus 168–80, 183
header 72, 74, 77–8, 83, 84, 85, 96, 227
Hidden Markov Model (HMM) 152, 162

ICE 7, 185, 188, 198, 220–3
induction model 131–2
information retrieval model 131

language
   acquisition 22–3, 32
   impairment, pathology, disorder 2, 113, 114, 116–27, 128–34
   spoken vs. written 37–8, 42, 43, 48, 70, 100, 104–6, 145, 164–6, 172, 184, 207
linearity 51, 56, 126, 184–5, 208, 219
LLC (London Lund Corpus) 9, 10, 86, 90, 93, 94, 183, 184, 186n, 187–202, 238
LOB (Lancaster Oslo Bergen Corpus) 113

mark-up (*see also* SGML, header, coding) 1, 2, 3, 4, 5, 6, 7, 15, 18, 19–34, 56–61, 66, 76–8, 82–98, 102, 109, 114, 115, 117, 119–27, 146–8, 163–5, 166–7, 178, 184, 185, 188–202, 204–6, 209–11, 213–18, 220–3
models 131–2, 225

NERC 99

orthographic representation 29, 34n, 38, 99, 114, 130, 145, 152, 176, 177–8, 190, 199, 209, 210, 211, 213, 214, 218, 222, 228, 231, 232, 235, 236, 238

participants 37, 38, 49–51, 52n, 83–4, 87, 136–8, 139–41, 163, 168, 171, 174, 176, 198, 222, 225, 227, 230
phonology 93–4, 171
principles 21–5, 30–2
prosody 24, 31, 56–61, 86, 96, 102, 114, 120, 149–60, 171, 187–8, 191–8, 199, 200–1, 204, 208, 209, 210, 211, 213, 214, 215–18, 231, 235, 237, 238–9, 240, 241

recording *see* DAT, CD-ROM, sampling rate

SALT (Systematic Analysis of Language Transcripts) 116
sampling rate 173–4
SEC (Spoken English Corpus) 10, 149–55, 158, 184, 185, 208–19
segmentation 26–7, 78, 86–7, 114, 120–1, 123–6
self-organizing model 131–2
sentence 120, 144, 171, 192, 228, 236, 237
SEU (Survey of English Usage) 94, 183, 184, 186n, 187–202
SGML 20–1, 69, 70, 71, 72, 73, 75, 76, 77, 81n, 107, 115, 161, 162, 163, 164, 165,
174, 176, 178, 179, 206, 222, 228
situation 37, 48–9, 83–4, 85
software 6, 32, 81n, 107, 108–9, 115, 128, 130, 133, 152, 156, 161–7, 174
spatial arrangement (*see also* format) 19, 24–5, 27–30, 51, 90
speech acts 2, 22
speech in action 67, 138, 143
standarization (*see also* ALEP, EAGLES, SGML, TEI, ToBI) 5, 31, 35, 69–81, 99, 100, 107–8, 121, 128, 130, 146, 179
stereotypes 132
story 138, 139–41, 143
SUMLARSP 116
System Life Cycle 63–5

tagging *see* coding
tape recording *see also* DAT, CD-ROM, 39, 67n, 101–2, 105–6, 168, 187, 225, 226
TEI (Text Encoding Initiative) 7, 9, 17, 18, 39–40, 69–81, 82–98, 102, 104, 107–9, 128, 130, 133, 161, 178, 179, 185, 203, 206, 207, 228, 235, 241
text 6, 37, 39, 40, 62–8, 72, 73–4, 75, 83, 86, 102, 139, 150–5, 162–4, 224–5, 227, 228, 236
TIMIT 5, 21, 150
ToBI 29, 155–60
transactional encounters 137, 141–2, 143
transcription issues (*see also* alignment, orthographic representation, segmentation, format)
   accent 227, 232
   code switching 144–8
   context 38, 43–4, 47
   doubt, uncertainty 36, 79, 95, 190
   incomplete utterances 114, 122–3, 130, 177, 205, 222, 231, 237, 240
   invariants 176–8
   laughter 46–7, 59, 145, 163, 177, 190, 223, 232–3, 237, 240
   non-speech sounds 24, 114, 177, 205, 223, 232–3, 237, 240
   normalisation 176–8, 204, 222, 232
   orthographic representation 34n, 38, 99, 114, 130, 145, 176, 177–8, 190, 199, 210, 213, 214, 222, 228, 231, 232, 236, 238
   overlapping speech and interruption 27, 36, 61, 64, 90–3, 96, 98n, 108, 130, 172, 176, 191, 198, 199, 205, 206, 222–3, 230–1, 237, 240
   paralinguistic features 16, 44–8, 52n, 88–9, 94, 149, 158, 187–8, 190, 201, 232
   participants 38, 49–51, 83, 87, 139–40, 174, 176, 198, 230
   pauses 22, 26, 31, 56, 57, 64, 82, 83, 88, 93, 98n, 114, 122, 163, 172, 176, 177, 190–1, 199, 222, 232, 237, 238, 240
   phonemic representation 34n, 39, 102, 152,

Subject Index

    155, 190, 199, 208, 213–14
  repetition 123, 130, 165–6, 176, 222, 241
  spelling out, reading out 233, 234
  use vs. mention 177
T-unit 120
turn 27, 86, 137, 138, 171, 176, 199, 204, 205, 206, 228, 230, 236
typography 16, 24, 71, 146–8, 202

utterance 28, 36, 118, 123–4, 163

word
  boundaries 210
  frequency counts 132
  morphemes 118
  unit of analysis 37, 38–42, 86, 210